# SON *of* MAN

## A BIOGRAPHY
### *of* JESUS

HENRY H HARRIS

Published 2015 by inChrist Press

ISBN 978-0-9963933-0-0 (Hardcover)
ISBN 978-0-9963933-1-7 (Paperback)

Edited by Susanne Lakin and Pennie Embry
Book design by Maureen Cutajar
Cover design by Dane Low
Cover image by Rembrandt (*Head of Christ*, circa 1656)

All Scripture quotations in the text are the author's translations, paraphrases, and harmonies of the Gospels of Matthew, Mark, Luke, and John.

*For Lauren, my wife and best friend*
*God has given me many gifts—you are the most precious*

# CONTENTS

# PROLOGUE

*"We did not follow cleverly devised myths when we made known to you the power and coming of our Lord Jesus Christ—we were eyewitnesses of his majesty."*

—2 Peter 1:16

I

# A Voice from the Wilderness

SPRING–AUTUMN, AD 29

*A voice cries out: "Clear a path in the wilderness. Make a straight highway in the desert for our God. Let every valley be filled and every mountain and hill be made flat. Let the crooked places be made straight and the rough places smooth. Then the glory of the Lord will appear for all to see. The Lord himself has promised this."*

—Isaiah 40:3–5

A RELIGIOUS STUPOR rests upon the land. Seven centuries have passed since the prophet Isaiah predicted a voice would call from the wilderness to prepare Israel for the Lord's arrival.

Most people believe the old prophecies shouldn't be taken literally, but some still look with prayerful anticipation toward the desolate lands west of the Salt Sea, where the prophets said a new exodus will begin. "I will lead her into the wilderness and speak tenderly to her there," the Lord told Hosea. "I will make the valley of trouble into a door of hope."

This is a tremendous promise, but hundreds of generations have come and gone, and only the names of the oppressors have changed. "How long, oh Lord?" is the question on the lips of many as the poor become poorer and the weak become helpless.

Recently there have been reports from the Jordan River of a Nazarite hermit who is reviving interest in the old predictions and announcing the arrival of the Messiah. "Repent," John bar Zechariah demands, "for the kingdom of heaven is at hand."

Like the prophets before him, his counsel is blunt: prepare to meet your God—He will be here soon. To the poor, who are convinced that only the Lord can deliver them from their hopeless situation, John's news is encouraging. To others, his words sound more like a warning. Maybe even a threat.

John's appearance is as startling as his message. He's in his early thirties, but years in the desert have weathered him. His dark skin is cracked and leathery, his beard is long and matted, and his hair is uncut and cascades down his back in thick coils. His body, lean from a diet of honey and locusts, is clothed in a coarse camel-hair cloak that is cinched at his waist with a leather tie.

John confines his ministry to the Jordan River Valley, but he is known in Jerusalem. His father was a priest in the Abijah division, and everyone assumed that one day John would take his father's place, but the son of Zechariah has a different destiny. Before John was born, the angel Gabriel proclaimed that he would be filled with the Holy Spirit from the womb and, like only Samson and Samuel before him, a Nazarite for life.

John proclaims the coming of the Messiah up and down the two hundred miles of switchbacking river that is compressed into a sixty-five-mile stretch between Lake Gennesaret and the Salt Sea.

Most who come to the Jordan are from Judea, and they travel the road the Romans built on the Ascent of Adumim. It is paved, but it is also steep and dangerous. While Jerusalem sits comfortably 2,500 feet above sea level, the Jordan Valley, just twenty miles away, is 1,500 feet below sea level and 4,000 feet below Jerusalem. To complicate matters, the remoteness of the Jericho road makes it appealing to thieves and robbers.

Rumors about the man known as "the Baptist" spring up in every town and village in Israel. Some believe he's the Messiah. Others note that John dresses like Elijah and has a similar message. He even ministers in the same location where the ancient prophet mounted a fiery chariot bound for heaven. Has Elijah returned?

Many go to the Jordan to judge for themselves. Unlike the lukewarm homilies they normally hear, the Baptist's messages are convicting.

John points them to God's Word, and when they confess their sins, he baptizes them and exhorts them to prepare for the coming of the one who will change everything.

John's baptism, like his appearance and message, is unorthodox. The rite itself is familiar. Every house of status has its own *mikveh* for ceremonial immersions, and Jewish communities throughout the land provide public pools. The Pharisees, Sadducees, and Essenes regularly immerse themselves to ensure their cleanliness before God, but John's baptism is administered one time only because it signifies something different. His baptism isn't another purification ritual—it's a public declaration by those being baptized that they will live obediently in anticipation of the Messiah. It is more like a proselyte baptism, but John is immersing repentant Israelites, not Gentiles seeking to convert to Judaism.

As the months pass, more and more people make pilgrimages to the Jordan, hoping to be made right with God, hoping that somehow life will be better after they hear John's message. Not everyone who comes, however, desires to be made right with God. Religious leaders descend from Jerusalem to challenge John's authority to administer rituals they are convinced are the prerogative of priests, not locust eaters. They stand warily on the fringes of the crowd, hoping to either get the Baptist into their camp or to discredit him.

John sees the men in the elegant robes but ignores them. He has been sent to proclaim God's salvation to the people the elite look down upon and dismiss as *am ha'aretz*—"people of the land"—the uneducated working poor who make up 90 percent of the population.

The religionists are convinced that the commoners are too rustic to keep the hundreds of laws and traditions necessary to remain blameless, yet it is the people of the land who are responding to John's invitation. Daily the banks of the river are lined with expectant faces, some traveling from as far away as Upper Galilee and Gaulanitis. Children play at the water's edge while their parents sit under the trees and listen to John explain what faithfulness looks like in everyday life.

This, too, was prophesied. Before John's birth the angel Gabriel declared, "He will turn many of the children of Israel to the Lord their

God, and he will go before him in the spirit and power of Elijah to turn the hearts of parents to the children and the disobedient to the wisdom of the just—to make ready for the Lord a people prepared."

As the months pass, the angel's prophecy is fulfilled.

One day when John is preaching near Bethany-by-the-Jordan, a large number of priests and teachers of the Law are in the audience. John turns to them, pauses long enough to be sure he has their attention, and says, "You children of vipers, who warned you to flee from the coming wrath?"

A popular legend describes how, during birthing, baby vipers will chew their way out of their mother's womb, killing her in the process. John accuses the religious leaders of doing the same to Israel. He knows what's in their hearts and will not pretend they are the high and holy men they want others to think they are.

"Produce the kind of fruit that demonstrates you have changed," the Baptist demands.

Knowing they rely on their heritage as a divinely chosen people to give them right standing with God, John warns, "Don't smugly think to yourself you can say, 'We have Abraham as our father,' for I tell you that God is able to raise up children for Abraham from these rocks. And even now the ax is lying at the root of the trees. Every tree that does not bear good fruit is cut down and thrown into the fire."

The Pharisees and Sadducees smolder and turn away, but the crowd overhears John's warning and is frightened. If the pious are doomed, what hope is there for the simple people? "What should we do then?" they ask.

John encourages them to live generously. "Let the one who has two tunics share with the one having none, and the one who has food should do the same."

Hearing John's instruction to live by faith, a tax collector then asks, "Teacher, what about us? What should we do?"

John won't condemn their occupation, but he knows they are allowed to keep any extra monies they can extort. "Collect nothing more than the amount you have been commanded to collect," he tells them.

Emboldened by John's gracious answer, another despised group asks the same question. "What about us—what should we do?" one of the Levite soldiers asks.

"Don't take money from anyone by force or accuse anyone falsely," John says, "and be content with your wages."

He speaks with such authority that some wonder aloud if he is the long-awaited Christ. The Messiah, the people of Israel are convinced, will be the answer to all their troubles. He will single-handedly crush their enemies, restore righteousness to the nation, and make Jerusalem the seat from which the world will be governed for all eternity.

The Baptist shakes his head at their speculations. "I baptize you with water to show that you have repented," John tells them, "but the one coming after me is stronger than I—I am not worthy to bend down and untie the strap of his sandal. I baptize you with water, but he will baptize you with the Holy Spirit and with fire. His winnowing fork is in his hand to clear his threshing floor, gathering the wheat into his barn but burning the chaff with unquenchable fire."

The crowd is familiar with the winnowing process, and the metaphor is disturbing. After threshing, the wheat (including husks, straw, and plant debris) is tossed high in the air with a shovel-like wooden fork. The heavy wheat kernel falls to the floor while the remaining debris—the chaff—is blown aside by the wind. And because Israel has few fuel resources, the chaff is often used for kindling. John says that people are like wheat. Some are grain and some are chaff. The grain will be blessed, but the chaff will be thrown into hell.

The priests and scholars scowl and walk away. They would like to lure the renegade prophet to Jerusalem to answer to the high priest, but John will not be diverted from his mission. He remains at the river, proclaiming the Messiah's coming and warning of impending judgment.

ONE DAY AS John is preaching and baptizing, a man quietly slips into the crowd and makes his way to the water's edge. He is clothed in Galilean homespun and appears to be in his early thirties. His height and weight are average—he's slightly over five feet tall and weighs about 120 pounds. His muscular build and rough hands give the impression of a workman, perhaps a *tekton* who builds with wood and stone. He's not a handsome man, but his smile is warm and his eyes sparkle with the inquisitiveness of a child. His hair is cut short and gently curls around his ears. Those who bother to look see a Jewish everyman from the northlands.

Jesus comes meekly and without fanfare, one of many seeking to be baptized, but as he walks toward the water, the Holy Spirit stirs in John. The Baptist wonders if he is in the presence of the Anointed One, but he's confused—if Jesus is the Messiah, why would he seek baptism? Why would he want to be identified with sinners?

When Jesus draws near, John pleads his inadequacy: "I need to be baptized by you, and yet you come to me?"

"Permit it at this time," Jesus says, "for in this way it is fitting for us to fulfill all righteousness."

John does not understand Jesus's reasoning, but when he's told it is fitting to do all things that are God's will, he immediately immerses the man. As Jesus rises from the water, he is praying. He opens his eyes and sees the Holy Spirit descending.

The Baptist also glimpses the Spirit, and all his questions are answered. Long before this day God had told him, "He on whom you see the Spirit descend and remain, this is he who baptizes with the Holy Spirit."

As John stands in the river allowing the significance of what has happened to wash over him, he hears a voice from heaven say to Jesus, "You are My son, the beloved—with you I am well pleased."

The words are from Psalm 2 and Isaiah 42, in which David describes the coronation of the Messiah and Isaiah identifies a righteous servant of God who will be beaten beyond recognition and killed. The Voice designates Jesus as both the servant and the king.

Jesus, his public anointing complete, immediately receives his first assignment from the Holy Spirit. With the Jordan's water still dripping from his tunic, he walks west into the wilderness. His first appointment will be with his oldest and most deadly adversary.

# INCEPTION

AUTUMN–WINTER, AD 29

*The old has passed away; behold, the new has come.*

—2 Corinthians 5:17

THE BROAD DESERTS and barren chalk peaks of the Judean wilderness are part of the legendary *midbar*—the dry lands east and south of Jerusalem where many of Israel's most painful memories are stored. The Torah records how God freed His people from Egypt and brought them to the land He promised to Abraham. Within weeks they were at the border, but the Israelites refused to enter. Their fear of the country's inhabitants was greater than their trust in the Lord. All but two of that faithless generation died in the desert, and forty years later their children followed Joshua and Caleb across the Jordan to claim their inheritance.

Isaiah prophesied that one day a deliverer would come from these dry lands to lead God's people in a new exodus, but until then the midbar would remain a feared place avoided by all but outlaws and ascetics. Moses, who lived in these wastelands for eighty years, described them as "a vast and terrifying wilderness with fiery serpents and scorpions and thirsty ground where there was no water." Other Scriptures describe the midbar as *horbah* (dry, desolate, ruined); *tsiyyah* (land of drought); *jeshimon* (desolation); and *tohu* (a chaotic void).

Here among the lions and leopards and snakes and scorpions, Jesus is to fast for forty days and contend with a powerful angel who has been carefully molding history into his own image for thousands of years. The angel has never met a mortal he could not enlist, deceive, or overpower, and if it were not for divine interference, the entire human race would by now be his slaves.

Over the years he has been known by many names. Once, as a leader in the special class of guardian angels known as *cherubim*, he was Helel ben Shachar (Shining Star, Son of the Dawn), but that was long ago. These days he only appears as an angel of light when it serves his purposes, and with Jesus there's no need for pretense.

Jesus fasts and prays for several weeks. The Devil is content to simply watch and wait. A month passes, and still Satan takes no action. This moment has been a long time coming, and he wants to savor it.

After forty days Jesus is starved and near exhaustion. The beguiler approaches meekly with concern in his eyes. Feigning worry about Jesus's health, he suggests, "Since you are the Son of God, tell these stones to become bread."

The recommendation sounds harmless, even compassionate. The man is obviously starving—why not use the resources at his command to help himself? But the suggestion is not as innocent as it appears. Jesus is being tempted to question God's provision. Satan is suggesting that Jesus will be better off if he takes care of himself rather than waiting for God to get around to it.

"It is written," Jesus says, "'Man does not live on bread alone, but on every word that comes from the mouth of God.'"

When the Devil realizes Jesus will not act independently of the Father, he supernaturally transports him to the top of the temple in Jerusalem and whispers in his ear, "Since you are the Son of God, throw yourself down from here, for it is written, 'He will command His angels to protect you,' and 'they will lift you in their hands so that you never hit your foot against a stone.'"

Jesus looks at the valley floor 450 feet below and reflects on the psalm the demon quoted from. The ninety-first psalm describes one who trusts in the Lord. Such a person is to be fearless. "When he calls to Me," God says, "I will answer him. I will be with him in trouble—I will rescue him and honor him."

The Devil hopes to persuade Jesus to test this promise. Surely his Father will not allow him to be hurt. Why not let go and let God confirm He is who He says He is?

"Again it is written," Jesus reminds the tempter, "'You shall not put the Lord your God to the test.'"

For a second time the account of the wilderness journey is called in as evidence. When God miraculously provided food for the Israelites, they weren't satisfied. Even though they had seen His deliverance with their own eyes and had tasted it daily with their own lips, they still doubted God's goodness and demanded, "Is the Lord among us or not?"

Jesus refuses to jump from the heights of the temple because he knows that same cynical challenge will be his if he forces God to rescue him. He chooses to trust without testing.

After his first two attempts fail, the Devil takes Jesus to a high mountain and shows him a vision of all the kingdoms of the world—the splendor of imperial Rome, the grandeur of ancient Greece, the beauty of the Mediterranean isles. "All these I will give you," Satan promises, "if you will bow down and worship me."

It's an offer of vast political power. Satan suggests that as king of the world, Jesus can eliminate injustice and poverty. Wars will cease. Laws can be made and enforced to ensure everyone is fed and well taken care of. And, as an added bonus, Jesus can have all of this now. No need to suffer to bring it about, and certainly no need for a cross. The world's problems can be solved politically if only the right leader will take the reins.

This is an incredibly appealing proposal, one Satan has been buying souls with for centuries, but Jesus has no interest in the Devil's bargain. While he can appreciate the positive changes a godly government would bring, Jesus also knows it would be a shallow, short-term fix. Saving people from hunger and injustice is not what they most need. What they most need is to be reconciled with God—something the painless solution offered by the evil one can never provide.

"Begone, Satan!" Jesus commands, "For it is written, 'You shall worship the Lord your God and Him only shall you serve.'"

When Jesus quotes the same command he is being tempted to break, the Devil realizes his first face-off with the Messiah has been a failure, but he knows there will be other opportunities. He retreats into the shadows as angels descend from heaven to care for Jesus.

AT THE JORDAN, six weeks have passed. John continues to proclaim the Messiah's arrival, and the nation's religious rulers grow increasingly alarmed with the prophet's popularity, especially among the poor. The leaders have seen the way the military responds when the Pax Romana is violated, and they can't afford to have a rogue prophet creating unrest. The high priest sends a delegation to gather evidence they can use to silence the Baptist.

When the priests and Pharisees reach John's camp, they ask probing questions about his identity. First and foremost they want to know if he claims to be the Christ.

"I am not the Messiah," John says.

"If you're not the Messiah, then who are you? Are you Elijah?"

"No, I am not."

"Then who? Are you the Prophet that Moses spoke of?"

"No."

The Baptist answers their questions but offers no further explanation, and eventually they tire of guessing. "Who are you?" they demand. "Give us an answer to take back to those who sent us from Jerusalem. What do you have to say about yourself?"

John replies with the words of the prophet Isaiah: "I am the voice of one shouting in the wilderness, 'Make straight the way for the Lord.'"

His answer only flusters them more. "If you're not the Messiah or Elijah or the Prophet, then why do you baptize people?"

Now their words betray their real concern—John is performing unsanctioned religious rituals.

John offers an enigmatic answer: "I baptize with water, but among you stands one you do not know. He is the one who comes after me, the thongs of whose sandals I'm not worthy to untie. This was he of whom I said, 'He who comes after me has surpassed me because he was before me.'"

What does that mean? the priests and Pharisees ask themselves. Frustrated with the prophet's unwillingness to give them a simple answer to a simple question, they return to Jerusalem.

They are, however, comforted by one thought: John is too outspoken for his own good. Especially promising is the Baptist's recent decision to confront Herod Antipas about his affair with his sister-in-law, the wife of Herod Philip. A quiet divorce had been arranged, but John is publicly rebuking Antipas and announcing God's opposition to the union. When Jerusalem's leaders reflect on this, some conclude that the prophet may one day go too far, and their problem will resolve itself.

John the Baptist is completely unconcerned about repercussions. He knows his part of the story is nearing its end. This was confirmed two months ago when the sky opened and he heard the voice of God. But where has the Messiah disappeared to and where is he now?

Then one day as John is teaching, Jesus walks by. John motions toward him and says, "Behold, the Lamb of God who takes away the sin of the world! This is the one I meant when I said, 'A man who comes after me has surpassed me because he was before me.' I myself did not know him, but the reason I came baptizing with water was that he might be revealed to Israel. I saw the Spirit come down from heaven as a dove and remain on him. I would not have known him, except that the One who sent me to baptize with water told me, 'The man on whom you see the Spirit come down and remain is he who will baptize with the Holy Spirit.'"

John pauses, looks into the eyes of his disciples, and says, "I have seen and I testify that this is the Chosen One of God."

For months the Baptist has been proclaiming the imminent arrival of an unknown Messiah. The Christ now has a face and a name.

The next afternoon John sees Jesus walking by and again says, "Behold, the Lamb of God!"

Two of his disciples, Andrew bar Jonah and John bar Zebedee, get up and begin walking behind Jesus, trusting the Baptist's testimony that the humbly dressed and unassuming man they are following is the Messiah.

When Jesus notices they are behind him, he turns and asks, "What do you want?"

The young men indicate their desire to become disciples with a simple question: "Rabbi, where are you staying?"

Jesus smiles and says, "Come, and you will see." Andrew and John follow Jesus to his lodgings and spend the remainder of the day with him.

By the time they leave, Andrew is convinced John the Baptist is right about Jesus. He runs and finds his brother, Simon, and exuberantly proclaims, "We've found the Messiah!"

Simon is fascinated by Andrew's story and even more impressed when he meets Jesus. He still has questions about how an ordinary-looking man from Nazareth could be the Messiah, but Simon can sense there is something profoundly different about this teacher.

Toward the end of their conversation, Jesus surprises Simon by giving him an Aramaic nickname: "You are Simon bar Jonah—you will be called *Kephas*."

Simon wonders why he will be known as "Rock" (which in Greek is *Petros*—Peter). He certainly doesn't feel like one, but the next day when Jesus announces he is leaving for Galilee, the new Rock and his companions follow. For Simon Peter, Andrew, and John, Capernaum is home. They are fishermen on the north shore of the harp-shaped Lake Gennesaret, recently renamed Lake Tiberias by Herod Antipas in honor of the emperor.

As the four men make their way toward the north shore, they meet Phillip, a friend from Simon and Andrew's childhood home of Bethsaida. He's a quiet man who, like many, wrestles with his faith, but he is greatly encouraged when he meets Jesus.

He is soon convinced that Jesus is the Messiah, and later, when he sees his friend Nathanael bar Tolmai sitting under a fig tree, he shares the good news with him: "We've found the one Moses wrote about in the Law and the Prophets. He's Jesus bar Joseph from Nazareth."

At the mention of Jesus's hometown, Nathanael becomes skeptical. He is from Cana, nine miles north of Nazareth, and has little positive to say about the village. "Can anything good come out of Nazareth?" he asks.

Philip laughs and says, "Come and see!"

Nathanael has his doubts, but his friend's enthusiasm is infectious, and soon they're looking for the new rabbi.

Jesus sees Nathanael approaching and says, "Behold, here is truly an Israelite in whom there is no deceit!"

Jesus contrasts Nathanael with his forefather Jacob, who regularly deceived people. Nathanael is startled. He has never met this man. "How do you know me?" he asks.

"I saw you while you were still under the fig tree before Philip called you."

Jesus says it casually, and his observation sounds innocuous to Philip and the others, but his words stun Nathanael. There is no way Jesus could have known that he was under the fig tree. Nathanael now sees why his friend became a follower. "Rabbi," he exclaims, "you are the Son of God— you are the King of Israel!"

"You believe because I told you I saw you under the fig tree," Jesus says. Then he turns to those who are following and adds, "You will see greater things than that. I tell you the truth, you will see heaven open and the angels of God ascending and descending on the Son of Man."

Jesus's words shock his new admirers. He is claiming to be the connection between heaven and earth, God and man. Jacob had named the place where he saw the vision of the ladder *Bethel*, "house of God." Jesus says God's house is no longer a place. Bethel has become flesh and dwells among them.

THE FIVE ARE still thinking about Jesus's words two days later when they travel to Nathanael's hometown of Cana for the wedding of a family friend. When they arrive they find Jesus's mother already there, helping coordinate the reception.

In small villages, weddings are the biggest local events of the year. The entire town turns out for the festivities. Traditionally, the ceremony begins with an evening processional: the groom, accompanied by his friends, walks to the home of the bride, takes her arm in his, and leads the wedding party back to his home for a reception that lasts for several days.

The wedding procession unfolds as planned, and the guests are noisily seated at tables filled with fine food and flagons of wine. All are enjoying themselves and the celebration is in full stride, when one of the servants realizes that the wine supply is inadequate.

Jesus's mother learns of the problem and knows that in a small town like Cana this will not only shame the couple, it will permanently tarnish their reputation. Mary finds Jesus and urgently whispers, "They have no wine."

Mary hopes her son will understand the gravity of the situation, but instead of responding sympathetically, Jesus mildly chastises her. "Woman, what does this have to do with me and you? My hour has not yet come."

Jesus gently lets his mother know that now his life must follow a different timetable. Mary doesn't understand her son's words but knows it is best to simply trust him. She turns to the servants and says, "Do whatever he tells you."

Jesus considers the circumstances and decides this could be a good teaching opportunity. Looking around, he sees six stone water jars that earlier were used by the wedding guests for rites of purification. Each jar holds two to three measures (sixteen to twenty-seven gallons), but the vessels have served their purpose and are now empty.

Jesus tells the servants, "Fill the jars with water."

The attendants think this is an unusual request, but they go to the well, and soon the receptacles are filled to the brim. Jesus tells one of the men, "Now draw some out and take it to the overseer of the feast."

The servant initially balks at the instructions. He fears what his busy boss will do when given a goblet of wash water to sample, but after a moment he dutifully delivers the drink and awaits the overseer's response. The attendant is surprised when his master does not ask the obvious question, and even more surprised to see that the cup he brought is now filled with red wine.

The banquet coordinator, a man well experienced at dealing with the complexities involved in supplying food and drink for multiday festivities, casually takes a sip of the wine. His eyebrows immediately shoot up. He looks to the attendant for an explanation, but the servant bows his head and says nothing, afraid to tell his master the wine had moments before been well water.

The wedding organizer, savoring the richness in his cup, loudly honors the bridegroom. "Everyone sets out the good wine first, and then, when people have become drunk, he sets out the cheaper wine. But you have kept the good wine until now."

The guests shout their approval, and the party continues. Only a handful of people see Jesus's first sign, but everyone at the wedding enjoys his gift. The prophet Amos predicted the Messiah's coming would be heralded by an abundance of wine in the land—"New wine will drip from the mountains and flow from all the hills"—and on this day a small village in Galilee has gotten a foretaste of that new wine and learned about a God who saves the best for last.

When the wedding celebration ends, Jesus invites his mother and brothers to travel to the lake with him and his new followers. The spring morning is pleasant, the road slopes gently downhill, and they make the sixteen-mile walk to Capernaum easily in a day.

Andrew, Simon, and John reunite with their families and tell them how the Baptist led them to Jesus and what happened in Cana. No one believes the wild story about water becoming wine, but the young fishermen know what they saw and tasted.

The teacher from Nazareth intrigues the men, and none of them are ready to return to their nets. Besides, it's time for Passover and the Feast of Unleavened Bread—eight of the most sacred days on the Jewish calendar. Jesus has announced he will be attending the festival, and his five followers can't wait to see what will happen. If water was turned into wine for an unimportant party in an out-of-the-way place like Cana, what might happen at one of the most important holidays of the year with the entire nation watching?

# 3

# THE FIRST PASSOVER

SPRING–SUMMER, AD 30

*Behold, I am sending my messenger to clear a path before me. Then the Lord whom you seek will suddenly come to his temple—even the messenger of the covenant in whom you delight—behold, he is coming, says the Lord of hosts. But who can endure the day of his coming, and who can stand when he appears? For he is like a refiner's fire and like a launderer's soap.*

—Malachi 3:1–2

THE MONTH OF Nisan has arrived. The cool rainy season has passed, and wildflowers blanket the land. The rose of Sharon mentioned in the Song of Solomon covers the sandy coastal plains, and the hills are speckled with brightly colored anemones, irises, and daffodils. Solomon described it as the season when "the flowers appear on the earth, the time of singing has come, and the voice of the turtledove is heard in our land."

Nature's time of renewal and rebirth also signals the start of the festival season. *Hag ha Pesah*, celebrated on Nisan 14, is followed by the weeklong *Hag ha Matzot*. Both commemorate the night Israel was liberated from slavery by the blood of a lamb.

The Law no longer requires the physical presence of every adult Jewish male, but all devout Jews want to be in Jerusalem for the Passover. Ships from faraway lands bring thousands into the ports of Caesarea,

Joppa, Ptolemais, and Dora. Caravans of boisterous pilgrims singing the Psalms of Ascent throng the roads to the capital.

By the second week of Nisan, Jerusalem is overflowing, and a large tent city has appeared on the plain outside the northern gates. Thousands of sheep and cattle dot the hillsides. Jerusalem, normally a city of 30,000, swells to a population of more than 150,000 during the feasts, creating major problems for those seeking food and lodging.

Preparation begins several weeks before the festival—roads to the city are repaired, bridges are reinforced, tombs near walkways are whitewashed so that pilgrims will not accidentally defile themselves, homes are scoured and scrubbed, food and drink reserves are set aside, and everything possible is done to beautify Jerusalem and the surrounding valleys for the eight-day commemoration.

For young men who travel light, Jerusalem is less than a four-day walk from Capernaum. Like most Jews coming from the north, Jesus and his new followers take the road along the Jordan. They arrive in Jericho in three days, and early the next morning they make the strenuous seven-hour climb up the Ascent of Adumim. The grade is steep, but the men are looking forward to the festival, and the hours pass quickly. By noon, the red hills are clothed in green. Soon after passing Bethany, they crest the Mount of Olives and get their first view of the holy city lying three hundred feet below them.

In the afternoon sun, Jerusalem, built of the same tawny limestone it rests upon, has the appearance of a rumpled old lion skin draped over four hills. The nearest hill, just across the Kidron Valley, is Mount Moriah. Purchased centuries ago by King David to be the site of a house dedicated to God, the original temple has been destroyed, but in its place is the ambitious building project of Herod the Great. What Ezra once described as an "open square before the house of God" is now twice that size—a massive thirty-seven-acre plaza enclosed by tall colonnaded porches.

Within an hour Jesus and his companions are standing on the temple mount in the Court of the Gentiles. Tables have been set up under one of the stoas to accommodate the money changers, who convert currency to the only coinage acceptable for the yearly temple tax—Tyrean shekels and half-shekels, chosen for their purity of silver. Each year the money changers are allowed to open for business a month before Passover in towns throughout Israel, and twenty days before the feast they are permitted to trade on the temple grounds.

Nearby are the stalls of the animal merchants. Stacked around the columns are cages filled with doves and pigeons. Livestock pens spill out into the plaza. The stench of fresh manure mingles with the aroma of frankincense and myrrh wafting down from the inner courts. Those in need of a sacrifice move from pen to pen in search of value, while the vendors extol the quality of their livestock.

In the past, the animal merchants were located under the trees east of town in the Kidron Valley. Viewed from one perspective, allowing the merchants and money changers into the temple precincts provides a convenient service for those attending the festival. Bringing an animal a long distance is difficult, and if it is deemed blemished, the expense and effort has been wasted. Thus it has become more pragmatic, even for those who live in Jerusalem, to buy the preapproved animals sold at the temple. Over the years, this has come to be seen as a mutually beneficial exchange. God gets an appropriate sacrifice, and the merchants make a nice profit.

Jesus watches the money changers weigh coins and haggle over everything from the weight and purity of the coins being exchanged to the amount of their fee (a surcharge of 4 to 8 percent is customary, the exact amount depending on the skills of the negotiators).

As Jesus takes in the sights, smells, and sounds around him, he reflects on the original purpose of the temple. The house of God was to be set apart for worship, but instead of the sound of prayer, there is the fearful bleating of sheep. Instead of reverent conversations about the greatness of God, there is haggling over mammon.

In his Father's house.

Jesus's new followers notice he is upset but fail to understand why. There is nothing out of the ordinary about this Passover. They are surprised when he walks over to one of the animal stalls, picks up a handful of cords, and twists them into a whip. They are even more surprised to see him take his newly formed scourge into the bazaar and begin overturning tables and opening livestock pens.

As he drives the animals from the stoa, he turns to the sellers of doves and gestures toward their cages. "Take these away!" he commands. "Do not turn my Father's house into a market!"

The Roman troops stationed in the Antonia Fortress overlooking the temple grounds notice the disturbance but assume it's just another religious squabble between rival Jewish sects. Since only a small area of the immense people-filled plaza is being disrupted, the soldiers ignore it.

In the courtyard, the money changers are scrabbling across the pavement and arguing violently over the gold and silver strewn on the ground. The merchants look helplessly at the temple police and wonder why the trouble-maker isn't being arrested. Yet the policemen, all Levites, hear Jesus calling the temple "my Father's house" and realize this is no ordinary agitator. They turn to the Sadducee priests, who provide oversight for the market.

The priests scowl at Jesus but do not give the order to arrest him. This is not the first time they have been opposed by those who believe the temple should be set apart solely for the worship of God. They have no interest in that debate. Rather than addressing Jesus's accusation, they challenge his authority to interfere with God's ordained leadership. "What sign do you show us for doing these things?" they demand.

Ironically, they ask for exactly what Jesus has just given them, so he gives them an even more obscure sign. "Destroy this temple," Jesus says, "and in three days I will raise it up."

The Jewish leaders scoff. "It has taken forty-six years to build this temple, and will you raise it up in three days?"

Jesus answers by turning and walking away.

The temple officials fume as they watch Jesus disappear into the crowd. The Galilean has attacked the financial machinery of the religious festival structure, and few threats are taken more seriously. The temple provides oversight and funding for every aspect of Jewish culture. Politics, religion, and law are virtually inseparable in the Jewish world, and Jesus has come to the center of that world during one of the biggest festivals and made a loud and symbolic protest. Property has been damaged, money has been scattered, and animals have been turned out into the streets. What Jesus has done isn't merely disrespect-ful—it's a major offense against the entire system.

Within hours the seventy members of the Great Sanhedrin gather to discuss how to deal with the false prophet. The ruling council is a diverse meld of aristocratic Sadducee priests, influential city elders, and ultraorthodox Pharisees, many of whom are lawyers and scholars known as scribes. Though severely limited in power by Rome, the Sanhedrin exerts tremendous influence over religious Jews, especially in Jerusalem.

After a heated discussion, all the councilmen are agreed that Jesus had no authority to do what he did, and all are agreed that his boast about being able to rebuild the temple in three days is absurd, but they are divided about the action he took with the money changers and animal merchants. The Sadducees reject Jesus's charge that the temple is being defiled; they are confident the bazaar is a blessing to both themselves and the people who buy there. Some of the Pharisees, however, are sympathetic. They, too, must pass the marketplace on their way to the temple. They, too, hear the frightened cries of the animals and the haggling over money. They, too, smell the manure. While none are willing to voice support for Jesus, some in the Sanhedrin secretly admire what the young man has done.

THE SEVEN-DAY FEAST of Unleavened Bread follows the Day of Passover. Jesus spends the week in the temple plaza, preaching to large crowds. Many praise him, but Jesus knows their flattery is insincere. Scribes and priests also regularly listen in; some come solely to gather evidence against him, but others come to hear what he has to say about God.

Among the curious is a scribe named Nicodemus. He is intrigued by Jesus's message and wants to hear more, but the temple mount is not the place for a high-ranking member of the Sanhedrin to have a conversation with an out-of-favor itinerant preacher. Still, there is something about Jesus that fascinates Nicodemus, and one evening he arranges a private meeting.

Wanting Jesus to know he is a potential friend, Nicodemus says, "Rabbi, we know you are a teacher come from God, for no one can do these signs that you do unless God is with him."

Jesus looks into the learned Pharisee's eyes and says, "Truly, truly I tell you, unless one is born again from above, he is not able to see the kingdom of God."

Nicodemus is confused; obviously Jesus is serious, but he speaks in riddles and demands the impossible. "How can a man be born when he is old?" Nicodemus asks. "Can he enter a second time into his mother's womb and be born?"

Jesus replies with an illustration from the Scriptures: "Truly, truly I tell you, unless one is born of water and Spirit, he cannot enter the kingdom of God. That which is born of the flesh is flesh, and that which is born of the Spirit is spirit. Do not be amazed that I said to you, 'You must be born again from above.' The wind blows where it will, and its sound you hear, but you do not know where it comes from or where it goes. So is everyone who is born of the Spirit."

Nicodemus now begins to understand. The prophets have long used water—so precious to those who live in a dry land—to represent the Holy Spirit. The wind is also a common metaphor for the Spirit, but Nicodemus can't make sense of how it all works in everyday life. "How can these things be?" he asks.

Jesus shakes his head and says, "You're the teacher of Israel, and you don't know these things?"

Nicodemus, stung by Jesus's observation, falls silent.

Jesus, knowing his words will eventually find a home in Nicodemus's heart, broadens his admonition to include the Pharisee's fellow Sanhedrists. "Truly, truly I tell you, that which we know, we speak, and that which we've seen, we bear witness to, but you don't receive our testimony. If you don't believe the earthly things I have told you, how will you believe if I tell you the heavenly things? No one has ascended into heaven except the one who descended from heaven, the Son of Man. And as Moses lifted up the serpent in the wilderness, so must the Son of Man be lifted up, so that whoever believes in him may have eternal life."

Nicodemus nods in partial understanding. Jesus is speaking of the brass serpent that saved those who looked to it for deliverance. But who is this son of man he speaks of, and how will he be raised up like the serpent on the pole? By the time their conversation is over and Nicodemus is walking home, his whole world has shifted.

A FEW DAYS later, when the Feast of Unleavened Bread is over, Jesus begins teaching in the many small villages that are suburbs to Jerusalem. Crowds gather everywhere he goes. Those who profess faith in Jesus are pointed to his disciples, who baptize them.

It's an amazing time for the people of Israel, for while Jesus is preaching in the hill towns of Judea, John the Baptist is teaching and baptizing at the springs near the town of Salim. Yet when Jesus begins attracting larger crowds, some of John's disciples grow resentful. The Baptist once was the premier prophet in the land. Now this carpenter from Nazareth, a mere candidate for baptism a few months ago, is eclipsing the master.

The more the Baptist's disciples think about the situation, the more indignant they become. One day they approach John and say, "Rabbi, the one who was with you on the other side of the Jordan, the one you talked about—behold, he is baptizing, and everyone is coming to him!"

John understands their bitterness. They remember when Jesus was a nobody from nowhere. They were surprised when John called Jesus the Lamb of God and encouraged them to give him their allegiance. A few Galilean fishermen had responded, but most chose to stay with the Baptist. They preferred a prophet to a lamb.

John knows that those who complain have never really understood his role. "A person cannot receive anything unless it has been given him from heaven," John tells them. "You yourselves can testify that I said, 'I am not the Messiah, but I have been sent ahead of him.' The one who has the bride is the bridegroom, but the friend of the bridegroom who stands and hears him rejoices greatly at the bridegroom's voice. Therefore this joy of mine has been made full."

The Baptist looks into the eyes of his disciples to see if his words are being received. He is delivering the same message he has been preaching for months. He is not here to draw attention to himself—he's here to announce the arrival of the Messiah.

The one they are jealous of is the very one for whom he came to prepare the way. John hopes the analogy helps them better understand his part in God's plan. The friend of the groom assures the wedding gets off to the right start—an important but limited role. John knows what his disciples want to hear, and his next words don't come easily. "Jesus must increase," he tells them, "but I must decrease."

John's followers are shocked to hear how resigned their master is to his dwindling popularity, but soon they have a greater concern. The Baptist's preaching has created powerful enemies, and one of the deadliest is Herodias, granddaughter of Herod the Great, and niece and new wife of Herod Antipas. She had once been married to his half-brother, Herod Phillip, but after a torrid affair with Antipas in Rome, she divorced Phillip and moved into his brother's palace in Galilee.

John is publicly denouncing the union. He will not pretend it is anything less than legitimized adultery.

Herodias is furious and wants to kill the brash seer, but her husband will not consent. Herod Antipas also wants to put John to death, but he fears public reaction. The people of the land have embraced the Baptist as a prophet from God, and silencing him must be done in a way that does not disturb the Pax Romana.

Antipas decides his best plan of attack is to eliminate the Baptist gradually. He sends his soldiers to the Jordan. John's disciples look on in horror as their master is arrested and unceremoniously taken south to a dungeon in Machaerus. Once little more than a rugged military outpost, the isolated peak is now the easternmost of Herod's renovated fortresses.

Word of John's imprisonment soon spreads throughout the land. The multitudes wonder what Jesus will do about John's arrest. Many are surprised when Jesus makes no strong pronouncements and delivers no ultimatums. Instead, it appears he wants to run from the conflict. He tells his disciples it is time they went back to Galilee.

Jesus knows there will be a day of reckoning, but that confrontation must wait. The Holy Spirit has prompted him to go north, but not by the route Jews prefer. Jesus is to take the road through Samaria.

4

# The God of all Clans

*"At that time," declares the Lord, "I will be the God of all the clans of Israel, and they shall be my people. . . . Again you shall plant vineyards on the mountains of Samaria; the planters shall plant and shall enjoy the fruit."*

—Jeremiah 31:1, 5

NINE HUNDRED YEARS before Jesus's birth, the hill country of Samaria was the heart of the northern kingdom of Israel. The once illustrious Way of the Patriarchs, the primary north-south highway in Israel, bisects the region. Father Abraham had travelled it, and near Shechem had been promised by God, "To your seed I will give this land." His grandson Jacob had not only travelled the road, he had owned the land. Then Jacob, renamed Israel, had given the land to his son Joseph.

Those were glorious days, but they are long past. Today the name of this region is spoken as a curse, if it is spoken at all. Pious Jews avoid even passing through it. Still, the highway through Samaria is the shortest route between Galilee and Jerusalem, and Jews often take the road despite their racial and religious bigotry.

It is a prejudice centuries in the making. After Solomon's death, the nation was divided. Jerusalem became the capital of the southern kingdom of Judah, and the city of Samaria became the capital of the northern kingdom of Israel. Neither was faithful to God, but the evil done in the northern kingdom by rulers like Ahab and Jezebel led Judah to sever all ties with Israel.

A few generations later, Assyria conquered the northern kingdom. Following their general conquest policy, the Assyrians deported all but the poorest Israelites. Their homes were given to refugees from other defeated territories: people from Babylon, Cuthah, Avva, Hamath, and Sepharvaim. The new residents brought their religious practices with them. A particularly grim ritual was central to the religion of the people of Sepharvaim. They worshipped a Babylonian sun god named Adrammelech and his consort, Anammelech—goddess of the moon. This couple, like their companion god, Molech, required child sacrifice. For a time, the land once home to Jacob and Joseph became home to dark lords who demanded babies as burnt offerings.

The Israelites who remained in the land ignored God's prohibition against marrying outside the faith, and within a few generations they were assimilated. These new people became known as Samaritans. In deference to the god of the land, they adopted the trappings of Judaism, and when Ezra and the Jews were allowed to return from exile to rebuild the temple, a number of Samaritans volunteered to help. When the Jews rejected their offer, the Samaritans built a temple on Mount Gerizim and discarded the writings of every forefather who had been sympathetic toward Jerusalem. The words of Samuel, David, and Solomon were stricken from their Scriptures, as were the prophets and chronicles of the kings. Ultimately only the Torah survived—Genesis, Exodus, Leviticus, Deuteronomy, and Numbers became the Samaritan Bible.

For centuries the hatred between the Jews and Samaritans simmered, occasionally erupting in bloodshed. When the Maccabean revolt freed Judea from Greek rule, the Jewish leader John Hyrcanus destroyed the city of Shechem and burned the temple on Mount Gerizim to the ground. This did not stop the Samaritans from worshipping on Gerizim, nor did it stop them from retaliating whenever the opportunity provided itself.

One Passover when Jesus was a boy, Samaritan grave robbers crept around the temple mount and littered it with human bones, rendering the area unusable for worship until ceremonially cleansed. These days the Pax Romana has reduced the violence, but the Jews and Samaritans still despise one another.

Jesus, who has been in Judea since the Passover, is prompted by the Holy Spirit to return to Galilee by way of Samaria. As he walks north, the road falls gently, and the mountains give way to rolling hills. By late morning, the cool air Jesus and his five companions enjoyed at dawn has vanished. They enter the region of Samaria tired, hungry, and thirsty.

At noon they arrive at Jacob's well—a major crossroad. To the west lie the plains of Sharon and the Mediterranean; to the north the road descends into Galilee. A short distance away is the village of Sychar. Peter, Andrew, John, Phillip, and Nathaniel go into town to buy food. Jesus decides to remain at the well and enjoy the lull of midday.

His solitude is interrupted by a lone woman with a water pot. Jesus immediately knows she is no ordinary woman. Otherwise, she would have come in the cool of the day with her neighbors. But the woman walking toward Jesus is not like the other women in town.

She notices a young Jewish man sitting on the well's limestone curb. She is surprised when he doesn't stand and walk away—this is no place for a man and woman to be alone. She approaches cautiously, expecting the man to ignore her, but when she draws near he says, "Give me a drink."

The woman jerks to a stop, and her eyes narrow. "How is it that you, a Jew, ask for a drink from me, a Samaritan woman?"

Jesus understands her confusion but refuses to be drawn into her world. He smiles and says, "If you knew the gift of God, and who it is that is saying to you, 'Give me a drink,' you would have asked him, and he would have given you living water."

The woman is skeptical. Living water—water that comes directly from God via rains and natural springs—is plentiful in Samaria, but she knows every water source near the village. And even if he did know of a secret spring, how could he give her a drink from it? "Sir," she points out, "you have nothing to draw water with, and the well is deep. Where do you get that living water? Are you greater than our father Jacob? He gave us the well and drank from it himself, as did his sons and his live-stock."

Jesus nods and says, "Everyone who drinks this water will thirst again, but whoever drinks the water that I will give him will never thirst again—the water that I will give him will become in him a spring of water gushing up to eternal life."

The woman shakes her head and laughs. "Sir, give me this water, so that I will not be thirsty or have to keep coming here to draw water."

"Go," Jesus says, "call your husband and come here."

The woman blushes, and her gaze falls to the ground. Her reply is just above a whisper. "I have no husband."

She says as little as possible, hoping the Jewish stranger will change the subject. He doesn't. "You're right in saying, 'I have no husband,'" Jesus says, "for you have had five husbands, and the one you have now is not your husband. What you have said is true."

His words are delivered gently and prefaced with praise for her honesty, but they remind her of all the promises made and broken, all the lies and deceit, all the anger and bitterness. And how, after five dead ends, she has given up on the covenant of marriage.

The woman looks into Jesus's eyes, expecting to find condemnation. She sees none. A spark of hope is kindled, but she is uncomfortable talking about her past. Too many memories. She politely attempts to change the subject. "Sir, I can see that you are a prophet. Our ancestors worshiped on this mountain, but you say that people ought to worship in Jerusalem."

Jesus refuses to be drawn into the ancient conflict. For him, it is irrelevant. As he had pointed out to the Jews in Jerusalem, the issue is not where to worship God, but how to worship Him. "Believe me, woman," Jesus says, "the time is coming when you will worship the Father neither on this mountain nor in Jerusalem. You Samaritans worship what you do not know. We worship what we know, for salvation is from the Jews. But the time is coming—indeed it has arrived—when the true worshipers will worship the Father in spirit and truth, for they are the kind of worshipers the Father is seeking. God is spirit, and those who worship Him must worship in spirit and truth."

The woman struggles to understand. The young Jew is speaking of the new age to be ushered in by the Prophet. God had said to Moses, "I will raise up for them a prophet like you from among their brothers, and I will put my words in his mouth, and he shall speak to them all that I command him." Moses then announced to God's people, "The Lord your God will raise up for you a prophet like me from among you, from your brothers—it is to him you shall listen."

The woman is familiar with the promise and longs for the arrival of the Prophet-like-Moses. He is the Messiah (Anointed) to the Jews and the *Taheb* (Restorer) to the Samaritans. The woman's Messiah is not a political or military leader like David but a teacher of righteousness like Moses. "I know that Messiah is coming," she says. "When he comes, he will tell us all things."

Like Nicodemus, the woman "knows" about the Messiah but can't recognize him when he is standing before her. "I am he," Jesus tells her. "The one speaking to you."

The conversation is interrupted by the men returning from town. As the disciples walk toward the well, they are shocked to see their rabbi talking cordially with a woman. History is full of stories about what can come from meetings between men and women at wells. Besides, rabbis are to have little or nothing to do with Samaritan women, all of whom are deemed unclean. "Menstruants from the cradle" is a coarse but popular description.

The woman does not speak or make eye contact with the men. She is lost in her thoughts. Had she met the Taheb? Is it possible the mighty Restorer would take the form of this gentle young man? But why would the Messiah, lord of the entire universe, be concerned about an unimportant person like her? Surely the Prophet had better ways to spend his day. None of it made sense. And yet, the man had told her secrets only God knew.

She is confused about Jesus's identity, but this is news she cannot keep to herself. Leaving her water pot at the well, she runs into Sychar and tells everyone she meets about the Jewish stranger. "Come," she says, "see a man who told me everything I ever did! Can this be the Messiah?"

The townspeople are wary but willing to investigate. A large delegation heads toward Jacob's well.

At the well, the disciples are sitting in the shade drinking cool water and enjoying the bread they bought in the village. One of the men turns to Jesus and says, "Rabbi, eat something."

Immersed in prayer and gazing into Samaria, Jesus says, "I have food to eat that you do not know about."

The men do not understand what he means and ask one another who might have given him food. Jesus interrupts their speculations: "My food is to do the will of the One who sent me and to accomplish His work. Don't you say, 'Four months more and then comes the harvest'? Look, I tell you, lift up your eyes and see that the fields are white for harvest. Even now the reaper receives wages and gathers a crop for eternal life, so that the sower and the reaper may rejoice together. For in this the saying is true, 'One sows and another reaps.' I sent you to reap what you have not worked for. Others have toiled, and you have reaped the benefit of their labor."

Peter, Andrew, John, Philip, and Nathaniel are familiar with the proverb about sowing and reaping, but Jesus has turned it upside down. The saying is derived from the common farming practice of hiring planters in the spring and harvesters in the fall. Those who plant do not see the fruit of their labors. Jesus says things are different in the kingdom of God. Here both sower and reaper experience joy because they share in the same blessing. There is no need to wait four months to see the fruit, Jesus says, because this is a radically different kind of farming. Kingdom agriculture is described in the Book of Amos: "'Behold, the days are coming,' declares the Lord, 'when the plowman will overtake the reaper and the treader of grapes him who sows the seed; the mountains will drip sweet wine, and all the hills will flow with it.'"

Jesus, like Amos, speaks of the time when Israel will be so prosperous that blessings will overlap one another. And Jesus says that time has already begun. It is, in his words, the time "to do the will of the One who sent me and to accomplish His work." And any doubt about what Jesus is speaking of disappears when the disciples see a large group of white-clad Samaritans walking toward them through the fields. Jesus greets them with a warm smile and begins teaching them.

Jesus's companions are amazed at the openness of the Samaritans to the Word of God, and they begin to understand what Jesus meant about the fields being ready to harvest immediately after being sown. Jesus spends two days proclaiming the good news to the Samaritans, and many put their faith in him, convinced that the long-awaited Taheb has come to his people in Samaria.

# 5

# GALILEE OF THE GENTILES

AUTUMN–WINTER, AD 30

*There will be a time in the future when Galilee of the Gentiles, which
lies along the road that runs between the Jordan and the sea, will be
filled with glory. The people who walk in darkness will see a great
light. For those who live in a land of deep darkness, a light will shine.*

—Isaiah 9:1–2, NLT

GALILEE IS THE northern border of Israel. In the days of Joshua, the region
was known as Galil Haggoyim because it was geographically *galil* (encircled)
by *goyim* (Gentiles). Nine hundred years ago, King Solomon was indebted to
King Hiram of Tyre and offered him twenty cities in Galilee as payment.
Hiram surveyed the land and told Solomon he deemed it worthless.

Many in Judea today would agree. They believe the foreign influ-
ences in Galilee produce Jews who are either liberals or revolutionaries.
The Romans, who have quelled several disturbances in the region over
the decades, are also suspicious of Galileans.

In truth, most of the people of Galil Haggoyim are faithful to God.
They study the Scriptures and teach them to their children. They keep
the Sabbath. They attend the festivals in Jerusalem. They live according
to the Law of Moses.

Tales of Jesus's exploits in Judea reach the hills of Galilee long before he
arrives. He travels slowly through the towns west of the lake preaching a

simple message: "The time has been fulfilled! The kingdom of God is near—repent and trust in the good news."

Jesus eventually arrives in Cana. A large crowd gathers and he begins teaching. A government official who works for Herod Antipas pushes through the throng. His voice quivers as he pleads with Jesus to return with him to Capernaum and heal his dying child.

The crowd listens carefully to the request, but Jesus knows they are more interested in his miracles than his message. He looks into the faces surrounding him and says, "Unless you see signs and wonders, you will not believe."

The Herodian official is desperate. "Sir," he begs, "come down before my child dies."

Jesus looks into the father's fear-filled eyes and says, "Go—your son lives."

The man is stunned by Jesus's confident pronouncement. His child is twenty miles away. Healings from that distance are unheard of, but the official believes that somehow Jesus has cured his son. He immediately sets off for home and walks until darkness forces him to stop. He continues at first light, and when he nears Capernaum, his servants greet him with good news—his son has made a miraculous recovery. The man asks a few questions and determines that the boy's health improved at the exact time Jesus pronounced him well.

Everyone in Capernaum knows about the healing of the Herodian official's son by the time Jesus arrives a few days later. The townspeople are excited to learn that the visiting teacher will be preaching at the synagogue, but Jesus has not come to visit—he plans to make Capernaum his home.

Built on a rich alluvial plain six hundred feet below sea level, Capernaum is a small but busy city on the north shore of Lake Gennesaret. Her thousand or so residents enjoy warm winters and long summers. Farmers plant and harvest a wide variety of crops ten months of the year, and as good as the farming is, the fishing is even better. Two miles west of town is the small cove of Tabgha. Warm mineral springs enter the lake here, creating plankton that draws large schools of *musht* (tilapia) in the cooler months.

Capernaum also benefits from its strategic location near the eastern frontier of Herod Antipas's tetrarchy (his half-brother, Herod Philip, rules the region east of the Jordan). Antipas has set up customs stations to tax everything that crosses the border and comes in from the lake. Taxes are also levied on merchants transporting goods on the ancient highway that skirts the northwestern edge of town. In olden days, it was called the Way of the Sea. Nowadays known by its Latin name, the *Via Maris* is one of the three major trade routes in Israel. It is in constant use by merchants from the west and south traveling across the Mediterranean plain to and from Damascus and the east.

There is a Roman garrison stationed east of Capernaum. The centurion who commands the troops built a synagogue for the city, and his patronage insures a cordial relationship with the city elders. He and his men live in well-appointed quarters that are large enough to include a *caldarium, tepidarium*, and *frigidarium*—a full Roman bath.

Capernaum's location and diverse population of farmers, fishermen, craftsmen, government workers, merchants, and soldiers creates an environment that is wholly Jewish, but with an international ambience.

Not only is Capernaum uniquely situated on the water and a major trade route—it is also visually striking. The city's black basalt construction stands in bold contrast to the blue lake and green hills surrounding it. An eight-foot-wide esplanade runs along the top of the seawall for 2,500 feet; several long piers extend from the walkway to accommodate the many boats that come and go daily. Shops line the waterfront. Broad boulevards radiate north from the lake into neighborhoods of rustic multifamily dwellings made of unhewn lava stone.

The synagogue, built from the same black volcanic rock, stands just behind the shops. Nearby is the large home of Simon Peter and Andrew. The brothers hail from Bethsaida, three miles to the east, but they relocated their families to Capernaum. Like the other residences in town, their home is what the Romans call an *insula*—a walled compound of small rooms clustered around an open courtyard. A narrow exterior stairway leads to the roof—additional living and working space in this climate where winters are mild and summers long and hot.

One morning while Jesus is walking by the lake, he sees two of his sometimes-disciples, Simon Peter and Andrew, fishing from the shore with cast nets. Twenty feet in diameter and weighted with lead, the large net must be thrown in a way that allows it to spread completely on the surface. A cast net is extremely effective, but only in the hands of a skilled fisherman.

Jesus walks over to where they are fishing, and the three men exchange greetings. "Come," Jesus tells them, "follow me, and I will make you fishers of people."

Simon Peter and Andrew are intrigued by Jesus's words. The prophet Jeremiah had spoken about fishers of people, but the context was God's judgment. The Lord promised to "send for many fishers" to catch those who "have polluted My land with the carcasses of their detestable idols, and have filled My inheritance with their abominations."

Simon and Andrew don't fully understand the invitation, but they leave their nets and follow Jesus. They continue down the lakeshore and come upon two more sometimes-disciples. James and John are near the shore in a boat with their father and the fishermen they employ. Jesus gives the sons of Zebedee the same cryptic invitation he gave the sons of Jonah. They immediately stop preparing their nets and make their way to shore, but, like Simon and Andrew, James and John only partially understand Jesus's invitation. How they will become fishers of people is not clear to them.

THE SUN RISES on the seventh day, and the town is quiet. The docks, normally filled with fish and fishermen, stand empty except for a few birds looking for breakfast. The townspeople are in their homes preparing for what is sure to be an exciting day. The new rabbi is preaching this morning.

The synagogue fills to overflowing. The worship service unfolds as usual—the congregation sings psalms and offers prayers, they recite the *Shema,* and there is a reading from the Law and a reading from the Prophets. Jesus then walks to the front, sits, and begins to teach. The audience usually hears messages about the traditions of the elders, but the new teacher has a different approach—the traditions are not even mentioned. Instead, he teaches directly from Scripture.

The people sit spellbound as Jesus proclaims the good news of the kingdom. But then, the message is interrupted by a loud shriek from someone in the audience. A murmur arises when the congregation discovers the frightening noise is coming from one of their neighbors.

The man's body is coiled and tense; his breathing is labored. "Let us alone!" He spits out the words. "What do you want with us, Jesus? Nazarene! Have you come to destroy us? I know who you are—the Holy One of God!"

The crowd gasps and steps back. Jesus is unmoved. He knows it is not the man who is taunting him but an ancient spiritual being who, until now, has been able to work in and through the man undetected. The demon's words are a threat—it says that if Jesus destroys it, the man in its possession will also die.

"Silence!" Jesus commands. "Come out from him!"

The man falls to the ground, writhing in convulsions. The congregation watches, speechless, as the loud cries diminish and the tremors subside. The exorcist walks over and helps the man to his feet. Those who see the expulsion shake their heads in disbelief. They have heard reports of elaborate rituals and incantations that can free a possessed soul, but here is one who can dispatch powerful demons with just a word. And Jesus not only banished the demon—he restored the man to health. "What is this?" they say to one another. "A new teaching—with authority! Even the unclean spirits obey his command."

Jesus walks out of the synagogue and up the street to Simon Peter's home. When he turns in to the courtyard, he is told that Simon's mother-in-law has a dangerously high fever. Jesus enters her room, touches her hand, and offers a word of rebuke to the fever that is similar to the word of rebuke he spoke to the evil spirit in the synagogue. The fever, like the demon, flees. The healing is so complete that she immediately gets up and, after profusely thanking Jesus, begins preparing lunch for them.

Her recovery, like the exorcism, becomes widely known. When the Sabbath ends at sundown and people can resume their normal activities, a crowd gathers at Peter's home. All evening the compound's two courtyards are filled with townspeople seeking healing, and Jesus heals all who come to him.

The new rabbi's fame spreads quickly. He becomes Capernaum's biggest celebrity. Locals brag to visitors about encounters they've had with Jesus, but few know him. Everyone loves to see him perform miracles, but most people ignore his calls to repentance. The crowds grow daily, and soon Jesus is in constant demand.

To prepare himself for the long days of ministry, Jesus often slips into the hills before dawn to pray. One morning he is late returning, and the throng demands that Peter, Andrew, James, and John retrieve him. The men dutifully search for Jesus and find him sitting quietly in prayer. "Everyone is looking for you!" they exclaim.

His disciples do not understand that this is one of the reasons Jesus sought solitude in the first place. "Let's go on to the neighboring towns so I can preach there also," Jesus tells them, "for that is why I came."

The men wonder why Jesus would want to leave Capernaum when things are going so well. When a group of townsfolk who followed the disciples arrive and plead with Jesus to return to Capernaum, he declines. "I must preach the good news of the kingdom of God to the other towns as well, for I was sent for this purpose."


JESUS LEAVES CAPERNAUM and takes his message into the towns and villages of Galilee. Demons are banished. Diseases are cured. The lame walk, the blind see, and the deaf hear.

When Jesus returns a few weeks later, Capernaum is filled with visitors hoping to see the new teacher. The crowds become so large that many are unable to get close enough to hear Jesus speak. One morning, when he is teaching by the lake, Jesus sees two boats sitting idle while their owners—Simon, Andrew, James, and John—clean their nets after a night of fishing. To take advantage of the natural amphitheater created by the water and surrounding hillsides, Jesus asks Simon Peter to row his boat a short distance offshore. The boat is large—more than twenty feet long and designed for a crew of four—but Peter skillfully maneuvers it to a place where the acoustics will allow the multitude to hear the message.

Jesus encourages his audience to change the way they think and to trust in God rather than in their own cleverness. The people are impressed by Jesus's teaching, but they can't imagine how they would survive if they depended completely on God. They don't disagree with Jesus's explanation of the Scriptures, but the new rabbi is too extreme in his application. How easy it is for a young single man to promote radical discipleship, but what do you say to your family when the crops fail or you catch no fish? Do you ask them to eat empty promises?

Words will never answer those kinds of questions, and Jesus doesn't try. Instead, he turns to Simon Peter and says, "Launch out into the deep and let down your nets for a catch."

To a professional fisherman, the request is absurd. Everyone knows fishing in the deep is done at night when the fish feed. During the day the fish in the deep hide under rocks, safe from nets. And even if there were fish in the deep, in the daylight they could see the layered net and easily avoid it. Simon has fished this lake his entire life. There is simply no value in going into the deep during the day with this kind of net. A cast net would work, but only in the shallows. A dragnet would work in the deep if there were enough men to pull it in, but the only net on board is the trammel.

The expert fisherman is blunt. "Master, we've worked hard all night and haven't caught anything."

Simon pauses, hoping for sympathy. Jesus does not reply, and Simon continues, "But at your word, I will let the nets down."

Simon rows toward the deep. James and John are surprised to see their partner going out again, and even more surprised when he beckons them to follow. John and James look at each other. They are being invited to go fishing in the wrong part of the lake at the wrong time of day with the wrong kind of net. The sons of Zebedee shake their heads, but they launch their boat and follow.

The lake bottom drops steeply. Simon is soon laying his net in deep water. James and John are surprised to see their partner's boat begin to list as the net is being set. The trammel net Simon Peter is extending is actually a compound of three nets; fish easily swim through a coarsely woven net, then into a fine mesh net, and then into another coarse net, forming a pocket. When the fish try to escape, they become hopelessly entangled in the three nets.

It is a wonderfully effective method for catching fish, but the net now trails behind them for hundreds of feet, and loud groans from the boat's timbers tell Simon they are in real danger—the fish can only be disentangled by hand, a slow process, and his boat will soon be pulled under by the weight gathering in the net.

He frantically motions to James and John. They quickly row over and begin pulling fish into their boat, but the net is so full that both boats nearly sink. By the time the net is out of the water, the boats are overflowing with fish and just above the waterline.

The object lesson has a profound effect on the fishermen, and particularly Simon Peter. He falls at Jesus's feet. "Go away from me, Lord, for I am a sinful man!"

Centuries earlier when God called Isaiah to be His spokesperson, Isaiah confessed he was an unclean man with unclean lips. Nevertheless, his response to God's call was, "Here I am Lord—send me." Jesus looks into Simon Peter's heart and sees the same willingness and zeal he saw in Isaiah. "Do not be afraid," Jesus tells him. "From now on you will be catching people."

Peter, Andrew, James, and John abandon their fishing careers and become full-time apprentices of Jesus. The profit from the two boat-loads of fish will be tremendous, and the monies will allow the men to provide for their families while they are away. Father Zebedee will oversee the fishing business. From this day forward, Peter, Andrew, John, and James have a new vocation: fishing for souls.

6

# Authority

*"Anyone who chooses to do the will of God will know whether my
teaching is from God or whether I am speaking on my own authority."*

—John 7:17

THE FIRST YEAR of Jesus's ministry draws to a close. He has spent most
of it in the two hundred small villages that dot the hills of Galilee. One
afternoon while walking between towns, Jesus and his four apprentices
are accosted by a leper.

Peter, Andrew, James, and John fall back in fright. No malady is
more feared by the Jews. Because leprosy is highly contagious, it is painful not only physically but socially as well. The Torah demands that
anyone who is afflicted with the disease be "set outside the camp." A
leper must "wear torn clothes, the hair of his head disheveled, and he
shall cover his mouth and cry out, 'Unclean, unclean.'"

These are only a few of the restrictions placed upon lepers. Con-
tracting leprosy means rapidly declining health, constant pain, no
family, no friends, no home, and exclusion from the community. Leprosy is essentially a living death sentence. Anyone who touches or comes
near a leper becomes ceremonially unclean and must go through the
same seven-day purification rites prescribed for those who come in contact with a corpse.

Lepers are treated as the living dead because people assume that leprosy is divine retribution. The story of God's punishment of Miriam is well known and often cited. People don't talk about being healed of leprosy; they speak of being cleansed, in the same manner one is cleansed of sin.

The man groveling at Jesus's feet pleads, "Lord, if you are willing, you can make me clean."

The leper believes Jesus has the power to make him whole, but he questions Jesus's willingness. Like his fellow Jews, the leper is more inclined to expect God's judgment than His mercy.

Jesus stoops to the ground and gently places his hands upon the ulcerated body prostrated before him. "I am willing," Jesus says. "Be cleansed."

The leper's eyes grow wide as he watches the oozing white sores that cover his body dry up and vanish.

The disciples are awed and confused. They believe only God can cure leprosy—but Jesus had not said, "God is willing." He said, "I am willing."

Jesus, who knows the heart of everyone he meets, knows the man he healed is ready to tell the world about his miraculous restoration. Jesus gives him a stern directive: "See that you say nothing to anyone, but go, show yourself to the priest, and make the offering that Moses commanded, as proof to them."

The man is told to follow the two-stage procedure outlined in the Torah. The ceremonial cleansing begins with a thorough physical examination by a priest. If there is no sign of the disease, two birds are presented as an offering to God. The person being cleansed sacrifices one of the birds. The living bird is then dipped in the blood of one slain. The priest sprinkles blood on the supplicant seven times and releases the bird that was washed in the blood.

The process is completed eight days later at the temple when the priest presents a guilt offering, sin offering, burnt offering, and grain offering on behalf of the supplicant. The four atonement rituals are rich in imagery that Jesus wants the man to grasp. The sacrifices have never been about the animals—they represent the person making the offering.

Jesus demands full obedience to the Mosaic Law for two reasons. The man will learn and experience the deeper significance of the rituals, and others will see God at work—particularly the priest who examines him.

The man healed of leprosy nods his head in agreement and departs, but he disobeys Jesus's instructions to tell only the priest. He shares his story with anyone who will listen. The multitudes coming to hear Jesus grow so large that he is forced to bypass the towns and preach in remote areas by the lake and on hillsides.

WHEN THE RAINY season arrives, Jesus goes home to Capernaum. Word of his return spreads quickly. Especially interested in the news is a group of men with a paralyzed friend. Doctors have been unable to help, but the men believe Jesus can heal him. They put their friend on a stretcher and walk toward the residence where Jesus is teaching, but when they draw near, the men realize they've underestimated Jesus's popularity. The insula is overflowing, and the crowd is spilling into the street. There's not enough room in the doorway for even a child to enter.

The men are discouraged but determined. They look around for an alternate entry and notice an exterior stairway to the rooftop.

Roofs in Capernaum are flat and supported by large wooden beams that span unmortared lava stone walls. The beams are interlaced with smaller poles and thatched with straw and reeds. Several inches of moist clay follow. The clay bakes in the sun and is compacted with a roof roller. The deck becomes an additional living and working space—a second story in the open air.

The men look from the congested street to the empty rooftop and have an idea. They find some rope and carry their friend up the stairway.

Jesus and a few of his disciples are in a room filled with townspeople and a large group of religious scholars who have come from throughout Judea and Galilee to investigate Jesus and condemn him as a false prophet. Jesus knows why the scribes are there, but he graciously responds to all their questions.

The discussion is interrupted when small pieces of dirt begin falling from the ceiling. Soon large clods of clay are raining down. The conversation ceases, and everyone stares at the rift widening above them. Hands are seen frantically removing thatch. An anguished face appears in the opening. He sees Jesus, and the men tear even harder at the sod. The reason for the demolition soon becomes clear—a stretcher is slowly lowered through the breach. The room grows quiet as a man whose body is twisted by paralysis comes to rest at the feet of Jesus.

Jesus smiles as he looks into the eyes of the paralytic and then up into the faces of his friends. The lawyers from Jerusalem approach faith as knowledge to be gained; the paralytic and his friends understand faith to be an active demonstration of trust.

But the men's faith doesn't prepare them for what happens next. Jesus says to the paralytic, "Be encouraged, child. Your sins are forgiven."

Jesus does not reply to the request for physical healing. Instead, he responds to the man's most urgent need. Unforgiven sin is far worse than the inability to walk, and Jesus knows the deeper truth—all suffering is rooted in humanity's separation from God.

The scribes are furious. "Why is this man speaking this way?" they murmur. "He is blaspheming. Who can forgive sins but God alone?"

The religious scholars believe Jesus is guilty of blaspheming God, an offense punishable by death under Mosaic Law. To blaspheme someone is to slander them. The lawyers think Jesus has slandered God by circumventing the only authorized method of forgiveness—securing God's pardon requires a priest and an appropriate sacrifice at the temple.

"Why do you harbor evil thoughts in your hearts?" Jesus asks. "Which is easier—to say, 'Your sins are forgiven,' or to say, 'Stand up and walk'? But so that you may know that the Son of Man has authority on earth to forgive sins . . . ." Jesus pauses and turns to the paralytic. "I say to you, rise. Take your mat and go home."

The man stands, picks up his mat, and walks out the door. Fear grips the room. One of the townspeople says, "We've never seen anything like this!" Another nods in agreement. "We've seen amazing things today."

Everyone in the audience is awestruck, but not everyone is praising God. Some are angry. They cannot understand how a blasphemer could perform such a miracle. The scribes are convinced that not even the Messiah will be able to forgive sins—only God can do that. Who is this son of man the Galilean claims has the authority to forgive sins?

JESUS DOES NOT stay to answer their questions. He makes his way out of the room, through the courtyard, and into the street. He walks south a few blocks to the international highway that skirts the town. A customs station is located here to collect taxes from fishermen coming in from the lake and merchants transporting goods on the Via Maris. The lucrative confluence of borders, waterways, and an international trade route requires several customs agents.

Tax collecting, introduced three centuries earlier by Ptolemy II, is part of a complicated system that ultimately demands nearly thirty percent of a working person's income.

There are two direct taxes: a land tax that is paid in grain at harvest and a poll tax that requires a regular census. These levies go directly to Rome, but the taxpayers tolerate them. People understand that building and maintaining roads, aqueducts, and a social infrastructure requires money.

There are also indirect taxes that vary by region. In Jerusalem, there are house levies and sales taxes. In Galilee, there are transportation tolls and fishing tariffs. These indirect taxes provide numerous opportunities for graft because corruption and bribery are built into the system. At the top is an emperor who wants peace in his empire and an uninterrupted supply of grain and tribute. He awards oversight of the tax collection to savvy individuals who convince him they can keep both the peace and the money coming in.

Once upon a time in Israel that person was the Edomite-turned-Jew—Herod. Before the client-king died, he obtained Caesar's permission to divide his kingdom among three of his sons. That was thirty years ago. His son Antipas has maintained the peace in Galilee and Perea. His son Philip has kept Gaulanitis, Trachonitis, Batanea, and Paneas quiet and prosperous. Herod's eldest son, Archelaus, was given the prized territories of Judea, Samaria, and Idumea. He was unable to maintain the Pax Romana, and in the tenth year of his reign he was stripped of his tetrarchy and exiled to Gaul.

Since then, governance of southern Israel has passed to the proconsul of Syria, but he and his troops are in Damascus, far to the north. To insure the Pax Romana in the south, a large military force is garrisoned on the coast at Caesarea Maritima. The troops are under the authority of a prefect—a civilian appointed by the emperor from the lower order of Roman aristocracy. Judea has been a notoriously difficult area to govern and has had five prefects in twenty years. The latest is a no-nonsense Italian of the Equestrian order named Pontius Pilate.

The Romans are aware of Jewish prejudice against Gentiles and never personally engage in the collection of taxes. In Judea, that responsibility is awarded to affluent members of the Sanhedrin, who then subcontract smaller areas to the highest bidders. The process is similar in the regions governed by Herod Antipas and Herod Phillip. Massive wealth is generated by leasing toll stations to affluent tax farmers.

The tax farmers hire subordinates to do the actual collecting. The customs agent is the lowest rung of the tax system, and thus its public face. Agents always work in the region they were recruited from; familiarity with the terrain and people assures a more comprehensive taxation.

The amount levied on merchants depends on the avarice of the taxman and the charm of the merchant. To the public, stopping people in the road, rifling through their belongings, and demanding money appears to be little more than government-sanctioned robbery. The fact that several tax offices are located along the same road, each demanding a different toll for the same goods, adds to the perception.

Moreover, because customs agents are required to come in contact with Gentiles and work on the Sabbath, they are considered unclean. Their status in the community is comparable to that of a thief or a money changer. Because a tax collector is unclean, he is excommunicated from the synagogue. Because he has no credibility in the community, he is barred from being a witness in court. He may be wealthy and have a home in the heart of the city, but culturally he is outside the camp.

The job demands a high price socially, but it pays well, and there are always people willing to trade a good reputation for a good-paying job.

Matthew Levi, sitting at his station in the Via Maris tax office, is just such a man.

Lately, however, Matthew has been rethinking not only his career choice but his entire life. He had been in the audience one day when Jesus preached about the kingdom of heaven. When Jesus said that God's grace extends even to outsiders, Matthew had felt something shift in his spirit, and he turned back to the God he had abandoned. Now Matthew comes to work each day wondering if the Lord might have any use for someone who traded his birthright for a bowl of porridge.

Matthew sees Jesus approaching and assumes he is on his way to the lake, but Jesus doesn't take his usual route. He walks up to the customs booth and tells the tax collector, "Follow me."

These are words an outsider would never expect to hear from a rabbi. Matthew is not even sure he heard the teacher correctly, but the look in Jesus's eyes tells him the invitation is sincere.

Matthew has a choice. He can remain a tax collector and serve God as best he can within the limitations of his job. He knows the teacher would not fault him for that. Like John the Baptist, Jesus has no problem with customs agents becoming his apprentices. What's important, Jesus says, is to be just and exercise integrity, whatever your job.

Matthew Levi, however, is struggling with something more significant than his livelihood—he's wrestling with his identity. He knows Jesus is offering him a new life, but the new life will require him to abandon his old one. For Matthew, it is no longer a difficult choice. He immediately resigns his position and becomes an apprentice of Jesus.

Soon the entire city is talking about Jesus inviting a tax collector to be his disciple. The religious leaders are convinced that being clean requires one to disassociate himself from sinners. Jesus disagrees. He believes the Scriptures describe a God who is so identified with sinners that the Messiah himself will be "numbered with the transgressors."

The upcoming feast in Jerusalem will provide an opportunity for that numbering to begin in earnest.

# 7

# LORD OF THE SABBATH

SPRING, AD 31

*"I will raise up for them a prophet like you from among their fellow Israelites, and I will put My words in his mouth. He will tell them everything I command him. Whoever refuses to listen to the words that prophet speaks in My name will answer to Me."*

—Deuteronomy 18:18–19

THE ANNUAL FEASTS that commemorate God's mighty acts are central to life in Israel. They are more than celebrations of God's grace; they are affirmations of the covenant He made with His people. When the people act out the prescribed liturgies of the various festivals, they are not simply remembering the event—in a sense, they are participating in it, declaring anew their identity as God's chosen people.

All the holy days are special, and some, like Passover and Tabernacles, are extra special, but none have the honor of being Israel's holiest day. That day does not come annually but weekly. Sabbath will forever be the most sacred day on the Jewish calendar. A hedge of laws and traditions protect it, and woe be to anyone who violates even the least of them.

Jesus is in Jerusalem for one of the feasts and is walking north of the temple plaza near the twin pools known singularly as the Pool of Bethesda. The religious elite never come here—too many unclean sinners—but the pools are popular with the sick and afflicted. Many believe that when the water stirs, it has the power to heal. This belief is rarely spoken of in public because the religious authorities condemn it, but the many infirm who gather daily near the waters cling to the superstition in hope of a cure.

Jesus winds his way through the crowd to the covered colonnades surrounding the pools. Hundreds of ailing people lie in the shade of the porticos and watch for any movement in the water. Among the sufferers is a dour-faced old man who has been disabled for thirty-eight years. Jesus walks over to where he is lying, stoops down so he can address the man face-to-face, and asks, "Do you want to be healed?"

The invalid's eyes narrow. Perhaps a polite reply will make the naive young man go away. "Sir," he explains, "I have no one to put me into the pool when the water is stirred up, and while I am going, another steps down ahead of me."

The hopeless man's answer doesn't surprise Jesus. Thirty-eight years of misery have taught him to expect little and trust no one. These days, the best he can do is position himself by the water, where he knows he will be unable to help himself.

The invalid's heart is as emaciated as his body. He has no faith in Jesus or anyone else. Jesus looks the shriveled man in the eye. "Get up," he commands. "Pick up your mat and walk."

As the words are spoken, the paralytic's legs, long atrophied into helpless twigs, begin to swell as new muscle and sinew forms. Energy courses through his body, and somehow, after thirty-eight years, he is able to stand. Those who are nearby gasp in disbelief.

The healed man is dumbfounded. He has spent almost four decades lying in the dust. He rolls up his straw mat and walks away from the pool. His first steps are awkward and unsure, but soon he is striding toward the stairs leading to the temple mount. He only goes a short distance before someone shouts, "It's the Sabbath, and it's not lawful for you to carry your mat."

Like many of the Sabbath traditions, the restriction concerning moving something "from one domain to another" began as an attempt to honor the Sabbath but devolved into legalism. Many feel the Sabbath laws are too restrictive, but no one is willing to challenge the traditions.

The man immediately stops and drops his bedroll. He had been so distracted that he had not realized the healer had commanded him to do something unlawful. The last thing the man wants is trouble with the authorities, and he knows how he can deflect their attention. "The man who healed me—he told me, 'Pick up your mat and walk.'"

This news shifts the interrogator's interest to the one guilty of the more grievous sin of enticing others to break the Sabbath. "Who is the man who told you, 'Pick up your mat and walk'?"

The old man confesses that he doesn't know; there had been shouting and confusion, and the physician slipped away unnoticed. The leaders are frustrated. Without a way to identify the healer, they can do nothing but warn the healed man and release him.

The former invalid makes his way to the temple mount and mingles with the thousands of pilgrims there for the feast. Surrounded by strangers, he immerses himself in the celebration.

Seemingly from nowhere Jesus walks up and says, "Behold—you are well. Stop sinning so that nothing worse happens to you."

The old man is stung by the implication. The healer somehow knows his long-kept secret—all his years of misery were self-inflicted, caused by sinful choices he alone had made. The "worse" he's being warned of is God's condemnation. The man becomes indignant and thinks this is quite a pronouncement from someone who himself is guilty of breaking God's laws. He excuses himself and hurries away to inform the authorities that he has learned the identity of the miracle-worker.

The religious leaders immediately recognize the name. The scribes find Jesus teaching in the plaza and begin persecuting him for violating the Sabbath.

"My Father is always working," Jesus tells them, "and I too am working."

The temple authorities bristle. The Galilean's presumption in calling God his father is shocking enough, but by claiming to work alongside God, he makes himself equal with God. The charge of undermining the Sabbath has now been eclipsed by a graver allegation: the charge of blasphemy.

Instead of tactfully meeting their objections, Jesus makes an even more alarming claim: "Truly, truly, I tell you, the Son can do nothing on his own, but only what he sees the Father doing—whatever the Father does, the Son also does. The Father loves the Son and shows him everything He is doing, and He will show him greater works than these, so that you will be amazed. For just as the Father raises the dead and gives them life, so also the Son gives life to whomever he wishes. The Father judges no one, but has given all judgment to the Son, so that all may honor the Son just as they honor the Father. Whoever does not honor the Son does not honor the Father who sent him.

"Truly, truly, I tell you, whoever hears my word and believes Him who sent me has eternal life and does not come into judgment but has passed from death into life.

"Truly, truly, I tell you that a time is coming—and is now here— when the dead will hear the voice of the Son of God, and those who hear will live. For just as the Father has life in Himself, so He has granted the Son also to have life in himself. And He has given him authority to execute judgment because he is the Son of Man. Do not be amazed at this, for an hour is coming when all who are in their graves will hear his voice and come out—those who have done good to a resurrection of life, and those who have done evil to a resurrection of judgment.

"I can do nothing on my own. As I hear, I judge, and my judgment is just, because I do not seek my own will but the will of Him who sent me."

Jesus pauses and gazes into the surprised faces surrounding him. No prophet has ever made claims like these, and the audience believes that not even the Messiah will have the ability to do the works Jesus says he will do. They understand Jesus to be speaking of having the kind of authority only God has.

Most in the audience reject his words because self-testimony is not considered acceptable. Jesus introduces a second witness: "If I testify on my own behalf, my testimony is not valid. There is another who testifies on my behalf, and I know that the testimony He gives about me is true.

"You sent messengers to John, and he testified to the truth. Not that I receive testimony from a human source, but I say these things so that you may be saved. John was a burning and shining lamp, and for a while you were willing to rejoice in his light, but my testimony is weightier than John's, for the works that the Father has given me to accomplish—the very works that I am doing—testify on my behalf that the Father has sent me. And the Father who sent me has Himself testified on my behalf."

The religious leaders are not being asked to take a blind leap of faith; they are being offered verifiable physical evidence—the testimony of John the Baptist and Jesus's miraculous works. Both speak clearly to his identity. Before their eyes he is doing things only God can do.

Sadly, most in the audience are deaf and blind. Jesus delivers a damning indictment: "You've never heard God's voice or seen His form, and you do not have His word abiding in you because you do not believe the one whom the Father sent. You search the Scriptures because you think that in them you have eternal life, and it is they that testify about me, yet you are unwilling to come to me to have life."

Jesus identifies the fatal mistake the religious authorities make—they worship the Scriptures rather than the one the Scriptures point to.

"I do not accept glory from people," Jesus tells them, "but I know you. I know that you do not have the love of God within you. I have come in my Father's name, and you do not accept me. If another comes in his own name, you will accept him. How can you believe when you accept glory from one another and do not seek the glory that comes from the only God?

"Do not think that I will accuse you before the Father. There is one who accuses you—Moses, in whom you have set your hope—if you believed Moses, you would believe me because he wrote about me. But if you do not believe his writings, how will you believe my words?"

Jesus leaves his question hanging in the air. No one responds, but there is little left to say. Jesus's claims are declarations of deity that leave his audience only two options: they can accept his claims, in which case he is to be worshipped and obeyed, or they can reject them, in which case he is to be branded a false prophet or dismissed as a madman.

THE FESTIVAL ENDS and Jesus returns to Galilee, but his words echo in the temple plaza for weeks. The Jewish leaders condemn him among themselves but say little about him in public. Jesus's popularity precludes any overt action, so they send emissaries to shadow him and collect evidence they can use to discredit him with the multitudes. They are convinced there is only one way to deal with the renegade prophet, and from this day forward the Jewish authorities plot to kill Jesus.

One Sabbath day in the late spring, Jesus and his disciples are walking on a path that separates two grain fields (thousands of acres of barley and wheat are planted in Galilee). Hungry, they pluck a few kernels, gently rub them in their hands to remove the chaff, and eat them. Pharisees who have been spying on them see the infraction and complain to Jesus, "Look, your disciples are doing what is not lawful to do on the Sabbath!"

The Pharisees are not accusing the disciples of stealing grain; Moses had made provision for travelers and the poor to glean from the fields. The accusation is that they worked on the Sabbath. In fact, according to the widely accepted "forty minus one" laws of what constitutes work on the Sabbath, the disciples were guilty of multiple violations: by plucking the grain they were reaping; by rubbing it between their fingers they were threshing; by blowing away the chaff they were winnowing.

Jesus has a different understanding of the Sabbath. Reasoning from the Scriptures, he asks the religious experts, "Haven't you read what David did when he and his companions were hungry, how he went into the house of God and ate the bread of the Presence, which it was not lawful for him or his companions to eat, but only for the priests?"

Jesus knows the Pharisees do not think David or the high priest sinned when they ate the showbread from the tabernacle. They are right about that, but they are mistaken about why there was no sin involved. They believe David was exempted from the Law because of a life-threatening situation. Jesus wants them to see the real reason. The high priest did not give them the bread because he had pity on starving men. This is clear from the account in the writings of Samuel: the priest first asked David if he and his men were ceremonially unclean. If that had been the case, the priest would not have given the holy bread to them no matter how hungry they were. David got the bread for one reason—he was acknowledged as an ambassador of the Lord on a royal mission.

The story of David isn't offered as an excuse but as a precedent. The religionists refuse to see any further than their traditions, and Jesus provides another illustration. "Or haven't you read in the Law how on the Sabbath the priests in the temple desecrate the Sabbath and are guiltless? But I tell you that something greater than the temple is here."

Jesus says that if priests can work on the Sabbath without incurring God's disapproval, so can his disciples. The religious leaders are infuriated, and Jesus rebukes them with the words of the prophet Hosea. "If you had known what this means, 'I want mercy, not sacrifice,' you would not have condemned the guiltless."

Key to Jesus's declaration is the biblical concept of *hesed* (translated "mercy" in Hosea). In the broadest sense, hesed is an active, positive concern for the good of others. Hosea identifies the religious leaders' problem—they are more interested in appearing righteous than in being righteous. Their attitude is shown not only in their lack of compassion but also in their inability to grasp the simplest truths of God's covenant.

Central to the covenant is God's hesed—His "forgiving lovingkindness" toward his people. If God had not adopted this merciful attitude, His covenant with Israel would have been broken by their first sin. By establishing the way of sacrifice, God provided a way for the relationship to continue.

The problem, Jesus says, is that hesed is not a part of these Pharisees' lives. They do not know God's forgiving loving-kindness and can only live within the rigid confines of the law. They are content to sacrifice animals and use Sabbath laws as boundary markers to point out who is in God's favor and who is out.

Jesus wants them to understand that God designed the Sabbath to be a servant, not a taskmaster. "The Sabbath was made for man, not man for the Sabbath," Jesus says. "So the Son of Man is Lord even of the Sabbath."

The Sabbath, according to the Scriptures, belongs to God alone. To claim authority over the Sabbath is akin to claiming equality with God. The religious leaders sense that Jesus is blaspheming, but they are frustrated—the Galilean cleverly couches his words and uses ambiguous phrases like "son of man." He's a sinner, but a wily one.

ON ANOTHER SABBATH, Jesus is teaching in the synagogue, and a man is there whose right hand is withered. The traditions of the elders decree that a physician can only work on the Sabbath when life is threatened; healing a deformed hand could easily be deferred. The Pharisees want to bait Jesus into violating the Sabbath traditions. One of the Pharisees motions toward the man with the paralyzed hand and asks Jesus, "Is it lawful to heal on the Sabbath?"

Jesus looks into their hard faces and smiles. "Which one of you who has a sheep, if it falls into a pit on the Sabbath, will not take hold of it and lift it out? How much more is a human being worth than a sheep? So it is lawful to do good on the Sabbath."

This application goes far beyond the question of what is lawful. Jesus reverses the prohibition and makes it a positive law: whatever is "good" to do is permissible.

The scribes find this a completely unacceptable notion. It leaves too many decisions in the hands of the people. People are like sheep—how would they survive without the Law and the traditions to shepherd them? The religionists are unfamiliar with a God who allows that much freedom; they confer with one another and glare at Jesus.

Jesus turns to the man with the withered hand and says, "Come and stand here."

The disabled man is startled; this is his worst nightmare. It's bad enough that every time he comes to worship and lifts his hands in prayer his fellow congregants can see his gnarled fist and speculate about what sin caused it, but now he is being called to the center of the synagogue to be put on display. The temptation to run away is strong, but the man courageously steps forward. There is something in Jesus's words that gives him hope.

With the man at his side, Jesus turns to the religious experts and poses a twofold question. "I ask you, is it lawful on the Sabbath to do good or to do harm? To save life or to destroy it?"

The first part of his question (whether it is lawful to do good or to do harm) refers to healing the man; the second part of the question (whether it is lawful on the Sabbath to save life or destroy it) is Jesus's way of telling the authorities that he knows they are plotting his death even on the Sabbath.

Jesus wants them to understand that simply professing concern for those who are hurting is not enough—human need must be addressed whenever and wherever it is found. Religion isn't about boundary-keeping; it's about showing God's love in tangible ways. The litmus test for all theology and morality is its response to the weakest and most vulnerable members of the community. Therefore, in Jesus's mind, it is not only permissible to heal on the Sabbath, it is the right and godly thing to do.

The scribes and Pharisees strongly disagree but find themselves in a dilemma because of the way Jesus has reframed the Sabbath issue. They say nothing, hoping Jesus will act.

Jesus, deeply distressed by their stubbornness, says to the man, "Stretch out your hand."

Again the man feels vulnerable. What he most fears is now before him, and a choice must be made—he can refuse and spare himself the humiliation, or he can risk embarrassment and obey. He chooses faith and offers his twisted fist to Jesus. He is immediately restored to health.

The congregation erupts in praise, but the religious leaders are enraged. The prophet from Galilee has crossed a boundary and must pay, in blood. They spend the afternoon plotting with members of the Herodian sect to kill Jesus. The Pharisees and Herodians—so named because of their deference to the royal family—are normally adversaries. The Pharisees view them as little more than starstruck sycophants, but the Herodians have the ear of the region's ruler and may prove valuable.

Aware of the plot to kill him, Jesus and his disciples leave Capernaum and make camp on the shore of Lake Gennesaret. While safe from the scribes and Pharisees here, Jesus is not safe from the multitudes. Initially, his audience is primarily Galileans, but later, people from all over Syria come to the lake to hear him preach and see him heal. And not just Jews.

As he begins his second year of public ministry, Jesus is incredibly popular, but he knows there's trouble on the horizon. His claims to be Lord of the Sabbath and greater than the temple are unforgivable sins in the eyes of the authorities. As the opposition mounts, Jesus continues to draw large crowds, but most come out of curiosity. Jesus decides the time has come to choose a smaller group for specialized training. His plan is simple but fraught with a dozen reasons to fail.

8

# The Divine Conspiracy

Spring, AD 31

*"Everyone then who hears these words of mine and puts them into practice will be like a wise man who built his house on the rock."*
—Matthew 7:24

THE RAINS CEASE, and spring comes to Galilee. It has been a year since Jesus announced his presence in Jerusalem by symbolically cleansing the temple. Since then he has violated numerous traditions and incurred the wrath of both sacred and secular authorities. Recent death threats in Capernaum have forced him to leave town. He and a large number of men and women are encamped in the hills above Tabgha, two miles west of Capernaum.

Jesus knows his time on earth will be brief. For his mission to succeed, he must train others to carry on his work. One evening he goes into the hills alone and spends the night in prayer. When morning comes, he returns to camp and chooses twelve men from among his apprentices to receive special instruction.

The number is parabolic. God called twelve tribes to be with Him and become His envoys to the nations; Jesus calls twelve men to be with him and become his envoys to the world. Apostles—sent-forth ones—is the name Jesus gives the group. They will be eyewitnesses to everything he does and have unlimited access to him.

There are two pairs of brothers in the twelve: Simon and Andrew bar Jonah, and their volatile fishing partners, James and John bar Zebedee. Jesus also calls Philip of Bethsaida, Nathanael bar Tolmai (Bartholomew) of Cana, Matthew Levi the tax collector, Thomas (also known as Didymus; both names mean "twin"), James bar Alphaeus, Simon the Cananaean ("zealous one"), and Judas Thaddaeus.

These eleven apostles are from Galilee, and all are *am ha'aretz*— uneducated people of the land. The twelfth apostle is the one non-Galilean. His name is Judas bar Simon. He is also known as Iscariot because he is from the town of Kerioth in southern Judea.

Jesus leads the newly appointed apostles down from the hills. The crowds who have been milling around the lakeshore see Jesus and begin walking up to meet him.

Jesus stops at a level place and allows the multitude to gather around him and the apostles. Some of the men and women are followers of Jesus, but most in the crowd are still evaluating the new rabbi. Jesus sits on the grass and explains what it means to follow him and live in the kingdom of heaven.

"Blessed are the poor in spirit, for theirs is the kingdom of heaven.

"Blessed are those who mourn, for they will be comforted.

"Blessed are the meek, for they will inherit the earth.

"Blessed are those who hunger and thirst for righteousness, for they will be filled.

"Blessed are those who show mercy, for they will be shown mercy.

"Blessed are the pure in heart, for they will see God.

"Blessed are the peacemakers, for they will be called God's children.

"Blessed are those who are persecuted because of righteousness, for theirs is the kingdom of heaven.

"Blessed are you when others hate you and exclude you and insult you and persecute you and make all sorts of false accusations against you because of the Son of Man. Rejoice and leap for joy! Great is your reward in heaven, for that is how their ancestors persecuted the prophets who came before you.

"But woe to you who are rich, for you are receiving your consolation in full.

"Woe to you who are well-fed now, for you will hunger.

"Woe to you who are laughing now, for you will mourn and weep.

"Woe to you when all people speak well of you, for that is how their ancestors treated the false prophets."

The people on the hillside are confused. Jesus's blessings and woes are contrary to what they have been taught all their lives. They believe wealth and power are signs of God's approval, but Jesus paints a radically different picture. He condemns those who trust in themselves and echoes God's declaration written in the scroll of Isaiah: "I dwell in the high and holy place, and also with those who are contrite and lowly in spirit."

Jesus looks into the faces of his apprentices and says, "You are the salt of the earth, but if the salt becomes flavorless, how can it be made salty again? It is no longer good for anything except to be thrown out and trampled under people's feet.

"You are the light of the world. A city set on a hill cannot be hidden. Nor do people light a lamp and put it under a basket—they put it on the lampstand so that it gives light to everyone in the house. In the same way, let your light shine before others so that they can see your good works and give glory to your Father in heaven.

"Do not suppose that I came to abolish the Law or the Prophets; I did not come to abolish them but to fulfill them. I tell you truly, until heaven and earth pass away, not the smallest letter or slightest stroke of the pen will pass away from the Law until everything is accomplished. Therefore, whoever sets aside one of the smallest of these commandments and teaches others to disregard them will be called the least in the kingdom of heaven, but whoever does them and teaches them will be called great in the kingdom of heaven. For I tell you that unless your righteousness goes far beyond that of the scribes and Pharisees, you will never enter the kingdom of heaven."

A puzzled look appears on the faces of the apostles. How could anyone be more devout than the religious elite?

The men are confused because they misunderstand the focus of the Scriptures. Like the scribes and Pharisees, they think righteousness is about external purity and appropriate behavior. Jesus says that righteousness is more internal than external. God is interested in matters of the heart—the attitudes that create the bad behaviors.

Jesus offers six examples of how this internal righteousness manifests itself.

"You have heard that it was said to those of old, 'You shall not murder,' and that whoever commits murder will be liable to judgment. But I tell you that everyone who is angry with his brother or sister without cause will be liable to judgment, whoever calls his brother or sister 'worthless' will be liable to a court trial, and whoever calls them 'fool' will be liable to the fires of hell.

"So if you are offering your gift at the altar and there remember that your brother or sister has something against you, leave your gift there in front of the altar—go first and be reconciled with your brother or sister— then come offer your gift.

"Reconcile quickly with your opponent in a lawsuit—while the two of you are still on the way to court—otherwise your accuser will hand you over to the judge, and the judge to the guard, and you will be thrown in prison. I tell you truly, you won't get out until you have repaid the last penny.

"You have heard that it was said, 'Do not commit adultery,' but I tell you that every man who looks at a woman who is not his wife and wants to have sex with her has already committed adultery with her in his heart. If your right eye causes you to stumble, tear it out and throw it away—you're better off losing one part of your body than having your whole body thrown into hell. And if your right hand causes you to stumble, cut it off and throw it away—you're better off losing one part of your body than having your whole body go to hell.

"It was said, 'Whoever divorces his wife must give her a certificate of divorce,' but I tell you that everyone who divorces his wife for any reason except sexual unfaithfulness makes her the victim of adultery, and anyone who marries a divorced woman himself commits adultery.

"Again, you have heard that it was said to people long ago, 'Do not swear falsely,' and 'Carry out the oaths you made to the Lord,' but I tell you, do not swear at all—neither by heaven, for it is God's throne, nor by the earth, for it is His footstool, nor by Jerusalem, for it is the city of the great king. And do not swear by your own head, for you cannot make a single hair white or black. Let what you say be simply 'Yes' or 'No.' Anything more than that comes from evil.

"You have heard that it was said, 'An eye for an eye and a tooth for a tooth,' but I tell you, do not resist an evil person. Instead, if anyone slaps you on the right cheek, turn the other cheek to him as well. And if anyone wants to sue you and take your tunic, give him your cloak as well. And if anyone conscripts you as his porter for one mile, go with him two miles. Give to the one who begs from you, and do not turn away from the one who wants to borrow from you. If anyone takes what belongs to you, do not demand it back.

"You have heard that it was said, 'Love your neighbor and hate your enemy,' but I tell you who are listening: love your enemies. Do good to those who hate you, bless those who curse you, and pray for those who mistreat you, so that you may show yourselves to be true children of your Father who is in heaven, for He makes His sun rise on both the evil and the good and sends rain on both the just and the unjust. If you love those who love you, what reward will you get? Don't even tax collectors do as much? And if you welcome only those of your own circle, what more are you doing than others? Don't even Gentiles do as much? Therefore, be perfect, as your heavenly Father is perfect."

The people on the hillside shake their heads in amazement. They are accustomed to hearing homilies that explain the letter of the Law. Jesus directs his followers to the spirit of the ancient Scriptures—to look beneath the surface and determine the source of the behavior. Addressing attitudes like anger and lust will eliminate murder and adultery and a host of other evils.

Jesus then describes what righteousness looks like when applied to the three cardinal disciplines of Judaism: almsgiving, prayer, and fasting.

"Be careful not to practice your righteousness in front of other people in order to be noticed by them, otherwise you have no reward from your Father, who is in heaven. So when you give to the needy, do not announce it with trumpets as the hypocrites do in the synagogues and the streets so that they will be esteemed by others. I tell you truly, they have received their reward. But when you give to the needy, don't let your left hand know what your right hand is doing, so that your almsgiving is in secret. Then your Father, who sees what is done in secret, will reward you.

"And when you pray, don't be like the hypocrites, for they love to pray standing in the synagogues and on the street corners so that people will notice them. I tell you truly, they have received their reward. But when you pray, go into your most private room, shut the door, and pray to your Father, who is in secret. Then your Father, who sees what is done in secret, will repay you.

"And when you pray, don't babble on like the Gentiles do—they think they will be heard because of their many words. Don't be like them, for your Father knows what you need before you ask Him. This, then, is how you should pray: 'Our Father, who is in heaven, may Your name be held in reverence. May Your kingdom come. May Your will be done on earth as it is in heaven. Give us today the bread we need for the coming day. And forgive us our debts, as we also have forgiven our debtors. And let us not be brought into temptation but rescue us from the evil one.'

"For if you forgive others for their offenses, your heavenly Father will forgive you as well, but if you do not forgive others, neither will your Father forgive your offenses.

"And when you fast, don't put on a gloomy face like the hypocrites do, for they neglect their appearance so that everyone will notice they are fasting. I tell you truly, they have received their reward. But as for you, when you fast, anoint your head and wash your face so that others can't see that you are fasting, but only your Father, who is in secret, can. Then your Father, who sees what is done in secret, will repay you."

The apostles nod and whisper to one another. Much of what Jesus says makes sense. God's children should reflect His character in their everyday activities.

Jesus then addresses two of people's greatest challenges: wealth and worry.

"Do not store up treasures for yourselves on earth, where moth and rust destroy and where thieves break in and steal. Instead, store up treasures for yourselves in heaven, where neither moth nor rust can ruin them, and no thieves can break in and steal them. For where your treasure is, there your heart will also be.

"The eye is the lamp of the body, so if your eye is healthy, your whole body will be full of light, but if your eye is bad, your whole body will be full of darkness. So if the light that is in you is darkness, how deep that darkness is!

"No one can be the slave of two masters—either he will hate the one and love the other or he will be devoted to one and despise the other. You cannot serve both God and *mammon*.

"That's why I tell you to not worry about the food and drink you need to live or about the clothes you need for your body. Isn't life more than food and the body more than clothing? Take a good look at the wild birds—they neither sow nor reap nor gather into barns, and yet your heavenly Father feeds them. Are you not worth more than birds? And who among you can add a single hour to his life by worrying?

"And why worry about clothing? Learn a lesson from the wildflowers and how they grow—they neither toil nor spin, yet I tell you that not even Solomon in all his splendor was dressed like one of these. If that's how God clothes the grass of the field, which is here today and thrown into the oven tomorrow, will he not do much more for you, O you of little faith?

"So don't be anxious, saying, 'What are we to eat?' or 'What are we to drink?' or 'What are we to wear?'—all these things the Gentiles strive for—your heavenly Father already knows that you need them. Seek first the kingdom of God and His righteousness, and all these things will be given to you as well. So don't worry about tomorrow; tomorrow will bring its own worries. Today's troubles are enough for today."

Jesus pauses to allow the audience to feel the weight of his instruction. He has taught about the disciple's relationship with God. Now he turns to an equally important subject—how his apprentices are to treat others.

"Be merciful, just as your Father is merciful. Judge not, and you will not be judged. Condemn not, and you will not be condemned. Forgive, and you will be forgiven. Give, and it will be given to you. Good measure—pressed down, shaken together, running over—will be put into your lap. You will be judged by the same standard by which you judge others, and the measure you give will be the measure you get back.

"Can the blind lead the blind? Will they not both fall into a pit? An apprentice is not above his teacher, but when he's fully trained, he will be like his teacher.

"Why do you see the speck in your brother's eye but fail to notice the log in your own eye? Or how can you say to your brother, 'Brother, let me take the speck out of your eye,' when all the time there is a log in your own eye? You hypocrite—first take the log out of your own eye, then you will see clearly enough to remove the speck out of your brother's eye.

"Don't give what is holy to dogs, and don't throw your pearls in front of pigs, lest they trample them underfoot and then turn and tear you to pieces.

"Ask, and it will be given to you; seek, and you will find; knock, and the door will be opened to you. For everyone who asks, receives, and everyone who seeks, finds, and to everyone who knocks, the door will be opened. Who is there among you who, if his son asks for a loaf of bread, will give him a stone? Or if the child asks for a fish, will he give him a snake? So if you, bad as you are, know how to give good gifts to your children, how much more will your Father in heaven give good things to those who ask Him!

"So whatever you would like others to do to you, do also to them, for this sums up the Law and the Prophets."

The people on the hillside can only shake their heads. Even the apostles are struggling to understand how they could survive if they adopted the lifestyle Jesus is describing. Jesus knows that most in the audience think his instructions are unrealistic, but he insists that there are only two paths.

"Enter through the narrow gate," Jesus says. "For wide is the gate and broad is the road that leads to destruction, and there are many who take it. But narrow is the gate and hard is the road that leads to life, and there are few who find it.

"Watch out for false prophets who come to you in sheep's clothing but inwardly are savage wolves. You will recognize them by their fruits. Every tree is known by the fruit it bears. Grapes aren't gathered from thorn bushes or figs from thistles, are they? In the same way, every healthy tree produces good fruit, but the diseased tree produces bad fruit. A healthy tree can't produce bad fruit, and a diseased tree can't produce good fruit. Every tree that does not bear good fruit is cut down and thrown into the fire. Thus you will recognize them by their fruits. The good person from the good treasure of his heart produces good, and the evil person from his evil treasure produces evil, for out of the abundance of the heart the mouth speaks.

"Why do you call me 'Lord, Lord,' and not do what I say? Not everyone who says to me, 'Lord! Lord!' will enter the kingdom of heaven but only the person who does the will of my Father who is in heaven. On that day, many will say to me, 'Lord! Lord! Did we not prophesy in your name, and cast out demons in your name, and do many mighty works in your name?' Then will I declare to them, 'I never knew you—depart from me, you evildoers.'

"Everyone who comes to me and hears my words and puts them into practice will be like a wise man building a house, who dug deep and laid the foundation on solid rock. The rain fell and the rivers flooded and the winds blew and beat against that house but could not shake it because it was built upon the rock. But everyone who hears my words and does not put them into practice will be like a foolish man who built his house on the sand. The rain fell and the rivers flooded and the winds blew and beat against that house, and immediately it collapsed, and the ruin of that house was great."

When Jesus stands to announce he is done, some on the hillside shake their heads and dismiss his words as fanciful and idealistic, but others try to imagine what life would be like in the kingdom Jesus describes.

9

# WISDOM'S CHILDREN

SPRING–AUTUMN, AD 31

*Does not wisdom cry out? Does not understanding raise her voice?*
*. . . . Blessed is the person who listens to me, watching daily at my*
*gates, waiting beside my doors. For whoever finds me finds life and*
*obtains favor from the Lord, but whoever fails to find me injures*
*himself—all who hate me love death.*

—Proverbs 8:1, 34–36

JESUS HAS CHOSEN twelve men and given them an overview of the apprentice life. Their training will begin immediately. Jesus and his new apostles come down from the hills above Tabgha and walk east toward Capernaum. When they arrive, they are met by a group of civic leaders who have come on behalf of one of the city's patrons, a Gentile centurion. His servant is paralyzed and in agony. The city elders ask Jesus to intercede. "He is worthy to have you do this for him, for he loves our nation, and it was he who built our synagogue."

Centurions are "commanders-of-a-hundred"—normally eighty infantrymen plus support personnel. Men are promoted to the rank because of their prowess on the battlefield, not because of their spiritual sensitivity and benevolence, but Jesus senses there is more to this centurion.

Still, this is a request from Jews, and Jews are rarely interested in helping Gentiles, so Jesus gently challenges them. "Shall I come and heal him?" His question is rhetorical and aimed at their prejudice.

Jesus, his disciples, and the city leaders walk toward the centurion's villa east of town. A small crowd of townspeople follows. Before they reach the military leader's home, they are met by another group of emissaries. The centurion has had second thoughts about the appropriateness of his initial request. Through his friends, the centurion says to Jesus, "Lord, do not trouble yourself, for I am not worthy to have you come under my roof. Neither do I now consider myself worthy to come to you."

The military officer understands authority and recognizes it in Jesus. "Just give the command, and my servant will be healed," he says. "For I, too, am a man under authority, with soldiers under me. And I say to one, 'Go,' and he goes, and to another, 'Come,' and he comes, and to my servant, 'Do this,' and he does it."

Jesus, moved by the centurion's poverty of spirit, turns to the crowd and says, "I tell you truly, I have not found anyone in Israel with faith like this. And I tell you that many will come from the east and west and recline at the table with Abraham, Isaac, and Jacob in the kingdom of heaven, while the sons of the kingdom will be thrown into the outer darkness—there will be weeping and gnashing of teeth."

The people begin murmuring. All are familiar with the messianic banquet Jesus is referring to. According to Isaiah, those at the celebration will enjoy "a feast of rich food, a feast of well-aged wine." Everyone in Israel longs to recline at that table, for an invitation to it means God's eternal blessing. Some of the teacher's words are comforting—Abraham, Isaac, and Jacob will have honored status at the head of the table—but surrounding them, Jesus said, would be Gentiles. The crowd, convinced that only Jews will be invited to the messianic banquet, scowl and shake their heads.

Jesus turns to the centurion's emissaries. "Go," he tells them. "As you believed, so let it be done for you."

The officer's friends thank Jesus and rush back to the villa, but when they arrive they find the servant healthy and talking with the centurion. When this news gets back to the crowd, their anger turns to awe and confusion. The evening ends without incident, but Jesus's words have enraged the townspeople and invigorated those who plot his death.

Jesus knows he is no longer safe in Capernaum, and early one morning he leaves town and travels west into the hills. His disciples and a crowd of the curious follow. Late in the afternoon, Jesus reaches the outskirts of Nain. A funeral procession is coming out of the city. In front is a bier bearing the body of a young man who had died earlier that day.

The two crowds meet near the city gate. Jesus looks beyond the bier to the boy's widowed mother, who is sobbing inconsolably. Her deepest fear has come to pass—death has robbed her of her entire family. Except for the mercies of God, she is alone in the world and helpless.

"Do not weep," Jesus tells the woman. He walks over to the wooden plank holding the body and touches it. Both crowds come to an immediate halt. The people who are following Jesus wonder why he's interfering with a funeral, and the mourners from Nain wonder why the procession has been interrupted.

But no one expects what happens next. Jesus speaks directly to the body on the bier. "Young man, I say to you, arise."

An audible gasp escapes the crowd as the once-dead man sits up and begins speaking. Those carrying the bier fall to the ground in fear. They had anointed his cold body for burial hours earlier—now he's alive and talking.

Jesus walks the young man over to his speechless mother, and the two crowds erupt in praise. "A great prophet has risen among us!" says one. "God has visited His people!" says another.

The revivification is seen by many, and soon everyone in Judea has heard about the prophet who, like Elijah, raised a widow's son from the dead. There are similarities between the two revivifications, but even more striking is the difference. Elijah prostrated himself before the Lord with prayers and supplication, and after a time God responded by reviving the dead man. With Jesus, the process was quite different—Jesus spoke directly to the corpse, and as the words were spoken, death became life. All who witnessed the miracle, and especially the new apostles, are wondering the same thing: Who is this man who can heal even the dead?

EVENTUALLY, THE STORIES about Jesus reach far down the Jordan Valley and into the bowels of Machaerus, Herod's desert fortress east of the Salt Sea, where John the Baptist is imprisoned. His months in the lightless dungeon have darkened his understanding. Where there had once been clarity, there is now doubt.

Some of the reports about Jesus are encouraging, but it appears to John that Jesus is content to simply roam the hills of Galilee as a healer and itinerant preacher. Where is the one who will come with his winnowing fork to sift and separate? Where is the one who will lay his ax to the root of the trees?

John, no longer certain, sends two of his disciples to Jesus with an urgent question. They immediately set out for Galilee, and a few days later they relay John's question to Jesus: "Are you the one who is coming, or are we to look for someone else?"

Jesus reflects on the question and the doubts that motivated it. John has been a faithful servant. He has done everything God has asked and has been rewarded with imprisonment in a rat-infested hole. John's confusion is understandable, but Jesus doesn't give him a direct answer. Instead, John is asked to consider how the Scriptures describe the work of Messiah. "Go and tell John what you have seen and heard," Jesus tells the Baptist's disciples. "The blind receive their sight, the lame walk, lepers are cleansed, the deaf hear, the dead are raised, and the poor have good news preached to them. And blessed is the one who does not stumble because of me."

Referencing the prophecies of Isaiah, Jesus offers implicit proof of his identity—proof John's disciples have been eyewitnesses to. But to John and those with ears to hear, Jesus has a more subtle answer: the passages he alluded to that speak of the good news also speak of God's judgment. Jesus would have John see that while he may not be meeting the Baptist's expectations, he is even now in the process of sifting and separating. John is gently admonished not to allow his expectations to trip him up.

John's disciples thank Jesus and begin the long trek south to Machaerus. As they walk away, Jesus turns to the crowd and says, "What did you go out into the wilderness to see? A reed wavering in the wind? What, then, did you go out to see? A man dressed in soft clothing? Behold, those who are beautifully clothed and live in luxury are in palaces. What, then, did you go out to see? A prophet? Yes, I tell you, and more than a prophet. This is the one about whom it is written, 'Behold, I send My messenger ahead of you, who will prepare your way before you.'

"I tell you, among those born of women, no one is greater than John, yet the one who is least in the kingdom of heaven is greater than he. From the days of John the Baptist until now the kingdom of heaven is subjected to violence, and the violent plunder it. For all the prophets and the Law prophesied until John, and if you are willing to accept it, he is the Elijah destined to come. Whoever has ears, let them hear."

Jesus is reminding the crowd of John's true identity. Until John, there had not been a prophet in Israel for four hundred years, only the *bat-kol,* the "daughter of a voice," but that all changed when John came in from the wilderness. God had sent them an Elijah-like prophet who was not only greater than Elijah, he was greater than all the prophets. John is greater not because he is more faithful than those before him but because of his role in ushering in the kingdom of heaven.

Nevertheless, a major transition is underway—the covenant God gave Moses is being fulfilled and will soon be superseded by the New Covenant. Meanwhile, the kingdom of heaven is being established on earth, and the difference between this kingdom and all others is so vast that even the most insignificant person in the new era will be greater than anyone in the old.

God told Jeremiah, "I will put My law in their minds and write it on their hearts. I will be their God, and they will be My people. No longer will a man teach his neighbor, or a man his brother, saying, 'Know the Lord,' because they will all know Me, from the least of them to the greatest, for I will forgive their wickedness and remember their sins no more."

The prophecy is being fulfilled. The New Covenant is coming in, but it must be ratified by blood, and Jesus knows that John will not live to see the gifts and revelations of that soon-coming day.

Much of John's confusion is due to his expectation that when the Messiah comes, all opposition will be swept away. Instead, as Jesus affirms, the introduction of God's kingdom is being met with fierce resistance—John is in prison; the nation's leaders are condemning Jesus; and most of the people, while enthusiastic about the miracles, resist his teaching.

Jesus identifies the source of the resistance. "To whom, then, shall I compare the people of this generation?" he asks. "What are they like? They are like children sitting in the marketplace and calling to one another, 'We played the flute for you, and you did not dance; we sang a dirge, and you did not weep.' For John the Baptist came eating no bread and drinking no wine, and you say, 'He has a demon.' The Son of Man has come eating and drinking, and you say, 'Look! A glutton and a drunkard, a friend of tax collectors and sinners!' Yet wisdom is justified by all her children."

Jesus describes his generation as people who want to play religious games but are never pleased with God's response. Because John does not dance to their tunes, he is slandered. Because Jesus will not respond to their laments, he is condemned. Jesus concludes that, despite the evidence, many will find excuses to reject him. As always, hard hearts give birth to invincible ignorance.

"Woe to you, Chorazin!" Jesus warns. "Woe to you, Bethsaida! For if the miracles that were done in you had been done in Tyre and Sidon, they would have repented long ago in sackcloth and ashes. And indeed I tell you, it will be more tolerable on the Day of Judgment for Tyre and Sidon than for you. And you, Capernaum—will you really be 'exalted to heaven'? No, rather, 'You will be brought down to Hades,' for if the miracles done in you had been done in Sodom, it would have remained until this day. And indeed I tell you all, it will be more tolerable on the Day of Judgment for the land of Sodom than for you."

*Woe* is a word that was often on the lips of the ancient prophets. It means "how greatly you will suffer!" Jesus condemns Capernaum, Chorazin, and Bethsaida because with greater privilege comes greater responsibility. Having seen Jesus do miracle after miracle in their presence, their responsibility is to turn humbly from their sins. Instead, they demand their agenda and condemn both John and Jesus.

Jesus assures them they will bear full responsibility for their sin. His bluntness is not born of anger, and his words are more lament than condemnation. Like those who made similar prophecies before him, his strong language is an attempt to awaken souls.

Many in the audience slumber in self-righteousness, but some are being roused. Jesus's next words are a prayer of thanks for those who are being awakened. Jesus opens his arms, lifts his eyes, and says, "I praise You, Father, Lord of heaven and earth, that You have hidden these things from the wise and learned and revealed them to little children; yes, Father, for such was Your gracious will."

Jesus pauses and surveys his audience. He wants no one to misunderstand his next words. "All things have been entrusted to me by my Father, and no one recognizes the Son except the Father—nor does anyone recognize the Father except the Son and anyone to whom the Son chooses to reveal Him."

The people once again begin murmuring. Jesus knows they are struggling with the exclusivity of his claim, and he assures them that God doesn't want any of them to perish. "Come to me," Jesus says, "all who are weary and heavy laden, and I will give you rest. Take my yoke upon you and learn from me, for I am meek and lowly in heart, and you will find rest for your souls, for my yoke is easy, and my burden is light."

Jesus promises them that God will embrace anyone who turns to him. His invitation stirs deep emotions in the listeners. All can identify with feelings of being tired and worn out. All struggle under various yokes, and particularly the "yoke of the Law," as it is called by the rabbis.

Jesus offers a different kind of yoke. He says that those who are willing to wear his yoke will learn the true meaning of rest. There will still be tragedy and heartache and death and disease, but his apprentices will be able to see the larger picture of how God works all things toward His good purposes in the lives of those who love Him.

Some in the audience accept Jesus's invitation, but most shake their heads and turn away.

NAIN, LIKE ALL towns in the region, has a few prominent citizens who belong to the party of the Pharisees. One is a man named Simon; he has listened intently to Jesus's claims and wants to hear more from the teacher who sounds like a blasphemer but can raise the dead. He organizes a banquet in his home, where he can question Jesus in a more controlled environment.

Simon's hastily offered invitations are quickly accepted. All are curious about the miracle-worker, and by the time the teacher and his apprentices arrive, Simon's home is filled with guests.

Jesus enters in through the doorway and makes eye contact with the host, but the Pharisee turns away without acknowledging him. A few minutes pass. Jesus and his disciples are not offered even the common courtesies all hosts are expected to provide. At a minimum, a guest can expect a greeting and a kiss from the host (either on the cheek, or, if the guest is a rabbi or distinguished person, on the hand), and some water and olive oil, which acts as a soap to remove the road dust. Servants would be standing by to wash the feet of valued guests.

Jesus and his disciples are ignored. It is an obvious slight, and everyone in the room notices immediately. The other guests whisper to one another and look nervously at the young rabbi standing near the door. When Jesus becomes aware that he is being dishonored, he says nothing and meekly takes his place at the table, where others are already reclining.

His gentle response is lost on no one in the room. There are about two dozen dinner guests, but there are also a number of the village poor sitting quietly against the back walls in the hope that at the end of the meal they will receive some of the leftovers. In this way, the host can demonstrate his generosity and prove his "door is open to God" because it is open to the poor.

One of the poor is a young woman who quietly watches Jesus being publicly disrespected. She knows a lot about how that feels—for her it's a daily occurrence. She has made many bad choices in her life, and everyone in town knows it. She understands her status, but what had Jesus done to deserve this? All he says and does is good and kind. Earlier she had heard his invitation to enter his rest and had accepted. Since that day, her life has made a dramatic turnaround. She no longer does the things that destroyed her integrity.

When she heard Jesus would be at the banquet, she saw an opportunity to express her appreciation. She brought an alabaster bottle of perfume to anoint him with, but her plan was undone by the unexpected behavior of the host. Jesus immediately reclined at the table, and only his feet are still reachable. But since they haven't been washed and she has no water or towel, she can't anoint even his feet.

Deep sobs well up in her chest; she closes her eyes and bites her lip to hold back the tears, but she is soon is weeping uncontrollably. No longer able to maintain her anonymity, she rises from the floor, walks over to Jesus, and collapses at his feet. There are no words that can express her love. There are no words that can communicate the hurt she is feeling for the way Jesus is being disrespected. She can only grasp his feet and weep.

The dinner party comes to a complete halt as all eyes turn to Jesus. They are curious about how he will respond to this obvious act of impropriety. Minutes pass and Jesus says nothing, apparently content to let the woman remain sobbing at his feet.

Eventually, the woman realizes her profuse tears have provided a way for her to honor her savior. She washes his feet with her tears and bathes them in kisses of gratitude. She has nothing to dry with, so she releases her long hair to serve as a towel. After several minutes of drying and more kisses, she breaks open her alabaster bottle, and the room is filled with a pungent sweetness. She pours out the perfume and begins to kiss and anoint the feet of Jesus.

The host is appalled as he watches the slow drama unfold. According to religious tradition, a woman who lets down her hair in public is guilty of sexual immorality (for, as the Scriptures note, a woman's hair is enticing). How can Jesus claim to be a holy man and allow this immoral woman to kiss and fondle his feet? Why doesn't he push this obvious sinner away? It is said that he is a prophet, but how can he be a prophet when he can't even identify a sinner? These questions and more are in the mind of the host.

Simon is an important man in this small town and knows everyone. He has seen the woman plying her trade in the village for years, but he has also seen the change in her since she began following Jesus. He knows she has walked away from her former life, yet he and his cronies have, thus far, refused to acknowledge her change of heart. Until they do, she will remain a pariah in her community.

Jesus wants to give Simon an opportunity to reconsider, but the Pharisee has already made up his mind. In his judgment, both Jesus and the woman are sinners, and Jesus is a fraud for claiming to be a prophet. Jesus knows that Simon is silently condemning him, and he answers the Pharisee's thoughts.

"Simon, I have something to say to you."

The brooding host is startled; Jesus used a phrase that often means "get ready to hear something you are not going to want to hear." But Simon no longer has much interest in what the self-styled prophet has to say and replies perfunctorily, "Say it, Teacher."

Jesus tells Simon a story he knows the wealthy man will be able to relate to: "A certain moneylender had two debtors. One owed five hundred denarii and the other fifty. When neither could repay him, he graciously forgave the debt of both." Jesus then follows up the short story with a question: "So which of them will love him more?"

This is a scenario a wealthy man like Simon knows well. His entire culture is built on a foundation of patronal ethics in which the generosity of a benefactor would help and thus obligate the receiver to return the favor in some way, even if it is only by being loyal to the patron.

Simon knows and uses this system well; in fact, this very banquet would obligate his guests. Because Jesus stays within the patronal system Simon is familiar with, the answer is obvious. "I suppose the one to whom he forgave more," Simon concedes.

"You have judged rightly," Jesus says. He is hoping to transform Simon's thinking about the whole concept of debt (which, in Aramaic, is also the word for "sin").

What Jesus is suggesting is revolutionary—if everyone were to adopt his philosophy of forgiveness, all the rules of interpersonal relationships would change. Discrimination and class privilege would disappear because everyone would be on the same level.

Jesus does not press this point to its logical conclusion. Instead, he keeps the conversation within the framework of the patronal system Simon embraces. In order to emphasize his point, Jesus turns his back to the Pharisee and faces the woman—but he continues to speak to Simon.

"Do you see this woman?" he asks. His question causes her to look up. When their eyes meet, she blushes and quickly bows her head.

Jesus continues to look lovingly at her while he rebukes the host. "I entered your house! You gave me no water for my feet, but she has wet my feet with her tears and wiped them with her hair. You gave me no kiss, but from the time I came in she has not ceased to kiss my feet. You did not anoint my head with oil, but she has anointed my feet with perfume. Therefore, I tell you, her sins—which are many—are forgiven, because she loved much. But he who is forgiven little, loves little."

The Pharisee bristles, but before he can speak, Jesus says to the woman, "Your sins are forgiven."

The table, quiet during the confrontation, now erupts in conversation. The guests ask one another, "Who is this, who even forgives sins?" It is incomprehensible that any man, even the Messiah, could offer to do that which is the prerogative of God alone.

Jesus knows their thoughts but ignores them. His primary concern is the poor and broken woman lying before him. He looks into her eyes and speaks a truth she has known since the day she repented and accepted his invitation: "Your faith has saved you."

Jesus doesn't excuse or minimize her sins, but, at the same time, he does not condemn her. Her outward actions make it clear that she has experienced an inward change of heart, and the only word Jesus has for her is a pronouncement of God's *shalom*. "Go in peace," he tells his new apprentice.

Jesus, his work in Nain complete, once again takes to the roads of Galilee. No village is too small to minister in, and many weeks are spent in the hills—Jesus working, his disciples watching. Then word comes from the south: John the Baptist is dead. The details are sketchy, but it is reported that he was beheaded at one of Herod's lavish parties.

Some say Herod was the mastermind, but others suggest the murder was orchestrated by his wife, Herodias, who passionately hated the prophet. It is rumored that she and her daughter devised a scheme that resulted in John's head on a platter, but Jesus knows who is behind the murder, and that one is not flesh and blood.

The one who would prepare the way for Messiah is now dead, but

Elijah has accomplished his mission. The way has been prepared. While his enemies celebrate and plot their next move, Jesus withdraws and awaits instructions from the Father.

# 10

# Dark Sayings from of Old

Autumn–Winter, AD 31

*Give ear, O my people, to my teaching; incline your ears to the words of my mouth! I will open my mouth in a parable—I will pour forth dark sayings from of old . . . . I will utter what has been hidden since the foundation of the world.*

—Psalm 78:1–2; Matthew 13:35

MONTHS PASS AS Jesus unhurriedly makes his way through the many villages in the hills west of Lake Gennesaret. Though he spends little time in Sepphoris and Tiberias, the region's two largest cities, his name is often heard in their streets, and his teachings have infiltrated even the palace. Joanna, the wealthy wife of Chuza, Herod's business manager, has become a devoted follower of Jesus. She slips away whenever he is teaching near Tiberias, and often gives money to the apostles to help meet the needs of the rabbi and those he has called to walk with him. Her husband is one of the most powerful men in the kingdom, and he shares the concerns of his master about the growing popularity of the prophet who is preaching to large crowds, sometimes just a short distance from the royal residence.

News about Jesus also regularly reaches the ruling council of the Jews in Jerusalem. As his fame grows, the Sanhedrin fears that the hysteria being stirred up in the north might spread to the entire nation and draw unwanted attention from Rome. They recall earlier uprisings that began in Galilee but created hardship for all Israel. After several evenings of long and heated discussion in the Hall of Hewn Stones, a plan is devised—a delegation of experts in the Law will make the three-day journey to the north shore of Lake Gennesaret. They are confident they can discredit the troublemaker and diffuse the potential crisis.

Within a week the legal team is in Capernaum. The lawyers meet with the local Pharisees and are soon current on the activities of their adversary. They learn Jesus has recently returned from the hills and is staying in the home of two fishermen. Every morning when Andrew and Simon Peter open their doors to the public, the religious scholars are waiting at the courtyard gate.

Reports about Jesus have also regularly made their way to his mother, brothers, and sisters in Nazareth. They learn how recent events in nearby Nain have swollen the crowds to the point that Jesus often no longer stops to eat. It is said he teaches and heals from early morning until late in the evening, then retreats alone into the hills for all-night prayer vigils. The more his family hears about his activities, the more concerned they become. Perhaps his popularity has gone to his head, or maybe he just doesn't know how to say no, but it appears to the family that the eldest son has lost his way and will do nothing to help himself.

After a long and difficult discussion, the family decides to intervene. His sisters will remain at home while his mother and brothers make the day-long journey to the lake to bring Jesus back to Nazareth—separate him from the hangers-on by force, if necessary.

Early one morning they set out for Capernaum. That morning finds Jesus doing what he does every day, all day—teaching about the kingdom and healing those who come to him. The scribes from Jerusalem sit in a far corner of the room observing. Morning becomes afternoon, and still the ailing come. Jesus turns none away.

One of the saddest cases that day is a man who is so helpless he must be carried in. He is a blind mute and would incite everyone's deepest pity—except he is also demon-possessed. He cannot speak, but he occasionally growls and makes menacing guttural sounds. The lawyers from Jerusalem whisper to one another, curious to see what the healer will do.

Jesus speaks a word. The man's sight is restored, and he shouts praises to God.

The crowd is amazed—who can restore sight and speech with just a word? This is the kind of mighty work the Scriptures say the Messiah will do. But how could this meek itinerant preacher and healer who spends all his time in insignificant Galilee be the Anointed One? Nothing is clear, but one in the room sees the Messianic possibility and tentatively says, "Surely this man is not the Son of David . . . . is he?"

The scribes and Pharisees from Jerusalem stir uncomfortably. This is not the conclusion they want the people to come to, but they must respond carefully. There have been hundreds of witnesses to dozens of miracles, and Jesus's authority over illness and demons cannot be denied. But while they can't deny he has power, they can challenge the source of his power. They unleash the plan crafted in the Hall of Hewn Stones. One of the lawyers points his finger accusingly at Jesus. "He is possessed by Beelzebul!"

Another nods in agreement and adds, "It is only by the power of Beelzebul, the ruler of the demons, that this man casts out demons."

Beelzebul, one of Satan's many nicknames, means "lord of the dwelling." They are accusing Jesus of being a sorcerer who heals and exorcises with powers he has received from the Devil.

Amazed at their hardness of heart, Jesus asks, "How can Satan cast out Satan? Every kingdom that is divided against itself is laid waste, and no city or household that is divided against itself will be able to survive. And if Satan casts out Satan, he is divided against himself. So then how could his kingdom survive? His end has come."

Jesus's reasoning is simple: demons are Satan's faithful servants. Why would the Devil give one of his servants the authority to destroy his other servants? Satan would be undermining his own kingdom.

The religious experts struggle to understand. They define the kingdom of heaven as a future event and the kingdom of Satan as an abstract concept—Jesus identifies both kingdoms as current realities that his miracles testify to. Jesus is suggesting that there is only one reasonable conclusion to draw from a work that frees a soul from demonic possession while restoring both sight and speech, but the Pharisees are not listening.

Jesus sharpens his point and makes it personal. "You say that I cast out demons by Beelzebul, but if it is by the power of Beelzebul that I cast out the demons, by whose power do your sons cast them out? Therefore, it is they who will be your judges. But if it is by the power of the Spirit of God that I cast out the demons, then the kingdom of God has come upon you."

Jesus is warning the religious scholars that if they claim his exorcisms are the results of sorcery, they will be forced to condemn all other Jewish exorcists as sorcerers as well—but if others are exorcising demons by the power of God, so is he.

Jesus recounts an ancient parable to help the lawyers grasp the profound truth he has demonstrated. "When a strong man, fully armed, guards his own dwelling, his possessions are secure. How can someone enter a strong man's house and steal his goods unless he first binds the strong man? But when one stronger than the strong man attacks and overcomes him, he takes the armor in which the man trusted and divides his spoils."

Jesus's words recall God's promise to personally rescue His people. The Lord told Isaiah, "Those who wait for Me shall not be put to shame. Can the prey be taken from the mighty? Can the captives of a tyrant be rescued? Even the captives of the mighty will be taken, and the prey of the tyrant will be rescued, for I will contend with those who contend with you, and I will save your children."

Jesus tells the parable of the strong man to demonstrate that not only is he not in collusion with the Devil, he is in an all-out war against him. The blind-mute demoniac had been one of the strong man's possessions. By healing him, Jesus had demonstrated to the "lord of the dwelling" who the true Lord is—he had entered Satan's kingdom, bound him, and repossessed a soul.

There is a choice before everyone in the room that afternoon, and the teacher's next words make it plain there is no neutral ground: "Whoever is not with me," Jesus says, "is against me, and whoever does not gather with me scatters.

"I tell you truly, people may be forgiven every other sin and blasphemy, but blasphemy against the Spirit will not be forgiven. And if anyone speaks a word against the Son of Man, they will be forgiven, but whoever speaks against the Holy Spirit will not be forgiven, either in this age or in the age to come, but is guilty of an eternal sin."

The lawyers sent by the Sanhedrin perceive Jesus is attempting to reverse their charge of blasphemy by accusing them of what Moses called sinning "with a high hand" (the image is of raising one's fist at God in deliberate defiance)—a sin the Jews believe is unforgivable. Jesus says God will forgive every sin but one—attributing the work of God to Satan—what Isaiah described as "calling evil good and good evil."

Jesus challenges them to decide who he really is. "Either make the tree good and its fruit good, or make the tree bad and its fruit bad, for the tree is known by its fruit." Jesus demands they make up their minds about him—either he is an evil person doing evil works, or he is a good person doing good works.

God is not the author of evil, and Satan isn't interested in doing good. Accusing Jesus of doing good by Satan's power is equivalent to attributing the work of the Holy Spirit to the Devil. This is a lethal mistake that cannot be forgiven because it cuts one off from the only means of salvation.

And there is no chance that Jesus has misjudged the important men from Jerusalem. It is by their own words they stand condemned. "You brood of vipers!" Jesus says. "How can you, being evil, say anything good? For out of the overflow of the heart the mouth speaks. The good person out of his good treasure brings forth good, and the evil person out of his evil treasure brings forth evil. I tell you, on the Day of Judgment people will give account for every empty word they speak—for by your words you will be justified, and by your words you will be condemned."

Jesus would have them see how words spoken in haste are often more revealing because they come straight from the heart. His warning falls on deaf ears. "Teacher," the lawyers say, "we want to see a sign from you."

Jesus is not interested in satisfying the whims of evil people who have already proven they will reject whatever sign they are given. "It's a wicked and adulterous generation that demands a sign," Jesus tells them. "But no sign will be given to it except the sign of the prophet Jonah—for just as Jonah was three days and three nights in the belly of the sea monster, so the Son of Man will be three days and three nights in the heart of the earth.

"The men of Ninevah will rise up at the judgment with this generation and condemn it, for they repented in response to Jonah's preaching, and behold—something greater than Jonah is here.

"The queen of the south will be raised up at the judgment with this generation and condemn it, for she came from the ends of the earth to hear the wisdom of Solomon, and behold—something greater than Solomon is here."

The religious scholars are not sure what Jesus is claiming, but he is clearly not honoring their request. He has chosen to respond with a counterchallenge. The idol-worshipping Queen of Sheba and the pagan people of Ninevah repented when God's messenger spoke to them, Jesus says, but the Jews remain obdurate despite hearing a much greater testimony.

He tells the scribes a darkly humorous story to underline his warning. "When the unclean spirit has been cast out of a person, it wanders through waterless places seeking rest, but finds none. Then it says, 'I will return to my house from which I was expelled.' And when it comes, it finds the house empty, swept, and put in order. Then it goes and recruits seven other spirits more wicked than itself, and together they enter and dwell there, and the final state of that person is worse than the first. And so it will be with this evil generation."

A Jewish superstition declares that demons like to dwell in desolate, arid places, but Jesus disagrees. He says demons much prefer a human home to one in the desert, and if the person they have been expelled from is not filled with obedience to another Spirit, the demon will return with a vengeance and make the person's situation much worse than before his halfhearted resolution.

One of the women in the room, moved by Jesus's words, says, "Blessed is the womb that bore you, and the breasts at which you nursed!"

Jesus shakes his head and says, "Blessed, rather, are those who hear the Word of God and obey it."

Someone comes to the door and announces the teacher's family has arrived from Nazareth and wishes to speak with him. Jesus knows his mother and brothers plan to force him to come home. His family's intentions are good, but their conclusions are similar to those of his enemies. Jesus looks around the room and asks, "Who is my mother, and who are my brothers?"

He pauses a few moments to allow the question to sink in, then motions toward the disciples seated around him and says, "Behold, here are my mother and my brothers! My mother and my brothers are those who hear the Word of God and do it. Anyone who does the will of my Father in heaven is my brother and sister and mother."

When his words are relayed to his family in the courtyard, they are hurt and confused, but say nothing. Jesus knows that the source of their confusion is their inability to grasp the nature of the kingdom of heaven. He wants to teach about the kingdom in depth, but he wants to share the message with a larger audience.

JESUS INVITES HIS listeners to the lake. They are joined by a crowd of townspeople. Hundreds press around Jesus at the water's edge. He steps into a small fishing boat and is rowed a short distance from the shore to take advantage of a natural amphitheater. He then begins teaching them about the kingdom of heaven in parables—stories that are "thrown alongside" a truth to make it more understandable.

"Listen," Jesus tells those gathered around him. "Once a sower went out to sow his seed. As he sowed, some fell along the path and was trampled underfoot, and the birds of the air came and devoured it. Some fell on rocky ground, where they did not have much soil. Immediately they sprang up because they had no depth of soil, and when the sun rose they were scorched because they had no moisture, and because they had no root they withered away. Some fell among thornbushes, and the thorns grew up and choked them, and they yielded no grain. And some fell into good soil and produced grain, growing up and increasing and yielding thirty-fold and sixty-fold and a hundredfold. He who has ears to hear, let him hear."

The audience is intrigued by the parable but has no idea what it means. At first it sounds like the story of a wasteful farmer who sows indiscriminately (three of the four areas he plants bear no crop), but the story has a surprising ending—the good ground is so fertile that it not only compensates for the farmer's profligate sowing, it also rewards him with an exceptional crop. A normal yield is less than tenfold. This farmer has at least tripled that. But who, the audience wonders, is the farmer? And what do the various soils point to?

Jesus sees their quizzical looks but doesn't explain the parable. Instead, he throws out another story. "The kingdom of God is like a man who scatters seed on the ground," Jesus says. "Night and day, whether he is asleep or awake, the seed still grows, but he does not know how it grows. On its own, the earth produces grain: first the blade, then the ear, then the full grain in the ear. But when the grain is ripe, he immediately sends forth the sickle because the harvest has come."

The images of the sickle and harvest are common references to the Day of the Lord. Most people in Israel expect the kingdom of God to come upon them like an earthquake. They believe the Messiah will one day dramatically appear to liberate his people. Jesus's parable warns against that kind of thinking and suggests the kingdom will come quietly.

God's kingdom will be established, but its growth will be mysterious. "The kingdom of heaven can be compared to a man who sowed good seed in his field," Jesus says. "But while his men were sleeping, his enemy came and sowed weeds among the wheat and went away. When the plants sprouted and produced a crop, then the weeds appeared also, and the servants of the master of the house came to him and said, 'Master, didn't you sow good seed in your field? How then does it have weeds?'

"'It is an enemy who has done this,' the master replied.

"So the servants said to him, 'Then do you want us to go and pull out the weeds?'

"But the master said, 'No, lest in gathering the weeds you root up the wheat along with them. Let both grow together until the harvest, and at harvesttime I will tell the reapers, 'First gather the weeds and tie them in bundles to be burned, but gather the wheat into my barn.'"

Jesus pauses and looks into the confused faces surrounding him. "With what can we compare the kingdom of God?" he asks. "What parable shall we use for it? It's like a grain of mustard seed that a man took and sowed in his field. It's the smallest of all seeds, yet, when it is sown, it springs up and grows larger than all the garden plants. It becomes a tree and puts out large branches so that the birds of the air come and roost in its shade.

"The kingdom of heaven is like leaven that a woman took and hid in three measures of flour until all the dough had risen."

"The kingdom of heaven is like treasure hidden in a field, which a man found and hid. Then in his joy he goes and sells all that he has and buys that field.

"Again, the kingdom of heaven is like a merchant in search of fine pearls, and when he had found one pearl of exceedingly great value, he went and sold all he had and bought it.

"Again, the kingdom of heaven is like a dragnet that was thrown into the sea and caught fish of every kind. When it was full, the fishermen pulled it ashore, sat down, and sorted the good into containers, but threw away those that were worthless. So it will be at the end of the age—the angels will come and separate the wicked from the righteous, and they will throw the wicked into the fiery furnace, where there will be weeping and gnashing of teeth."

Jesus shares parable after parable about the mysterious way the kingdom grows, but he explains none of them. When Jesus is finished and the crowd disperses, he and his followers share a meal and rest by the lakeside. The conversation turns to the teaching earlier that afternoon. One of the disciples asks, "Why do you speak to them in parables?"

Jesus pauses long enough to ensure he has his apprentices' full attention, then says, "Because to you it has been given to know the mysteries of the kingdom of heaven, but to them it has not been given. The secret of the kingdom of God has been given to you, but for those outside everything comes in parables, so that 'they may be ever seeing but never perceiving, and ever hearing but never understanding. Otherwise, they might turn and be forgiven.'

"In them the prophecy of Isaiah is fulfilled that says, 'You will be ever hearing but never understanding—you will be ever seeing but never perceiving, for this people's heart has become calloused. They can barely hear with their ears, and they have closed their eyes. Otherwise, they would see with their eyes, hear with their ears, understand with their heart, and turn so that I might heal them.'

"But blessed are your eyes, because they see, and your ears, because they hear. I tell you truly that many prophets and righteous people longed to see what you see and did not see it, and to hear what you hear and did not hear it."

Jesus says that some will hear God's invitation and turn to Him, but others, no matter how often they hear the truth, will refuse to repent and be healed.

The disciples smile and nod in agreement, but they are confused about the meaning of the stories. They ask Jesus to explain the parable of the sower.

"Do you not understand this parable?" Jesus asks. "How, then, will you understand any of the parables? Hear then the meaning of the parable of the sower. The seed is the Word of God. The sower sows the Word. Some people are like seed along the path where the Word is sown. When anyone hears the message of the kingdom and does not understand it, the evil one comes and immediately snatches away the Word from their heart so that they may not believe and be saved.

"The ones on the rocky ground are those who hear the Word and immediately receive it with joy, but they are rootless and don't last very long—when trouble or persecution arises on account of the Word, they immediately fall away.

"The ones sown among thorns are those who hear the Word, but the worries of this world and the false allure of wealth and the desires for other things come in and choke the Word, and it proves unfruitful.

"But those sown in the good soil are those who understand and accept the Word. These are those who, when they hear the Word, hold it fast in an honest and good heart and bear fruit with patient endurance. These do indeed produce a crop—thirty, sixty, or even one hundred times what was sown."

Jesus's apprentices begin to understand—there is one message but many results. The soils represent the different responses people have to the message of the kingdom, and the disciples are already familiar with all of them. Often they meet people who hear God's Word but give little thought to it. Often they see people who are initially filled with joy but walk away at the first sign of adversity. Often they talk with those who are distracted by wealth and its attendant worries. As for the good soil, the apostles need look no further than their own experiences to understand the fruitfulness Jesus speaks of.

Why does the parable sound so simple when the master explains it?

Emboldened by Jesus's willingness to explain the parable of the sower, they ask about another confusing image. "Explain to us the parable of the weeds of the field."

"The one who sows the good seed," Jesus says, "is the Son of Man. The field is the world, and the good seed are the children of the kingdom. The weeds are the children of the evil one, and the enemy who sowed them is the Devil. The harvest is the end of the age, and the reapers are angels.

"Just as the weeds are gathered and burned in the fire, so will it be at the end of the age. The Son of Man will send his angels, and they will gather out of his kingdom all the stumbling blocks and all lawbreakers and throw them into the fiery furnace, where there will be weeping and gnashing of teeth. Then the righteous will shine like the sun in the kingdom of their Father. He who has ears, let him hear."

The disciples nod thoughtfully as Jesus explains the parable. Ultimately there are but two paths—each person is walking either toward the light or into the darkness. One day all those who reject God will be judged. Until then, Jesus's followers will grow up alongside the children of the evil one.

This is why it is imperative his apprentices respond to God's Word. "No one lights a lamp and then covers it with a bowl or puts it under a bed," Jesus tells them. "A lamp is put on a stand, so that those who enter may see the light. For nothing is hidden that will not be revealed, nor is anything concealed that will not be known and come to light. If anyone has ears to hear, let him hear."

"Pay close attention to what you hear—the measure you give will be the measure you get, and still more will be added. For to the one who has, more will be given, and from the one who has not, even what he thinks he has will be taken away."

Jesus slowly looks around the circle and into the heart of each disciple. He knows a fuller understanding of the parables will require time and prayerful reflection, but his followers must at least have a basic grasp of each parable's meaning, so Jesus asks, "Have you understood all these things?"

The apprentices realize there is still much to learn, but regarding today's lessons, they think they understand and collectively respond, "Yes."

Jesus nods and challenges them to teach others what they have learned from him. "Therefore every scribe who has become a disciple of the kingdom of heaven is like a master of a house who brings out of his treasure chest things new and old."

# IDENTITY

AUTUMN–WINTER, AD 31

*And they will give him the name God-with-Us.*

—Isaiah 7:14

JESUS HAS SPENT the afternoon teaching parables about the kingdom of God. After the crowds leave, Jesus and the apostles share a meal, and he tells them they will spend the night traveling to the Decapolis. This will be a new experience for the apprentices; until now they have only ministered in the Jewish villages west of the lake. The Decapolis, named in honor of the region's ten most important cities, is on the eastern shore of the lake and predominantly Gentile.

Soon the men are heading southeast in one of the fishermen's boats. The evening is mild, the lake is flat, and the trip promises to be uneventful. As the boat pulls away from the shore, Jesus, exhausted after a long day, makes his way to the stern and is soon sleeping soundly.

The trip is pleasant until darkness falls and the boat is far from shore. Then the wind begins to build. The professional fishermen look up nervously as clouds fill the sky. Located in a basin nearly seven hundred feet below sea level, the lake is usually calm, but occasionally cool winds roll over the mountains and clash with the warm air on the lake's surface, and fierce squalls can arise quickly. The fishermen see the weather changing and are reminded why the lake is often called the "sea" of Galilee—within a matter of minutes the gentle breeze they enjoyed while leaving the western shore has been transformed into a low whistling howl that is spawning six-foot swells.

As the boat dips in and out of deep troughs of black water, it begins taking on water faster than the men can bail it out. The apostles become convinced they are about to drown. They turn to Jesus but find him still asleep in the stern.

"Master, Master," one of the disciples cries out, "we're perishing!"

Another shouts, "Save us, Lord!"

A third asks the question brewing in all their minds, "Teacher, don't you care that we're perishing?"

Their clamor awakens Jesus. He sees the fear in their faces and shouts above the tempest, "Why are you afraid, O you of little faith?"

The disciples look at one another in exasperation but say nothing. Isn't it obvious why they are afraid?

Jesus stands and addresses the storm: "Quiet!" he commands. "Be still!"

As the words are spoken, the winds cease, and the surface becomes calm. The change is so instantaneous and so complete that the apostles become more afraid of Jesus than they were of the storm. They turn to one another and ask, "What sort of man is this that he commands even the winds and the sea, and they obey him?" And behind that question is a deeper one—who but God has that kind of authority?

In the morning, they land near the Roman settlement of Gergesa. The apostles are thankful to reach shore safely, but they are soon wondering why they came—as they step out of the boat they see two naked, obviously deranged, Gentiles running toward them. They have a reckless and violent look about them, and the disciples conclude they are about to be attacked by madmen, but when they look to their master for guidance, they see Jesus is calmly awaiting the men's arrival.

The two were once respected members of the community, but nowadays are feared and avoided by all. Family and former friends are convinced the two are under the control of demons. Attempts to incarcerate and restrain them have been futile—they are possessed by a superhuman strength that can break through even iron chains.

Lately, the men have taken up residence in a graveyard north of town. Burial caves have been cut into the stone hillside that are large enough to hold several ossuaries and still provide shelter to anyone desperate enough to need it. The men no longer terrorize the town, but the demons who possess the men exact their price. They menace all who pass their way, and when there are no hapless travelers to intimidate, the demons turn on the two bodies they possess, tormenting them into cutting themselves with sharp rocks.

The dark forces amassed in the two men running down the hill are like none the disciples have encountered. The twelve brace themselves for an assault. Instead, the two wild-eyed men fall writhing at Jesus's feet.

The apostles still aren't clear about the identity of the one they follow, but the demons know whose presence they are in, and tremble.

Jesus knows his adversaries are not the two men but a multitude of fallen angels who indwell them. He addresses them as one. "Come out of the man, you unclean spirit!"

The demons beg him to leave them alone. "What have you to do with us, Jesus, Son of the Most High God? I adjure you in God's name, do not torment us. Have you come here to torment us before the time?"

The demons fear Jesus because they know he not only has the power to evict them from the two men, if he chooses, he can banish them to eternal torture in a bottomless abyss. Seeking another option, any option, the demons see a large herd of swine on a nearby slope. "If you're going to cast us out," they plead, "send us into the herd of pigs."

It is a curious request, but one Jesus determines he can use to demonstrate what is taking place here—two more souls are being repossessed from the strong man. Jesus looks into the eyes of the men and addresses the spirits within. "What is your name?"

The demons, still trying to avoid destruction, answer evasively, offering a number rather than a name. "My name is Legion, for we are many."

The disciples now better understand the confrontation they are witnessing. "Legion" is a military number approximating six thousand.

"Go!" Jesus tells the demons.

As he speaks, the two men fall to the ground and become still, but bedlam breaks out on the hillside—loud, tortured squeals and snorts erupt from the herd. The pigs begin jostling, biting, and kicking one another. Then, as one, the possessed swine stampede. The pigs hurtle headlong down the steep embankment and into the lake, where they all drown.

Everyone watching is stunned. They walk to the embankment and stare into the roiling waters. The swine herders are at first mystified, but soon begin piecing together what happened. They see Jesus kneeling beside the two demoniacs, talking quietly with them and treating their wounds, and the herdsmen realize they are in the presence of a powerful exorcist. Terrified of Jesus's abilities and afraid they will somehow be blamed for what happened, the pig herders scatter, some to the towns and others to nearby farms. They tell everyone they meet about the strange occurrence at the lake.

Those who hear the account find the story too incredible to be true. How could an exorcism and the mishap with the swine be connected? Hundreds travel to the lake to see for themselves. When they arrive, they are surprised to find the two men who were once the bane of the territory now calmly sitting at Jesus's feet with his other disciples. The two are clean, clothed, and acting peaceably.

The fearful herdsmen again recount the story. The Gerasenes listen thoughtfully and walk to the embankment to view the carcasses in the water. They determine the story of the herdsmen is true. Then they, too, become afraid. What kind of man has such authority? What might the powerful Jewish sorcerer do next?

The region's residents don't want to find out. They ask Jesus to get back in his boat and return to wherever he came from. Some are distraught about the financial loss from the destruction of the herd. Others are more concerned about the intentions of the Jewish magician—unlike their own gods, this fellow is assertive and unpredictable and does not appear open to negotiation.

Jesus nods and tells the Gerasenes he will respect their wishes. He directs his disciples to ready the boat; they will leave immediately. The two men who have been restored do not want to be separated from Jesus and beg him to take them with him, but their new master has a different mission for them. "Go home to your friends, and tell them how much God has done for you, and how He has had mercy on you."

The men are disappointed that they will not be able to accompany Jesus, but they are excited about the opportunity to proclaim God's goodness. As Jesus enters the boat, he knows he will not return to Gergesa, but he also knows the region will not be without a witness. History will record little of it, but many souls will come to know Jesus through the testimony of two men who were once home to a legion of demons.

SOON AFTER JESUS returns to Capernaum, Matthew Levi hosts a banquet to introduce his old tax collector friends to his new master. Dinner invitations are rare for customs agents. No one in respectable society will socialize with them. Their only friends are others like themselves, and they are intrigued by the notion of a holy man who will share a meal with tax collectors.

Other townspeople are annoyed. They can't understand why Jesus is openly defying the sacred traditions by eating with sinners. They view tax collectors as worse than even lepers—the leper, at least, does not choose his condition.

The evening arrives. Tax collectors from all over the region make their way to the party. A wonderful meal is served, and Matthew's guests find Jesus fascinating to talk with. He's humorous and full of intriguing stories, and by the time the celebration ends, the customs agents have a completely different perspective. According to Jesus, God is loving toward all and willing to accept anyone—even tax collectors.

Jesus's gentle treatment of society's outcasts kindles deep feelings in the hearts of the tax collectors but infuriates the local Pharisees. They are tempted to confront Jesus with his sin, but experience has taught them that directly challenging the Nazarene doesn't end well. They approach the apostles and ask, "Why does your teacher eat with tax collectors and sinners?"

The disciples, who have wondered the same thing at times, take the question to their master. Jesus recognizes the significance of the query; in a shame-based culture, a public complaint like this is a challenge. The Pharisees want to shame and censor Jesus, and they will succeed if he can't provide an acceptable answer to their charge.

Jesus offers a simple proverb. "Those who are well have no need of a physician, but those who are sick do." Jesus points out that a spiritual teacher who avoids sinners would be as foolish as a doctor who avoids those who are ill.

Jesus then turns the tables on the religionists by shaming them with the words of the prophet Hosea. He tells the Pharisees, "Go and learn what this means: 'I desire mercy, and not sacrifice.' For I came to call not the righteous but sinners to repentance."

The issue, Jesus explains, is much bigger than observing boundary markers like table fellowship and remaining ceremonially clean. Relationships always take precedence over ritual—beginning first and foremost with one's relationship with God.

In Hosea's day, God's people were more attentive to religious rites than to the needs of others. Those ancient people focused on ceremonial pomp and purity but ignored the heart of worship: God's *hesed*, the forgiving loving-kindness his people are to both enjoy and reflect. Mere outward conformity to God's Law and ceremonial correctness will never do, Jesus says, and any righteousness that places ritual above mercy is no righteousness at all.

The disciples report Jesus's words to the Pharisees. The religious teachers scoff and walk away, vowing to one day silence the quick-witted false prophet who somehow seems to come up with one clever answer after another.

Jesus is not surprised by the Pharisees' unwillingness to acknowledge their sin. Because they have no godly sorrow, they see no need for repentance, and the way to their salvation remains hidden.

Several days pass, and gossip about Matthew's party continues to circulate. Much of the talk is about Jesus's religious laxity. His casual approach to the fences erected to protect God's Law is causing deep concern among the pious. Some disciples of John the Baptist come with a question about one of Judaism's most prominent boundary markers. "Why do we and the Pharisees fast, but your disciples do not fast?"

Fasting, along with prayer and almsgiving, is one of the three pillars of Judaism and a widely respected worship practice. The Mosaic Law requires the nation to fast one day a year on *Yom Kippur*, but fasting is popular in every season and is deemed appropriate whenever one is dissatisfied with life. Sometimes one fasts in response to a loss, sometimes to signify repentance, and at other times to plead for God's intercession, but fasting is always to be an act of worship.

The Pharisees zealously fast every Monday and Thursday. John's disciples also fast frequently, as do the Essenes, Sadducees, and others who are serious about their religion. In their minds, it is inconceivable that a rabbi would not teach his disciples to fast. If Jesus wants to be taken seriously, he must honor the sacred traditions.

Jesus answers their question by identifying why people fast in the first place—fasting signifies that one is dissatisfied with something in themselves or their world. Jesus then explains why he and his disciples do not fast often. "Surely the wedding guests are not to mourn while the bridegroom is with them, are they?"

His question mines one of the richest veins of Jewish life. There are appropriate seasons for mourning and dissatisfaction with the status quo, but wedding celebrations are times for feasting, not fasting. The wedding imagery makes sense to those listening, but according to the Scriptures, the bridegroom is not a man. The groom is God.

As the people reflect on the wedding image, Jesus says, "But the days will come when the bridegroom is taken away from them—then they will fast."

The audience doesn't understand why the groom would be expelled from his own wedding. Jesus offers two parables and a proverb that may help.

"No one tears a piece of cloth from a new garment and patches it on an old garment," Jesus says. "The new piece will pull away from the old and a worse tear will be made, and the patch from the new will not match the old.

"And no one puts new wine into old wineskins. If he does, the new wine will burst the skins, spilling the wine and destroying the skins. No, new wine must be put into fresh wineskins.

"And no one after drinking old wine desires new wine, for he says, 'The old is good.'"

Jesus's observations about patches and wine are simplistic when applied to tailoring and winemaking but profound when applied in the realm of the spirit. Jesus has given them a timeless principle—the new cannot be put on or into the old without disastrous results. The religious establishment is attempting to shame Jesus into keeping the traditions, but he knows the expanding fermentation of the gospel will require a much larger and more adaptable container than Judaism.

Jesus is not criticizing the Old Covenant; he is simply saying that the Mosaic Law, like an intact old wineskin, has admirably served its purpose—it has prepared the way for the gospel—but the new must have a fresh container.

Many in the audience shake their heads and turn away. If Jesus wants to be accepted, he needs to patch his teachings onto those of the venerable elders. The new way is unfamiliar and ignores the sacred tenets and traditions. Why abandon those? The old is good.


JUST THEN, THE door bursts open and a man collapses in tears at Jesus's feet. His name is Jairus, and he is known to Jesus and everyone in the room. He organizes worship at the synagogue and is one of Capernaum's most prominent citizens. His twelve-year-old child is gravely ill, and physicians have been unable to cure her. "My little daughter is at the point of death," Jairus sobs. "Come and lay your hands on her so that she may be made well and live."

Jesus immediately stands and walks with Jairus out the door and into a large crowd that is gathered in the street. Jesus finds it difficult to make his way through the jostling throng; everyone wants to be near him. One in particular is a woman who has a gynecological bleeding disorder that has rendered her ceremonially unclean. She has suffered for twelve years and has spent her entire life savings seeking a cure, but to no avail. She has no hope in physicians, but she believes Jesus can heal her—if only she can get close enough.

She sees Jesus come out of a house with another man and walk away. Her heart quickens. She feels she cannot wait another day and begins forcing her way through the hundreds of people between her and the healer. Getting close to him is difficult, but she will not be denied. Ducking, squeezing, and crawling, she comes within a few feet of Jesus, but he, too, is pushing through the crowd. It appears he is on an urgent mission.

The woman sees her opportunity slipping away and desperately reasons that perhaps this holy man of God, like the altar of the Tabernacle, can make holy anything that touches him. Stretching out her hand, she can reach but the hem of his garment. Instantly she feels a change within and knows she has been healed.

Jesus stops, turns, and scans the crowd. "Who touched my garments?" he asks.

Simon Peter shrugs and says, "You see the crowd pressing around you, and yet you say, 'Who touched me?'"

"Someone touched me," Jesus explains, "for I know that power has gone out from me."

The healer continues to stand in the middle of the street surveying the crowd and asking who touched him. He asks not because he doesn't know who touched him but so that the woman might feel the full impact of her restoration.

The woman he healed is rejoicing that her life-destroying condition has disappeared, but she is also afraid. The healer somehow knows it was her, and she is about to be exposed. Her fear grows, and soon she is trembling uncontrollably. She throws herself at Jesus's feet and confesses. She tells everyone why she touched his garment and how she was healed.

The crowd begins murmuring. The woman has admitted her uncleanness. She should not even be here. The woman steels herself to receive the healer's wrath, but rather than reprimanding her, Jesus says, "Daughter, your faith has made you well—go in peace and be healed of your affliction."

The woman's heart leaps within her, but her joy is dampened when word comes from Jairus's home that Jesus is too late. "Your daughter is dead," Jairus is told. "Why trouble the teacher any further?"

Jairus's chin falls to his chest. He nods sadly and turns to thank Jesus for his willingness to come, but the healer tells Jairus to ignore the news. "Do not fear," Jesus says. "Only believe, and she will be well."

The synagogue leader is confused but does not question Jesus. They soon arrive at his home. Dozens are gathered. Loud wails and moans can be heard from within. When Jairus's wife sees them enter the court-yard, she runs to her husband and falls into his arms, sobbing.

Jesus instructs everyone to remain outside except the child's parents and three of the apostles. They enter the house and find singers from the mourner's guild weeping and chanting dirges. Several flutists provide a haunting accompaniment.

"Why are you making a commotion and weeping?" Jesus asks. Then he turns to the child's mother and comforts her. "Do not weep, for she is not dead, only sleeping."

When the professional mourners hear Jesus's pronouncement, they laugh derisively. They've been around death long enough to know it when they see it. The girl isn't sleeping. She's dead.

Jesus tells the mourners to leave and walks into the room where the body lies. He goes directly to the child's bed, takes her small cold hand in his, and says, "Little girl, I say to you, arise."

Immediately the child sits up and looks into the eyes of the kind-faced stranger who is holding her hand. Her parents gasp in disbelief and clutch each other tightly. The girl sees her parents' tears but doesn't understand why they are crying. Jesus tells the child's mother to prepare her some food and charges both parents to keep what happened a secret.

His work accomplished, Jesus walks home with a large throng following. In the crowd are two blind men who are convinced Jesus is the Messiah. As they stumble along behind him, they shout, "Have mercy on us, Son of David."

Jesus hears their cries, but he has already performed two very public miracles and doesn't want to stir the crowd up further, so he walks home without acknowledging them. The men, however, are persistent. They know the Messiah will be able to heal blindness, and their faith in Jesus is so strong that they follow him through the front door of his home.

Once inside and out of sight of the crowd, Jesus asks, "Do you believe that I have the power to do this?"

The men reply in unison, "Yes, Lord."

Jesus lays his hands on their eyes and says, "In response to your faith, be it done for you."

As the word is spoken, their sight returns. Jesus sternly warns them, "See that no one knows about it."

Jesus walks back into the street. There are still dozens of people milling around, wondering if anything else will happen. A few men walk up the street carrying a mute who is demon possessed. Jesus dispatches the evil spirit and restores the man's ability to speak. Those who see the exorcism proclaim, "Never was anything like this seen in Israel."

A Pharisee in the crowd attempts to dampen their amazement. "He casts out demons by the prince of demons."

Again Jesus hears his enemies' favorite allegation. Jesus ignores the taunt. His words and deeds are sufficient testimony to his identity—let those who have eyes see.

# HOMECOMING

WINTER, AD 31–32

*"He's just a carpenter—Mary's boy. We've known him since he was a kid. We know his brothers, James, Justus, Jude, and Simon, and his sisters. Who does he think he is?"*

—Mark 6:3 The Message

OF THE MORE than two-hundred towns in Galilee, none are more special to Jesus than the one he grew up in, yet in two years of public ministry he has not taught in his hometown. As Jesus and his disciples enter Nazareth, he knows the challenges that await him.

When it's announced that he will be speaking on the coming Sabbath, all his former neighbors make plans to attend. They have heard much about his exploits, and many have known Jesus since he was a child, but the rumors circulating about him do not sound at all like the gentle boy they once knew.

Sabbath arrives. When the call to worship is given, the building is filled to overflowing. The services open, as always, with prayers of confession led by one of the elders. After prayer, the revered *Shema* (hear!) is recited by the congregation in unison. It opens with six powerful words that go to the heart of their faith: *Shema Yisrael, Adonai Elohainu, Adoni Echad.* HEAR ISRAEL—the LORD our GOD, the LORD is ONE. The Shema is followed by more prayer.

As the congregation prays, the synagogue attendant prepares for the next part of the liturgy: he brings a scroll containing a portion of the Torah to the table in front. One of Jesus's old neighbors comes forward, reads from the Law, and returns the scroll to the attendant, who puts it back in its place and removes a scroll with writings from one of the prophets.

Jesus moves to the reading table and is given a scroll containing the prophecies of Isaiah. He unfurls the sheepskin and reads a familiar passage. "The Spirit of the Lord is upon me because he has anointed me to preach good news to the poor. He has sent me to proclaim release to the captives and recovery of sight to the blind, to set free those who are oppressed, to proclaim the year of the Lord's favor . . . ."

Jesus stops reading in the middle of Isaiah's prophecy and carefully rolls up the scroll. All eyes are fixed on the young rabbi as he returns the writings to the attendant and sits down to teach. Jesus surveys the faces of people who have known him for almost thirty years. He smiles and says, "Today this Scripture has been fulfilled in your hearing."

Jesus then begins teaching them what Isaiah was referring to in the passage he read, and as he reveals the meaning of the Scriptures, the men and women turn to one another in astonishment. Where had he learned these deep truths? And he presents them so confidently! Isn't this Joseph's son?

His neighbors are impressed with his ability to teach, but Jesus knows they do not believe his claim that the Day of the Lord has begun. Isaiah's words about the Messiah's work should have prompted everyone in the synagogue to consider the implications of Jesus's claim to be the prophecy's fulfillment. The promised "year of the Lord's favor" would also be a "year of Jubilee," when all debts were to be forgiven and all slaves freed. Moses and the prophets had spoken of such a year, and Jesus says it is now here—he has brought it.

The people of Nazareth shake their heads in disbelief. How could this meek young man possess that kind of power? The townsfolk are more interested in why Jesus has not done the kinds of miracles in Nazareth he has done in other places—if those stories are even true. The people will need more proof. They want an unmistakable sign from heaven.

Knowing their thoughts, Jesus says, "Surely you will quote me that proverb, 'Physician, heal yourself'—everything we have heard you did at Capernaum, do here in your hometown as well."

Jesus is aware of the fears and prejudices that motivate their beliefs. He responds not with a sign but with a rebuke and a history lesson. "I tell you truly, no prophet is accepted in his homeland."

The congregation winces at the reminder. The persecution of prophets in Israel is well documented, and Jesus offers an embarrassing example. "In truth I tell you that there were many widows in Israel in Elijah's day when the heavens were shut for three years and six months, and a severe famine came over all the land—yet Elijah was sent to none of them, but only to a widow in Zarephath, in the land of Sidon."

Jesus has pulled a story from some of Israel's darkest days. Back then the nation was divided. The southern kingdom was the land of Judea. The northern kingdom, which included Samaria and Galilee, retained the name Israel, and was ruled by an evil king named Ahab and his queen, Jezebel. They led Israel to trade the God of their fathers for a storm god named Baal. This created a deep rift not only between them and the people of Judea but also between them and God. His response to their idolatry was a drought and famine that lasted three and a half years. Daily the people prayed for the storm god to bring rain, but not a drop came, not even the morning dew. Thousands died in Israel, but God's prophet was sent only to a Gentile woman in Phoenicia.

The people in the synagogue know their history and are insulted by the suggestion that they are like their forefathers. Jesus responds with an even more offensive example. "There were many lepers in Israel in the time of Elisha the prophet," Jesus reminds them, "and none of them were cleansed—only Naaman the Syrian was."

Jesus mentions an event he knows will infuriate every Jew in the synagogue. Leprosy and other skin diseases are understood to be outward manifestations of inward corruption, so, to a Jew, to be cleansed of leprosy is equivalent to being cleansed of sin. In Elijah's day, many Jews suffered from incurable skin diseases. God healed none of them. Instead, He cleansed a Gentile—and not just any Gentile. He healed the general of the Syrian army that was at war with Israel.

There is no mistaking Jesus's message: the people of Nazareth are not entitled to special treatment just because he grew up there. God is not a respecter of persons and is more interested in where a person's heart is than where he lives. Jesus wants his old neighbors to see it is not God's will that they seek blessings only for those who look and think and act like them. He would have them understand that God is more than a regional Savior. As Isaiah said long ago, the Messiah would come not just to the Jews but to every nation. Particularly galling to the Nazarenes is Jesus's insistence that, as in the cases of the Phoenician widow and the Syrian general, receiving God's blessings is a matter of faith, not ancestry.

As the implications of Jesus's words sink in, the synagogue erupts in protest; the angry villagers resent being told they are worse off than Gentile women and lepers. There is shouting and shoving as the townspeople force Jesus out of the building and toward a rocky cliff on the outskirts of town. Many are ready to execute judgment on the infuriating prophet immediately, but in the commotion and confusion Jesus slips away. Where he has gone, they do not know, but his words will be long remembered.

UNDAUNTED BY HIS rejection in Nazareth, Jesus continues to travel from town to town in Galilee. He works from early morning until evening, but the number of those in need continues to grow. His compassion for the harassed and helpless of Israel is boundless, but physically he has an obvious limitation—he can only be in one place at a time. Jesus, however, has known all along that his mission is not his alone.

"The harvest is plentiful," he tells those who follow him, "but the workers are few. Therefore ask the Lord of the harvest to send out workers into His harvest."

The harvest, Jesus says, is the work of the Creator. Ultimately, it is God who draws souls to Himself. Nevertheless, those who follow Jesus are to pray for more workers because the Lord has chosen to give His people key roles in His work. Some will plant, others will water, and God will give the increase.

The apostles are divided into six pairs and told to prepare for a missionary journey. Jesus then gives them specific instructions about where to go and what to do. "Do not go among the Gentiles and enter no town of the Samaritans, but go instead to the lost sheep of the house of Israel. As you go, proclaim this message: 'The kingdom of heaven has arrived.' Heal the sick, raise the dead, cleanse the lepers, cast out demons."

To the apostles, the mission Jesus describes sounds like the one they have been on for two years, with one significant difference—until now, their role has been to watch and learn from their master's example. Now it will be their hands God uses to heal, their commands that awaken the dead and banish demons, and their preaching that God uses to save souls.

The apostles struggle to understand the breadth of the commission, and Jesus reminds them that they will be offering only what they themselves were given. "Freely you received," Jesus says. "Freely give."

According to Jesus, God has a different strategy for their sustenance, and His provision is so generous, there will be no need to bring money or supplies. The clothes on their back and the sandals on their feet will be sufficient. The staff they leave with will bring them home. "Take nothing for your journey," Jesus tells them. "Don't take gold or silver or copper in your money belts. Don't take bread or bag or sandals or staff or a second tunic, for the worker is worthy of his keep."

Traveling light will allow them to respond quickly to the Spirit's leading. More importantly, his apprentices will learn to rely upon God and one another for every necessity. Jesus explains, "Whatever town or village you enter, make inquiries as to who in it is worthy, and stay with them until you leave. As you enter the house, wish peace upon it, and if that household is worthy of it, let your peace come upon it. But if it is not worthy, let your peace return to you. And if anyone will not welcome you and listen to your message, as you go out of that house or town, shake off the dust from your feet as a testimony against them. I tell you truly, on the Day of Judgment it will be more bearable for the land of Sodom and Gomorrah than for that town.

"Behold, I am sending you out as sheep in the midst of wolves, so be as wise as serpents and as innocent as doves. Be cautious of people, for they will hand you over to the courts and flog you in their synagogues, and you will be brought before governors and kings because of me, as a witness to them and the Gentiles. When they hand you over, don't worry about what to say or how to say it. What you are to say will be given to you at that time, for it is not you who speak but the Spirit of your Father speaking through you.

"A brother will hand over his brother to be killed, and a father his child. Children will rise against their parents and have them put to death. You will be hated by all because of my name, but it is the person who remains faithful to the end who will be saved. When they persecute you in one town, flee to the next, for I tell you truly, you will not have gone through all the towns of Israel before the Son of Man comes.

"A disciple is not above his teacher, nor a servant above his master. It is enough for the disciple to become like his teacher, and the servant like his master. If they have called the master of the house Beelzebul, how much more the members of his household?

"So have no fear of them, for nothing is covered that will not be uncovered, or hidden that will not be known. What I tell you in the dark, you are to speak in the light, and what you hear whispered, you are to proclaim from the rooftops.

"And do not fear those who kill the body but cannot kill the soul. Instead, fear the One who can destroy both soul and body in hell."

Jesus's knowledge of eternity creates an urgency in his invitation. He wants the twelve to know what is at stake. Hell is not an abstract doctrine or children's tale; it is an eternal shop of horrors.

But Jesus says there is good news—because of the Father's love and provision for His creation, there is no need for anyone to go to perdition. "Are not two sparrows sold for a penny?" Jesus asks. "Yet not one of them will fall to the ground without your Father's knowledge. Indeed, even the hairs of your head are all numbered. So fear not—you are worth more than many sparrows!"

But Jesus wants the twelve to know that every soul they encounter has a choice to make. "Everyone who acknowledges me before others, I also will acknowledge before my Father who is in heaven," Jesus says. "But whoever denies me before others, I also will deny before my Father who is in heaven.

"Do not think that I have come to bring peace on the earth—I have not come to bring peace but a sword. Indeed, I have come to set a man against his father, and a daughter against her mother, and a daughter-in-law against her mother-in-law—a person's enemies will be those of his own household. Whoever loves father or mother more than me is not worthy of me, and whoever loves son or daughter more than me is not worthy of me. And whoever does not take his cross and follow me is not worthy of me. Whoever finds his life will lose it, and whoever loses his life for my sake will find it.

"Whoever welcomes you, welcomes me, and whoever welcomes me, welcomes the One who sent me. Anyone who welcomes a prophet because he is a prophet will receive a prophet's reward, and anyone who welcomes a righteous person because he is a righteous person will receive a righteous person's reward. And whoever gives even a cup of cold water to one of these little ones because he is a disciple, I tell you truly, he will by no means lose his reward."

When Jesus concludes his teaching, the apostles know he has told them truths that reach far beyond the current mission, but they have been given more than enough instruction about where to go and what to do on this assignment.

As Jesus and his followers move to the next town, the six teams scatter in different directions. For weeks they travel throughout the region telling people about Jesus and healing those who are ill and oppressed.

The exploits of Jesus and the apostles are often discussed in the palace of Herod Antipas. Tiberias is the largest port on the lake, and the docks resound with stories of miracles happening all over Galilee. Everyone is interested in news about Jesus, and none more than Antipas. Most alarming to Herod is the persistent rumor that John the Baptist has returned from the dead.

13

# THE BREAD OF LIFE

SPRING, AD 32

*"Oh, for some meat! We remember the fish we used to eat for free in Egypt, and the cucumbers, melons, leeks, onions, and garlic. But now our appetite has dried up. All we ever see is this manna!"*

—Numbers 11:4–6

THE SPRING RAINS make the hills green and the roads muddy, yet nothing can dampen the success of the twelve who were sent into the countryside to preach and heal. From all over the land come stories of miracles wrought by the apostles. The blind see, the deaf hear, the lame walk, lepers are healed, and the demon-possessed are set free. There are even far-fetched tales of people being raised from the dead.

This last rumor is particularly disturbing to the region's ruler. Herod Antipas is not a Jew and is more superstitious than religious, but he believes in the resurrection of the dead and is haunted by his decision to kill John the Baptist. Antipas knows John was a prophet and fears God will punish him, but the tetrarch fears Rome more than he fears God. He is concerned about reports that Jesus is announcing the arrival of a new kingdom. Kingdoms require kings, and Galilee has long been a birthplace of revolutionaries. If Rome interprets Jesus's preaching as politically motivated, there could be serious consequences.

Jesus knows that Antipas is paranoid, and he's seen how the ruler responds to perceived threats. With the return of the apostles from their mission, the hundreds who once followed Jesus from town to town now number in the thousands. Further, the large crowds are so demanding that he and his apostles often miss meals and lose sleep. The apostles don't complain, but Jesus can see the price they are paying and decides that now would be a good time to retreat for some much-needed rest. One morning he gathers the twelve and says, "Come away by yourselves to a desolate place and rest awhile."

The crowd is dismissed, and the thirteen get in a boat and begin rowing north along the shore. The crowd, however, refuses to disperse. They can see the boat Jesus is in and simply walk along the shore following it. When the boat reaches the north shore, Jesus instructs those rowing to head east toward the Golan Mountains. Located just east of the Jordan in the tetrarchy of Phillip, Gaulanitis is a wilderness area ideal for solitude and rest, but by the time they arrive there is a crowd the size of a small city. In addition to those who followed the boat around the lake, a large multitude of locals arrive.

It becomes clear to Jesus that his plan to rest must wait; he instructs the rowers to make for shore. More than fifteen thousand people await them. Jesus is hungry and exhausted, but his compassion compels him to teach and heal all afternoon. When evening approaches, the twelve, sensitive to the size of the multitude and fearing a crisis is developing, come to Jesus and say, "This is a desolate place, and the hour is now late. Send the crowd away into the surrounding countryside and villages to find lodging and buy themselves something to eat."

Given the remote location, the request is reasonable, but rather than alleviating the crisis, Jesus says "They don't need to go away—you give them something to eat."

Seeing the stunned look on the apostles' faces and wanting to stretch their faith, Jesus turns to Phillip and casually asks, "Where can we buy bread so that these people may eat?"

Phillip, who grew up in nearby Bethsaida, is flummoxed by the question. Surely Jesus knows that buying bread would be impossible at this late hour. Besides, even if food were available, where would they get the money to buy it? Phillip throws up his hands in exasperation and says, "Two hundred denarii worth of bread would not be enough for each of them to get even a little."

Jesus nods and asks, "How many loaves do you have? Go and see."

Soon Andrew returns and reports, "There is a boy here who has five barley loaves and two fish, but what are they for so many?"

"Bring them here to me," Jesus replies. He then tells the apostles to organize the crowd to facilitate serving. "Have them sit down in groups of about fifty each."

The apostles make their way through the multitude, and soon all are seated in groups on the lush green carpet provided by the spring rains. Jesus then says a prayer of thanksgiving to the Father and gives the bread and fish to the apostles to distribute. The five barley loaves are the size of a saucer and finger-thick, and the two fish are hand-size. When divided into twelve baskets, the provision looks impossibly inadequate, but the twelve do as they are told. They are shocked as person after person reaches into the baskets and retrieves bread and fish. Thousands are not only fed but filled.

When everyone has eaten all they want, Jesus tells the apostles, "Gather up the leftover fragments so that nothing may be lost."

When they collect the leftover bread and fish, they bring it to Jesus. The twelve large baskets are now filled with food. The disciples are reminded of two passages in the Scriptures. One tells the story of how Elisha miraculously provided food to fill a hundred men from twenty small barley loaves, but even more striking is the parallel with the accounts in the Torah and the Psalms that recall the time when God "gave them bread from heaven in abundance."

Those who were miraculously fed by Jesus see the connection and proclaim, "This is indeed the prophet who is to come into the world!" They are alluding to "the prophet like Moses" foretold in Deuteronomy who would lead God's people to freedom in a new exodus.

Jesus knows that populist and revolutionary sentiments burn passionately in the crowd, and he perceives that if he were to reject their offer, they could easily start a rebellion, publicly declare him their guerrilla king, and thus conscript him. There are already in the crowd five thousand men ready to swear allegiance to the cause, and if they recruit in Galilee, birthplace of the passionate Zealot movement, they could easily raise a large army.

However, Jesus has no interest in such a kingship; it would defeat his mission. He tells the apostles to get in the boat and go west toward Bethsaida until he can free himself from the crowd. He assures them he will join them later, but they must leave immediately. The apostles hastily board the boat and row away. Jesus turns again to the multitude. There is nothing he can say or do to change their mind, so he doesn't try. He determines that his time would be better spent in prayer, and there is much he needs to talk with his Father about.

Jesus quietly walks toward the mountains. Most in the crowd do not see him climb into the Golan Heights and disappear into the night.

AS THE APOSTLES row across the lake, they discuss the amazing day and wonder aloud why Jesus sent them away so hurriedly. They are soon off the coast of Bethsaida, where Jesus had instructed them to wait. When Jesus doesn't arrive, the fishermen see the weather deteriorating and decide to continue toward Capernaum.

They row back across the lake, but their progress is slowed by a fierce west wind. They labor at the oars for hours with little progress. The headwind grows into a tempest. The howling gale and rough seas remind the apostles of a similarly frightening storm they were in earlier, but with one significant difference—Jesus isn't in the boat with them this time.

Their master, however, has not abandoned them. From the heights where he is praying, Jesus sees the storm develop and knows the apostles are far from shore, but he also knows his apprentices are in the caring hands of his Father. He senses no urgency and remains in prayer until the dead of night.

A few hours before dawn, Jesus walks down from the mountain and onto the water. The apostles, more than three miles ahead and far from shore, continue to struggle, hope ebbing in the rising gale. They suspect the waves have tossed them off course and strain to find their bearings. Peering into the predawn darkness, they wonder if their eyes are playing tricks on them—they see a man-shaped apparition walking on the water.

They shudder. All have heard tales of maritime assaults by night specters and the spirits of men drowned at sea. One cries out, "It's a ghost!"

The apparition answers with a familiar voice, "Take courage. I am here. Do not be afraid."

The disciples are terrified. How can this be? Men cannot walk on waves. Simon Peter impetuously responds, "Lord, if it's you, command me to come to you on the water."

To his surprise, Jesus says, "Come."

Peter steps out of the boat and onto the water. When he does not sink into the sea, he begins walking tentatively toward his master. All is well until he takes his eyes off Jesus, and his faith turns to fear. As he sinks under the waves, Simon Peter cries, "Lord, save me!"

Jesus reaches out his hand, takes hold of him, and says, "You of little faith, why did you doubt?"

As Jesus speaks the words, Peter rises and is soon standing beside Jesus on the surface of the lake. Hand in hand, they walk through the tempest to the boat. When they step inside, the wind immediately ceases, and the water becomes calm. The men are astounded and fall to their knees, confessing, "Truly you are the Son of God."

Their words profess his deity, but Jesus knows they only have a partial understanding of the one they worship. None of them have grasped the message bound in the feeding of the multitude. They are in awe, but it is an awe born of misunderstanding. Knowing they will later comprehend the meaning of what they have seen, Jesus says nothing.

The shoreline appears, and they see they are approaching the plain of Gennesaret a few miles southwest of Capernaum. As they moor the boat, they are recognized by several on the shore. Jesus is a renowned healer, and soon many who are ill are headed toward the lake. Jesus heals all who come to him, then returns to Capernaum.

On the other side of the lake are thousands of people who wake up hungry and find Jesus gone. They know he had come to the region by boat, but they had also seen his disciples leave without him the night before. The crowd knows that Jesus lives in Capernaum; they assume he slipped away in the darkness and walked home.

Most return to their homes, but hundreds of people head toward Capernaum. They find Jesus at the synagogue. They want more of what they received the day before but do not know how to ask. Seeking to start a conversation, one of the men says, "Rabbi, when did you come here?"

Jesus nods and says, "Truly, truly, I tell you, you are seeking me not because you saw signs but because you ate your fill of the loaves. Work not for the food that perishes but for the food that sticks with you and nourishes eternal life, which the Son of Man will give to you. For on him God the Father has set His seal."

The crowd is stung by Jesus's knowledge of their true intent but encouraged by his discussion of works they might do in order to obtain God's favor. They ask, "What must we do to do the works God requires?"

They want a precise definition of how one is made right with God, but Jesus knows they are steeped in a tradition that says they must earn their salvation by good works. He answers enigmatically, "This is the work of God—that you believe in the one He has sent."

The audience is stunned. Jesus's answer runs contrary to everything they have been taught. Just believe in him? What about the Law of Moses and the sacred traditions? By what authority does he make such pronouncements?

One in the crowd challenges Jesus. "Then what sign will you perform that we may see it and believe you? What will you do? Our fathers ate the manna in the wilderness; as it is written, 'He gave them bread from heaven to eat.'"

The irony of their request is not lost on Jesus. Many in the crowd had seen (and were filled by) just such a sign the day before. Moreover, they completely miss the point of the wilderness account they reference. Jesus says, "Truly, truly, I tell you, it was not Moses who gave you the bread from heaven but my Father who gives you the true bread from heaven. For the bread of God is he who comes down from heaven and gives life to the world."

The audience is intrigued but lacks understanding. "Sir," they say, "give us this bread always."

Jesus smiles and says, "I am the bread of life. Whoever comes to me will never hunger, and whoever believes in me will never thirst. But as I told you, you have seen me and still you do not believe. Everyone the Father gives me will come to me, and whoever comes to me I will never cast out, for I have come down from heaven not to do my own will but the will of the One who sent me. And this is the will of the One who sent me: that I lose none of all that He has given me but raise it up on the last day. This is the will of my Father: that everyone who looks on the Son and believes in him will have eternal life, and I will raise him up on the last day."

When the audience realizes that Jesus is claiming to have come from heaven, they begin grumbling, "Is this not Jesus, the son of Joseph, whose father and mother we know? How can he now say, 'I have come down from heaven'?"

Jesus hears the murmuring and says, "Do not grumble among yourselves. No one can come to me unless the Father who sent me draws him, and I will raise him up on the last day. It is written in the Prophets, 'And they will all be taught by God.' Everyone who has heard from the Father and has learned comes to me—not that anyone has seen the Father except the one who is from God; only he has seen the Father.

"Truly, truly, I tell you, whoever believes has eternal life. I am the bread of life. Your fathers ate the manna in the wilderness, yet they died. This is the bread that comes down from heaven, so that one may eat of it and not die. I am the living bread that came down from heaven. Anyone who eats this bread will live forever, and the bread that I will give for the life of the world is my flesh."

The murmuring grows louder as the people quarrel about the meaning of Jesus's words. It's obvious that he's not talking about cannibalism, but if his words are figurative, what do they represent? For most, the metaphor is impenetrable—hardness of heart prevents them from recognizing that Jesus is comparing feeding to faith.

Jesus, however, does not explain the metaphor. Instead, he intensifies it. "Truly, truly, I tell you, unless you eat the flesh of the Son of Man and drink his blood, you have no life in you. Whoever eats my flesh and drinks my blood has eternal life, and I will raise him up on the last day, for my flesh is true food, and my blood is true drink. Whoever eats my flesh and drinks my blood abides in me, and I in him. Just as the living Father sent me and I live because of the Father, so the one who feeds on me will live because of me. This is the bread that came down from heaven; it is not like the bread your fathers ate. They later died. But whoever eats this bread will live forever."

The grumbling grows louder. Someone in the audience says, "This is a harsh message," and many nod their heads in agreement. They find the teacher's words not only obscure but offensive.

"Does this cause you to stumble?" Jesus asks. "Then what if you see the Son of Man ascend to where he was before? It is the Spirit who gives life; the flesh accomplishes nothing. The words that I have spoken to you are spirit and are life, yet there are some of you who do not believe. This is why I told you that no one can come to me unless it is given to him by the Father."

When Jesus concludes his message, some of his disciples know they have heard deep truth that must be carefully unpacked, but many shake their heads in disgust and walk away. There is no need to follow this teacher any longer—he makes outlandish claims and refuses to substantiate them. He promises food that can eternally satisfy, yet their stomachs still growl. He asserts he is greater than Moses but rejects those who would crown him king. He says the only work that will meet God's requirements is to believe in him, yet he offers no corroborating proof from heaven. At best, this fellow is filled with empty words.

Within a few days, it becomes obvious that a dramatic shift has taken place. The multitudes who once followed Jesus are now nowhere to be found. No longer is he celebrated in Capernaum, or even wanted. Jesus sees the effect this is having on the twelve. He gathers them together and asks, "Do you want to go away as well?"

Simon Peter answers, "Lord, to whom shall we go? You have the words of eternal life, and we have come to believe and know that you are the Holy One of God."

Jesus knows his apprentices well and senses a note of superiority in the response. Peter is pretentiously claiming that the apostles are not like those who left. Jesus wants to remind them it was he who chose them, not the other way around. Further, there is nothing superior about them or their knowledge. His next words are carefully chosen to wake them up.

"Did I not choose you, the twelve?" he asks. "Yet one of you is a devil."

# 14

# TRADITION

*Depart, depart, go out from there—touch no unclean thing . . . .*
*purify yourselves.*

—Isaiah 52:11

TWO HUNDRED YEARS before the birth of Jesus, Israel was being assimilated into a Greek culture that had already enveloped most of the world.
Hellenist philosophy, art, architecture, and language eclipsed even the Romans, who had defeated them. No country was beyond their influence,
including Israel. Attitudes and practices that had long distinguished the
Jews from other nationalities were becoming blurred, and Israel would have
been Hellenized like the lands around them except for the resistance of a
small group of faithful Jews known as the *Hassidim*—the Pious Ones.

The Hassidim were dedicated to preserving the distinctive character-
istics of Judaism and aligned themselves with the priest, Mattathias,
who started a revolt against the rule of the vicious anti-Semitic king of
Syria, Antiochus IV. When the old priest died, his sons continued the
fight, and Israel was eventually liberated.

The victory of the Maccabees ushered in eighty years of independence. The Hassidim restored temple worship and reinstituted the Law
of Moses. Politically, the nation was led by the *Hasmoneans*, a dynasty of
priest-kings named in honor of Mattathias's great-grandfather.

The Hassidim and the Hasmoneans were allies until the powerful influence of Hellenization again enticed the nation's rulers to promote Greek culture and values. By this time, however, there was theological and political dissension within the Hassidim.

Some advocated complete physical separation from Gentiles. They identified themselves as *Essenes* and withdrew from society to live in their own neighborhoods in Jerusalem and other large cities. Some of the more zealous Essenes took vows of celibacy and established Qumran, an ascetic monastic community in the wilderness near the Salt Sea.

Others within the Hassidim preferred a less radical approach. They, too, insisted on separation but chose to work within the system to effect the changes they sought. This faction, known as the *Pharisees*, was willing, to a degree, to do business and interact with the non-devout. This brought condemnation from the Essenes, who labeled them "seekers after smooth things," but the Pharisees weren't lax—they simply took a different route to holiness. To insulate themselves from the lure of Hellenization, they established rules and traditions.

Their focus was ritual purity; thus, many of their injunctions addressed how to remain ceremonially clean while surrounded by Gentiles and Jews who did not obey the Torah. They built a fence of oral laws around the written Law to protect it from possible infringements. These oral laws became known as the traditions of the elders. The desire to protect the Torah from being corrupted was admirable, but pharisaical zeal often took their precautions to absurd lengths.

Nevertheless, throughout Jesus's lifetime the Pharisees have been the largest and most respected of the five major Jewish sects. Pharisaic practices are deeply entrenched throughout Israel and viewed by the majority of pious Jews as nonnegotiable. To violate the traditions of the elders is to rebel against God—and here the Pharisees come into direct conflict with Jesus.

In the two years Jesus has been in public ministry, he has violated the oral laws hundreds of times. The Sanhedrin decides it is time for a reckoning. A group of scribes and Pharisees are sent from Jerusalem to rebuke Jesus for his lack of respect for the traditions.

Shortly after they arrive in Capernaum, the lawyers observe the apostles ignoring the oral laws concerning ritual hand washing. They ask Jesus, "Why do your disciples violate the tradition of the elders? They eat with impure hands."

Jesus shakes his head and says, "Why do you violate the commandment of God for the sake of your tradition? You hypocrites! Isaiah prophesied rightly about you when he said, 'These people honor Me with their lips, but their heart is far from Me; in vain do they worship Me—their teachings are but rules taught by men.'

"You have skillfully set aside the commandment of God in order to observe your tradition. For God said, 'Honor your father and your mother,' and, 'Whoever speaks evil of his father or mother must surely die.' But you say that if someone tells his father or his mother, 'Any help you might have expected from me is corban,' then you no longer permit him to honor his parents. Thus you cancel out the Word of God by the tradition you pass down—and you do many similar things."

The Pharisees wince when they hear the word *corban*. Jesus is accusing them of ignoring a law of primary importance—the fifth commandment—in order to keep one of secondary importance: the law of honoring vows. Leviticus and Numbers define corban as a sacrificial offering to God. When someone designates a portion of their property as corban, it is no longer theirs; it belongs to God. In practice, that means it belongs to the temple treasury. What makes the tradition so attractive is how it is enforced—the Pharisees allow the donor to defer giving the gift as long as he chooses. Thus a selfish person can simultaneously protect his property, shirk his responsibility to honor his parents, and appear to be righteous.

Jesus says this tradition not only circumvents the Law, it nullifies it.

There is no response from the Pharisees; they are not interested in discussing the merits of the traditions. Besides, Jesus has not answered their question—why does he refuse to teach his disciples to cleanse themselves of impurity?

Jesus hasn't forgotten their question. It is of great importance. Purity is one of the major tenets of the faith, but the Pharisees have completely misunderstood why God instituted purity laws. They believe the purpose of the laws is to protect God's people from outside evils.

"Hear me, all of you, and understand," Jesus says. "It isn't what goes into the mouth that makes a person unclean but what comes out of the mouth—this is what makes a person unclean."

The Pharisees scoff and walk away. With the confrontation over and the day spent, Jesus and his disciples head home, but the afternoon's heated discussion still occupies their thoughts. The twelve fear that Jesus has crossed a dangerous line with the nation's spiritual leaders. One of the men timidly asks, "Do you know that the Pharisees were offended by what you said?"

Jesus nods and says, "Every plant that my heavenly Father has not planted will be uprooted. Leave them—they are blind guides, and if the blind lead the blind, both will fall into a pit."

When Simon Peter realizes that Jesus is adamant about the irrelevancy of the Pharisees, he changes the subject. He has strong convictions about ritual purity and is struggling with what Jesus said about what defiles a person. "Explain the parable to us," he asks.

Jesus looks into the faces of the disciples and says, "Are you still without understanding? Don't you see that nothing that enters a person from the outside can make him unclean? For whatever goes into his mouth doesn't go to his heart but into his stomach and is expelled. But what comes out of the mouth comes from the heart, and these are the things that make a person unclean. For from within, out of people's hearts, come evil thoughts, sexual immorality, theft, murder, adultery, covetousness, wickedness, deceit, lewdness, envy, slander, pride, foolishness, and false testimony. It is these things that make a person unclean, but to eat with unwashed hands does not defile anyone."

Jesus says the source of uncleanness is the heart, and it begins with evil thoughts. The traditions of the elders focus on behavior, but Jesus says people must first change the way they think—they must repent. Until there is genuine change in the way a person understands who he is in relation to God and others, any attempt to draw close to God is futile.

FOR TWO YEARS, Jesus has walked the hills of Galilee proclaiming the good news. It's time to take the gospel outside the boundaries of Israel. Jesus announces they will leave immediately for Syria.

They walk northwest toward the coastal city of Tyre, twenty-five miles away. Located in a bustling port on the Mediterranean, Tyre is the southernmost city in Syria and is world-renowned for three things: the purple dye they make from the shells of murex snails, the purity of their silver coins (Tyrian silver is the only coin deemed acceptable for Jerusalem's annual temple tax), and their worship of the Greek hero Heracles, whom the Romans call Hercules.

The city is crowded and busy, but the hills surrounding it are quiet and isolated. It is here Jesus wants to spend time training his apprentices, but even in this remote country his fame precedes him. One woman, a lifelong resident of Tyre, is convinced Jesus has come in answer to her prayers. When she hears Jesus has entered the region, she walks toward the border to find him. Later that day she sees a dozen or so Jewish men in the distance and knows she has found Jesus.

"Have mercy on me, O Lord, Son of David," she cries out. "My daughter is severely oppressed by a demon. Have mercy on me, O Lord, Son of David!"

The twelve assume their master will quiet the Canaanite woman, but Jesus continues walking as if he hears nothing. The woman's pleas grow louder and more insistent. "Have mercy on me, O Lord, Son of David!"

Jesus knows his disciples see no value in the woman. His recent lesson about what God defines as unclean fell on deaf ears. This Gentile woman is shouting her acknowledgement of Jesus as the Messiah, but the apostles only see Jesus ignoring the plea of an obnoxious idolator. As he should. Godly rabbis are to talk with neither women nor Gentiles.

"Send her away," they tell Jesus. "For she is crying out after us."

When Jesus hears the request to get rid of her, he stops and waits for the woman to catch up with them. When she draws near, Jesus turns to his disciples and says, "I was sent only to the lost sheep of the house of Israel."

His answer appears to affirm his followers' prejudice. Their racism is deeply ingrained, and Jesus knows it will take more than a verbal reprimand to change their thinking. He wants to provide them with a living parable and stretch the woman's faith at the same time.

The woman falls at Jesus's feet with a simple but fervent plea: "Lord, help me!"

"Let the children be fed first," Jesus replies, "for it is not right to take the children's bread and throw it to the dogs."

The disciples wince when they hear their prejudices verbalized. Like most Jews, they are convinced Gentiles are dogs (the analogy is so common it has become proverbial), but hearing the proverb applied to a humble woman who is pleading for her daughter's life is unsettling.

The woman humbly acknowledges her status and responds with a proverb of her own. "Yes, Lord," she says. "Yet even the dogs under the table eat the children's crumbs."

Jesus is delighted with her answer, and the apostles are amazed at the wit and wisdom demonstrated by someone they had judged to be little better than a wild dog. "O woman," Jesus exclaims, "great is your faith! Let it be done for you as you desire—the demon has left your daughter."

The mother rejoices and runs home. The disciples are embarrassed by the lesson and realize there is much they need to learn.


JESUS SPENDS SEVERAL weeks in Syria teaching the apostles. He travels north toward Sidon, then turns eastward. Some still come to Jesus for healing, but the isolated locations afford him the time he needs to train his disciples. They walk east until they come to the arid heights of the Golan Mountains in the Decapolis. They were here weeks earlier, but this time there are no crowds following from Galilee, and the people they meet are mostly Gentiles.

They, too, have heard of Jesus. Crowds gather, hoping he will do for them what he has done among the Jews. Jesus does not disappoint. The lame walk, the blind see, demons are displaced, and the Gentiles praise the God of Israel.

Among those brought for healing is a man who is both deaf and mute. Jesus ordinarily heals such people with just a word, but this time he chooses a more visible demonstration: he touches the deaf man's ears, then applies some of his saliva to the mute's tongue. Lifting his eyes, Jesus commands, "Be opened!" and instantly the man is made whole.

The crowd is overjoyed. They know how severe the man's condition was and recognize how much power resides in the healer. "He has done all things well," they say to one another. "He even makes the deaf hear and the mute speak."

The number of Gentiles coming to Jesus astonishes his disciples. What he did among the children of Israel he now does among the Gentiles. After Jesus has been in the region for several days, the multitude swells to nearly ten thousand men, women, and children. They have little in the way of provisions but refuse to leave because Jesus is among them.

Jesus calls his disciples together and says, "I have compassion on the multitude. They've already stayed here with me for three days, and they have nothing to eat. If I send them home hungry, they will collapse on the way, and some of them have come a long distance."

The apostles are caught off guard by Jesus's statement and ask, "Where could we get enough bread in such a desolate place to feed so great a crowd?"

"How many loaves do you have?" Jesus asks.

"Seven, and a few small fish."

Jesus asks the twelve to seat the crowd on the ground and have them prepare to eat. He then takes the bread, gives thanks to the Father, and divides the seven loaves into seven large baskets, each with a portion of the fish. As his disciples share the food, they realize there is enough for everyone to eat their fill. Jesus has again miraculously multiplied the meager resources of his followers.

When the people finish eating, the disciples gather the remainder and fill the seven baskets. Jesus tells them to pack the baskets into their boat. They will be traveling back west to Magdala. As they row away, hundreds of Gentiles wave to them from the shore. The apostles reflect on the surprising new direction Jesus has taken and wonder how they will be received when they return to Galilee.

They come to shore a few miles north of Tiberias in the fishing village of Magdala. News of Jesus's arrival travels quickly. He has many enemies in the area and is soon accosted by a group of Pharisees and Sadducees. Hoping to discredit him, they demand he show them a sign from heaven.

Jesus offers them a lesson from the weather instead. "When it's evening you say, 'It will be fair weather, for the sky is red,' and in the morning you say, 'It will be stormy today because the sky is red and threatening.' You know how to interpret the appearance of the sky, but you can't interpret the signs of the times. Why does this generation seek a sign? I tell you truly, no sign will be given to this generation except the sign of Jonah."

Jesus offers no further explanation, and the religionists are left to ponder the meaning of the sign of Jonah. Jesus has said all he has to say to Galilee's religious leaders. He directs the apostles back into the boat, and they row north toward Bethsaida.

Near the end of the crossing, the twelve realize that in their haste to leave Magdala they forgot to bring food for the trip. Jesus overhears them discussing the lack of bread and says, "Watch out—beware of the leaven of the Pharisees and Sadducees and that of Herod."

Jesus is reminding them of the confrontation just hours earlier, but the disciples can think only of their growing hunger. They conclude that Jesus's comment about leaven is his way of chastising them for forgetting to bring food.

Jesus shakes his head and says, "You of little faith, why are you talking about having no bread? Do you still not perceive or understand? Have your hearts become hardened? Having eyes, do you not see? Having ears, do you not hear? And do you not remember? When I broke the five loaves for the five thousand, how many basketfuls of pieces did you pick up?"

"Twelve."

"And when I broke the seven loaves for the four thousand, how many basketfuls of pieces did you pick up?"

"Seven."

Jesus nods and says, "How can you still not understand that I wasn't talking to you about loaves of bread? But be on your guard against the yeast of the Pharisees and Sadducees."

The teacher looks into their eyes and is encouraged. The twelve are beginning to understand.

When they reach the shore, they moor the boat and walk toward Bethsaida. Shortly after they enter the town, a blind man is brought to

Jesus. The healer takes him by the hand and leads him outside the village. The twelve watch Jesus spit in the man's eyes and then rub the spittle in with his hands. "Do you see anything?" Jesus asks.

The man blinks a few times and squints. "I see people," he says, "but they look like trees, walking."

The one touch by Jesus has only partially restored his sight. Jesus again places his hands on the man's eyes, and his sight is fully restored. Jesus then tells the man to go home without broadcasting his healing.

As the man walks away, Jesus looks into the faces of his followers to see if they have understood the lesson. Like the man healed by Jesus, the apostles must move from blindness to full sight—they must move from no understanding of their master's identity to full comprehension.

And this, as Jesus intimated in the lesson, will take more than one touch. Ultimately, it will require an empty tomb.

# 15

# THE TURNING POINT

SUMMER, AD 32

*"Who do you say I am?"*

—Matthew 16:15

ALMOST THREE YEARS have passed since Jesus was anointed by John in the Jordan. The large crowds that once followed him have dwindled. His diminishing acclaim is due, in part, to the efforts of the nation's religious leaders to discredit him, but more damaging to Jesus's reputation is the message he brings. His teaching goes against the grain of some of Judaism's most honored beliefs and practices.

Jesus is undeterred. He expected his gospel to be widely misunderstood and knew there would be fierce opposition. But while there are no surprises for Jesus, there is the realization that his ministry in Galilee has come to an end. In a few months, it will be Passover; Jesus must prepare his apprentices for what will happen to him in Jerusalem and what awaits them afterward.

From Bethsaida, they walk twenty-five miles into Traconitis, the northern boundary of ancient Israel at the base of Mount Hermon. Once home to the tribe of Dan, the area has long been populated by Gentiles.

The region's tetrarch, Herod Phillip, recently renamed the primary city Caesarea Phillipi as a tribute to Caesar and himself, but for many generations the city has been known as Paneas, in honor of its most popular deity: the half-man, half-goat god Pan.

Seventeen hundred feet above the lake and overlooking the north end of the Jordan River Valley, the region's appeal to Jesus is its isolation; the sparsely populated area will allow him time to teach uninterrupted.

After a hike up the mountainside, the disciples stop for the evening. After dinner, Jesus asks the twelve, "Who do people say that I am?"

The apostles reply, "Some say John the Baptist, others say Elijah, and others say Jeremiah or one of the prophets of old has risen."

"But who do you say I am?"

The men look at one another, hesitant to speak. Finally, Simon Peter confesses what most of them believe: "You are the Christ—the Son of the living God."

Jesus nods and says, "Blessed are you, Simon bar Jonah, for flesh and blood has not revealed this to you but my Father who is in heaven has."

Peter is not the first of the twelve to call Jesus the Messiah, and recently all the disciples acknowledged him as the Christ when he came to them walking on the water. But something important is being missed.

The apostles, like the crowds, only understand the coming of the Messiah in a political context—a "Son of David" who will liberate Israel from her oppressors and restore the prosperity she enjoyed during the reign of the first David. Peter and the other disciples cannot comprehend a Christ who will suffer and die. This is simply not his role.

Jesus's apprentices do not grasp the nature of his mission, but they have reached a watershed in their understanding—they know he is the Messiah. Now they must learn how the Son of David and the Suffering Servant are the same man.

This will take time. The belief in a militaristic Messiah is deeply entrenched in the Jewish mind-set, and Jesus knows that changing this way of thinking will not happen in isolation. There must be a community. There must be participation. Only by partnering with God and others on the path will they come to understanding.

Jesus responds to Peter's declaration with one of his own. "And I tell you, you are Peter, and on this rock I will build my church, and the gates of Hades shall not prevail against it. I will give you the keys of the kingdom of heaven, and whatever you bind on earth shall have been bound in heaven, and whatever you loose on earth shall have been loosed in heaven."

Jesus says that Simon Peter—Rocky—will become a foundation stone in God's house, the church.

The apostles understand little of Jesus's teaching, but the concepts are familiar. *Ekklesia* (church) is the word the Septuagint translators chose to replace the Hebrew word *qahal*—the community of God's covenant people during the exodus. The apostles have been appointed to lead a faithful remnant in a new qahal, and Jesus promises that even the gates of Hades (a common Semitic metaphor for death) will not prevail against his church. In Christ, God's community will be eternally unstoppable.

Even more surprising to the apostles is the role they are to play in the new qahal. Peter will be given "the keys to the kingdom." Keys are a familiar symbol of authority. They open and close doors. They control who has access and who does not.

Later Jesus will confer this role on the entire church, but Peter will be the kingdom's chief steward and lead administrative officer. He will be like the one God told the prophet Isaiah about. "I will place on his shoulder the key to the house of David. What he opens, none shall shut—what he shuts, none shall open. I will fasten him like a peg in a secure place."

Essential to Peter's role as chief steward is mindfulness of whose kingdom he holds the keys to. First and foremost, stewards are servants. All the authority they wield is delegated. Stewards do not determine who is let in or put out; they simply obey their master's decrees. As Jesus said, that which the church binds or looses on earth must be that which has already been bound or loosed by God. Peter and the apostles are to function as ambassadors of the kingdom of heaven.

The twelve hear Jesus for the first time affirm he is the long-awaited Messiah, but he tells them that for now this information must be kept secret. He charges them to not use the title in public, partly because it will stir up notions of nationalism, but also because the disciples are still attached to false ideas about the Messiah.

The people of Israel have been confused about the Messiah for centuries. In ancient Israel, a person appointed to a special task was sometimes anointed with oil as a symbol of God's blessing. They would be deemed a messiah—an "anointed one." Over the course of many generations, the term came to identify a particular person—a coming king who would free God's people and establish a kingdom of righteousness. Particularly influential in the development of this concept were the *Psalms of Solomon*, a collection of extra-biblical writings that prophesied the Messiah would restore David's kingdom to its former glory. The only image the disciples have of the Messiah is one of a conquering liberator.

Jesus tells them, "It is necessary for the Son of Man to suffer much and be rejected by the elders and chief priests and scribes and be killed and on the third day be raised."

The twelve are dumbfounded. Jesus believes his death is somehow necessary? The rabbi is obviously confused about the arc of the Messiah.

Simon Peter takes Jesus by the arm and walks him away from the circle. "God forbid, Lord!" he whispers. "This shall never happen to you."

Moments earlier Peter had spoken for God; now he speaks for the enemy. Jesus confronts the source of the suggestion. "Get behind me, Satan!" he tells Peter. "You are a stumbling block to me, for you are not setting your mind on the things of God but on the things of man."

Peter's declaration promises the same political shortcut the Devil proposed in the wilderness, and Jesus knows that so long as the rock upon whom the church is to be built holds that belief, he will be a stumbling stone. Thus the admonition to "get behind" and assume the appropriate position of an apprentice.

"If anyone wishes to come behind me," Jesus says, "let him deny himself, take up his cross daily, and follow me—for whoever wishes to save his life will lose it, but whoever loses his life for my sake will save it."

Jesus wants his followers to understand that discipleship is more than a decision—it is a way of life. It's about choosing obedience to God even when faithfulness leads into harm's way. Jesus says it's about following him down a path that ends at a cross.

"What does it profit a person to gain the whole world only to lose or forfeit his soul?" Jesus asks. "For what can a person give in exchange for his soul?"

Jesus admonishes his followers to take the long view: today's decisions will have eternal consequences.

"Whoever is ashamed of me and of my words in this adulterous and sinful generation, the Son of Man will also be ashamed of when he comes in the glory of the Father with the holy angels. Then he will repay each person according to what that person has done."

Jesus speaks of a day of reckoning when all accounts will be settled. Then he adds enigmatically, "But I tell you truly, there are some standing here who will not taste death before they see the kingdom of God come with power."

JESUS KNOWS HIS revelation has not been understood, and he spends the next six days alone with the apostles, reinforcing his teaching about what awaits him in Jerusalem. Late one afternoon, they make camp at the base of a mountain, and Jesus invites Peter, James, and John to climb into the heights with him for prayer. They near the summit as darkness falls and begin praying, but the apostles are exhausted after a long day and fall asleep.

The sound of voices awakens them. They lift their heads and rub their eyes to be sure they are not dreaming—the Jesus they know has been transformed. His face is shining, and his clothing is radiating light.

As their heads clear, the disciples realize their master is talking with two men. From the conversation, they learn they are in the presence of Moses and Elijah, two of Israel's preeminent prophets. Moses foretold the coming of a final prophet who would lead God's people to a new kingdom, and it was prophesied that before that day came, Elijah would return and "turn the hearts of fathers to their children and the hearts of children to their fathers." This restoration of relationships was understood to be the harbinger of the restoration of all things.

The conversation is concluding, but the disciples hear enough to know that Jesus, Moses, and Elijah are discussing the suffering Jesus will experience in Jerusalem. The topic frightens the three apostles, and none are willing to ask for more information, but when the two prophets prepare to leave, Peter wants to extend the meeting.

Not knowing what to say, he suggests the disciples do something to commemorate the occasion. "Rabbi," he says, "it is good that we're here. Let us make three tents, one for you and one for Moses and one for Elijah."

Peter's intention is good; he wants to honor three of the most important people in Israel's history, but he is misinterpreting what he sees—this is not a conversation between three prophets.

As Peter speaks, an unnaturally radiant cloud envelopes the mountaintop. From the cloud comes a voice. "This is My beloved Son, My chosen one. With him I am well pleased—listen to him."

At Jesus's baptism, the Father had quoted Psalm 2 and the prophet Isaiah to identify the Son as both the Messiah and the Suffering Servant. The Father repeats those two references and adds "listen to him." These three words point to a third title for Jesus. Peter, James, and John are seeing the fulfillment of Moses's prophecy in Deuteronomy: "The Lord your God will raise up for you a prophet like me from among you, from your brothers—you must listen to him."

The disciples understand the significance of the prediction. To listen to God is to comprehend what He is saying, but listening doesn't end there. Ultimately, to listen to God is to obey Him. Hence God's admonition following Moses's prophecy: "I will put My words in his mouth, and he will tell them everything I command him. Whoever refuses to listen to My words that he shall speak in My name will answer to Me."

Peter, James, and John are familiar with the Scriptures that surround the command and realize that God has transferred all of Moses's authority to Jesus. And more, for the one spoken of by Moses is the final prophet who will usher in the consummation of the age. When the three hear this pronouncement, they tremble and fall facedown on the ground.

Jesus walks over to his terrified disciples and touches them. "Rise," he says, "and have no fear."

When they lift their heads, they see they are alone with Jesus. Moses, Elijah, and the luminous cloud have all vanished. The Jesus they know has returned.

Morning breaks, and they walk down the mountain to rejoin the others. On the way, Jesus says, "Don't tell anyone what you have seen until the Son of Man has been raised from the dead."

Peter, James, and John readily agree, but they have no idea what Jesus is talking about and are afraid to ask. As they walk, the three exchange confused whispers about the mysterious reference to being raised from the dead and wonder if Jesus has told them another parable.

Particularly troubling to the disciples is their inability to reconcile Jesus's words with what they have been taught all their life about the chronology of the eschaton. The prophet Malachi closed the canon of Scripture with God's promise to "send Elijah the prophet before the great and awesome Day of the Lord." Jesus had just spoken with Elijah. Is what they saw on the mountain a fulfillment of that prophecy?

Further, it was commonly taught that Elijah would "restore all things" before the Messiah arrives, but how could the Messiah be killed in an environment in which justice and righteousness have been restored? Jesus's reasoning doesn't make sense.

The disciples ask, "Why do the scribes say that first Elijah must come?"

Jesus responds with a rhetorical question that frames the disciples' dilemma. "Elijah does indeed come first to restore all things," he tells them. "Yet how is it written concerning the Son of Man that he should suffer many things and be treated with contempt? But I tell you that Elijah has already come, and they did not recognize him but did to him whatever they wanted. In the same way, the Son of Man is destined to suffer at their hands."

Jesus acknowledges Elijah's role in the restoration of righteousness, but he reminds them that the Scriptures also speak of a righteous sufferer who will come before Earth's ultimate restoration. Isaiah called him "the Servant of the Lord" and predicted he would be despised and rejected by men, a man of sorrows who would bear the sins of many—a man who would ultimately be "pierced for our transgressions and crushed for our iniquities."

Jesus is asking his followers to reconsider Isaiah's prophecy, and particularly what it says about the necessity of the Servant's death—even though the Servant will be innocent of any wrongdoing, he will be "numbered with the transgressors," and it will be "the will of the Lord to crush him."

It is essential that Jesus's apprentices grasp this truth. All they can think about is the victorious reign of the Messiah, but there can be no exaltation of the Messiah until there has been a humiliation of the Servant. The two are inseparably linked, for it is the Servant's sacrificial death that makes the Messiah's reign possible in the first place.

Jesus is saying that the disciples' interpretation of the Scriptures is right, but their history is wrong. Elijah has already fulfilled his mission. He was rewarded with rejection and martyrdom—the same destiny Jesus expects for himself.

The three nod knowingly; Jesus is speaking about John the Baptist. That much they understand.

JESUS, PETER, JAMES, and John reach the foot of the mountain and find the other apostles embroiled in a dispute with a group of religious scholars.

When the crowd sees Jesus approaching, they run to greet him, but Jesus continues walking toward the nine, who are being accosted by the scribes.

"What are you arguing about with them?" Jesus asks.

Before anyone can answer, a man steps out of the crowd, kneels before Jesus, and says, "Lord, have mercy on my son, my only child, for he is possessed by a spirit that makes him mute. He has seizures and suffers terribly. Whenever the spirit seizes him, he screams and is thrown to the ground in convulsions. He foams at the mouth and grinds his teeth and becomes rigid. It scarcely ever leaves and is destroying him. I brought him to your disciples and asked them to cast it out, but they could not."

Jesus realizes he has walked in on a failed exorcism attempt and says, "You faithless and perverted generation, how long must I stay with you and put up with you?"

Jesus pauses to allow his question to sink in, and then turns to the boy's father. "Bring your son to me."

When the boy is brought to Jesus, the demon within the child recognizes the Christ and attempts to intimidate him. The spirit throws the boy to the ground. He begins convulsing and rolling in the dirt, foam bubbling from his mouth.

Jesus watches the behavior for a few moments, then asks the boy's father, "How long has he been like this?"

"From childhood," the man replies. "And it has often cast him into fire and water, to destroy him."

The father pauses to consider his next words. Earlier he had boldly asked Jesus's apprentices to exorcise the demon, and they were unable. Why would their master fare any better? The boy seems possessed by an inexorable force. Still, any assistance would be appreciated.

"If you can do anything," the father pleads, "have compassion on us and help us."

The father's faith is tentative. Once hopeful of a complete cure, he will now settle for whatever help he can get. Jesus knows the man's faith is small and wants to stretch it. He uses the man's own words to do it.

"'If you can'?" Jesus replies. "All things are possible for the one who believes."

Immediately the man cries out, "I believe—help my unbelief!"

Jesus looks at the child writhing on the ground but speaks to the malevolent spirit within. "Mute and deaf spirit, I command you: come out of him and never enter him again."

As the words are spoken, an unearthly shriek comes from deep within the boy. He shudders violently and goes into convulsions. Then the screaming and shaking stops. The boy's body lies limp and still in the dust. To the onlookers, it appears the exorcism has gone terribly wrong.

Word spreads through the crowd: "The boy is dead."

The exorcist responds by taking the boy by the hand, lifting him up, and walking him over to his father. The crowd is astonished and shouts praises. Jesus bids them farewell and walks south.

The apostles who failed to exorcise the demon are thankful for the way things turned out but bothered by their lack of success. "Why were we not able to cast it out?" they ask.

"Because of your little faith," Jesus says. "For I tell you truly, if you have faith the size of a mustard seed, you will say to this mountain, 'Move from here to there,' and it will move. Nothing will be impossible for you. But this kind cannot be cast out by anything but prayer."

Jesus is telling the twelve that their faith is virtually nonexistent. Worse, what little faith they do have is misdirected. They had been given the authority to heal, but had treated the gift like it was a magical ability they could apply at will.

Jesus points out that an apprentice's power lies not in incantations but in his relationship with God. God does not demand exceptional faith—even a minuscule amount is sufficient to move a mountain—but at the heart of "mustard seed" faith is a willingness to obey God. Having a title, even one as lofty as apostle, is of no value if one is not regularly receiving God's guidance and implementing it.

And this is precisely the challenge Jesus faces. His disciples believe their problems are sins and bad habits, but the source is much deeper— they are unwilling to trust God's Word enough to live by its principles.

Jesus knows there is much work to be done in the hearts of his apprentices, but he also knows his hour is rapidly approaching.

In a few short months, he will be dead.

# 16

# A Kingdom of Children

SUMMER–AUTUMN, AD 32

*"Unless you turn and become like children, you will never get into the kingdom of heaven."*

—Matthew 18:3

JESUS AND THE apostles return to Galilee after several weeks in the region of Caesarea Phillipi. In the past, he has drawn large crowds. Now he bypasses the towns and villages. There are no miraculous healings, no exorcisms, no sermons—his teaching is limited to the twelve and focused on what lies ahead. Jesus must prepare his followers for a future they cannot begin to imagine.

"Let these words sink into your ears," Jesus tells them. "The Son of Man is destined to be betrayed into the hands of people who will kill him, and on the third day he will be raised."

The words are plain, and the disciples now understand that what Jesus told them earlier was not a parable; he is prophesying his death. What they can't understand is how this could be part of God's plan. And who except God is mighty enough to deliver the Messiah to death? And what does a resurrection have to do with any of this? The twelve have no answers but are afraid to ask.

Jesus and his apprentices walk south toward the lake and eventually arrive in Capernaum. The town is quiet, and the men inconspicuously

145

make their way to the home of Peter and Andrew.

They do not, however, escape the notice of the townspeople. The Levites who collect the temple tax have no record of Jesus paying, so when they see Peter in the street one day, they ask, "Does your teacher not pay the tax?"

They are not asking about a civil tax but one that, since the days of the Maccabees, has been annually requested of every Jewish male between the ages of twenty and fifty. Its purpose is honorable—the maintenance and beautification of the temple—but the tax is controversial.

While most Jews pay the levy, two small but vocal minorities do not. The party of the Sadducees reject it as a modern invention of the Pharisees, and the Essenes, in keeping with the Scriptures that mention the tax, instruct their followers to pay it only once in their lifetime.

The temple tax is sourced in the Exodus account of a half-shekel required of every male member of the community when the census was taken. The Scriptures describe each Israelite's offering as "a ransom for his life" to be used for the upkeep of the Lord's tabernacle in the wilderness, "that it may bring the people of Israel to remembrance before the Lord."

The levy is a wellspring of Jewish pride and is viewed by most as a patriotic duty. The religious representatives would be content with a "no" to their question—a refusal could be useful in undermining the prophet's popularity. But Peter answers yes. Of course Jesus will pay the tax.

Peter's reply comes quickly, but as he walks away he is less sure of his answer, and when he returns home, he is startled when Jesus says, "What do you think, Simon? The kings of the earth—from whom do they levy duties and tax? From their own sons or from others?"

The apostle is at a loss for words. The master is obviously addressing what happened earlier, but how could he know about that conversation?

"From others," Simon stammers.

Jesus smiles and says, "Well, then, the sons are exempt. But so that we don't cause them to stumble, go down to the lake and cast a hook. Take the first fish that comes up; when you open its mouth, you will find a coin. Take that and give it to them for you and me."

Jesus is convinced that he and the children of the King are free from obligation, but he's happy to surrender personal privileges when they become stumbling blocks. The apostles' attitudes are different. Their inclination is to think of themselves first. Arguments often break out among the twelve about who is the greatest apostle. They may be an elite group, but all of them are insecure and competitive.

One day after a particularly heated quarrel, the apostles approach Jesus meekly and ask, "Who is the greatest in the kingdom of heaven?"

The question sounds innocent, but Jesus knows what motivates it and asks, "What were you arguing about on the way?"

The men say nothing and stare at the ground. Jesus sits down and asks his apprentices to gather around him. "If anyone wishes to be first," Jesus tells them, "he must be last of all and servant of all."

Jesus calls a young child to come to him. Embracing the child, he addresses his followers. "I tell you truly, unless you turn and become like children, you will never get into the kingdom of heaven. Anyone who will take the lowly position of this child is the greatest in the kingdom of heaven.

"Whoever receives a little child like this in my name receives me, and whoever receives me, receives not just me but the One who sent me. For whoever is the least among you is the greatest."

The apostles are concerned about their place in the heavenly pecking order. Jesus wants them to strive for greatness, but he warns them that God's definition of greatness is different from theirs—in God's economy, the ones awarded the highest positions are those who serve others and give no thought to rank and privilege.

Jesus's recommendation to seek the status of a child is hard for the twelve to receive. A child has no status—all he is and all he has comes from his parents. Jesus says life in the kingdom is the same way.

The apostles hear little of Jesus's instruction; their thoughts are focused on how they can gain stature in the church. "Teacher," John says, "we saw someone casting out demons in your name, and we tried to stop him because he's not following us."

Jesus shakes his head and says, "Do not stop him, for no one who does a miracle in my name will be able soon afterward to speak evil of me. Whoever is not against us is for us. For I tell you truly, whoever gives you a cup of water to drink because you belong to Christ will by no means lose his reward.

"But whoever causes one of these little ones who believe in me to stumble, it would be better for him to have a heavy millstone hung around his neck and to be drowned in the depths of the sea. Woe to the world because of stumbling blocks, for stumbling blocks are bound to come, but woe to the one through whom the stumbling block comes!"

Jesus then admonishes those who allow their behavior to trip them up. "If your hand causes you to stumble," Jesus says, "cut it off and throw it away. It is better for you to enter life crippled than with two hands to go to Gehenna, to the unquenchable fire. And if your foot causes you to stumble, cut it off. It is better for you to enter life lame than with two feet to be thrown into Gehenna. And if your eye causes you to stumble, tear it out. It is better for you to enter the kingdom of God one-eyed than to have two eyes and be thrown into Gehenna, 'where their worm does not die, and the fire is not quenched.'"

The word pictures are as memorable as they are gruesome. Jesus quotes Isaiah's prophecy about *Gehenna*, the final abode of people who rebel against God.

Gehenna (a compound word meaning *valley of Hinnom*) was originally the southern border of the city of Jerusalem. The prophet Jeremiah identified it as a pagan holy place where children were sacrificed to the god Molech. King Josiah ended that by desecrating the valley and turning it into a refuse dump. It became the destination for things that had no value. Human excrement, animal carcasses, and other rubbish were dumped there. The fires in the valley constantly burned, and over the years the site became symbolic of the place of divine punishment. "Gehenna" became a place of endless torment with no hope of relief. Gehenna represents the eternal hell of all who refuse to accept God's invitation to life.

Jesus solemnly warns the twelve to stop trivializing and misinterpreting what it means to be an apprentice. It's about obedience and servanthood, not status and privilege.

"For everyone," Jesus tells them, "will be salted with fire."

The apostles are not sure what Jesus is referring to. Salt and fire are widely used metaphors, but the only place they are used together is in sacrificial worship—salt is a symbol of the covenant and is applied to every sacrifice before it is consumed by the fire.

The prophet Malachi had said the Messiah would be "like a refiner's fire" and would "purify the sons of Levi and refine them like gold and silver." John the Baptist, drawing on Malachi's words, had prophesied that the Messiah would baptize with the Holy Spirit and with fire.

In the Scriptures, fire often refers to trials that God uses to make His people fit for the kingdom. Believers, however, are far from passive victims in the process. "Salt is good," Jesus tells his apprentices, "but if the salt has lost its saltiness, how can you make it salty again? Have salt in yourselves, and be at peace with one another."

Salt means different things to different people. To the homemaker it is a preservative; to the cook it is a flavor enhancer; to those before the altar it speaks of purity; to the rabbis, salt symbolizes wisdom. But there is no need for the disciples to choose between these options—all are relevant to the work Jesus is calling them to.

Jesus's admonition to be at peace with one another reminds the apostles how the conversation began—they were squabbling about status. "See to it that you do not despise one of these little ones," he tells the future leaders of his church. "For I tell you that their angels in heaven continually see the face of my Father who is in heaven."

The message is clear—the least matter much to God, and He is always watching over them.

"What do you think?" Jesus asks. "If someone has a hundred sheep and one of them wanders away, won't he leave the ninety-nine on the hillsides and go in search of the one that went astray? And if he manages to find it, I tell you truly that he rejoices over it more than over the ninety-nine that never went astray. In the same way, it is not the will of your Father in heaven that one of these little ones should perish."

The parable is carefully chosen. Jesus knows the day will come when his church will have to resolve her conflicts without his physical presence, and the parable of the one and ninety-nine is taught to prepare his people to help one another when that day arrives. Everyone falls out of step with God at times, and there must be a path for reconciliation.

Jesus teaches his disciples four progressive steps to take when a fellow church member wanders away from God.

"If your brother sins," Jesus says, "go and tell him his fault, between you and him alone. If he listens to you, you have gained your brother. But if he does not listen, take one or two others along with you, so that 'every charge may be established by the evidence of two or three witnesses.' If he refuses to listen to them, tell it to the church. And if he refuses to listen even to the church, let him be to you as a Gentile and a tax collector."

Jesus's teaching echoes the command from the Torah to "reason frankly with your neighbor so you will not share in his guilt." If one disciple sees another disciple wandering from the truth, the first course of action is to, in a spirit of gentleness, personally and privately speak with the wanderer. If the one-on-one conversation results in repentance and reconciliation, that is to be the end of it.

But if the person refuses to listen, Jesus says to follow God's instruction in Deuteronomy—a second meeting takes place in the presence of objective witnesses. Perhaps the additional counselors can help both parties become clear about God's will. And, again, if there is repentance, the matter is to be closed.

But if there is still hardness of heart, a third step is to be taken—the entire church is informed. Hopefully a multitude of witnesses will persuade the wandering soul to return, but if there is still no repentance, one last drastic step is to be taken—the community of faith is to dissociate herself from the person. The one who refuses to turn back to God is to be treated like "a Gentile and a tax collector." In the Torah, this was called being "cut off" from the assembly.

In Christ's community of faith, believers are to teach, encourage, and admonish one another, but this is impossible when a person refuses to listen to Jesus. He is to be excluded from the church.

But even this final step is not about retribution—it speaks to rehabilitation and reconciliation. No animosity is to be shown toward the one set outside; he is to be loved and prayed for. The hope of the church is that the Holy Spirit will use the severance to convict the wanderer's heart and lead him to repent and return to the fold.

The church, however, is to take an active role in the process. "I tell you truly," Jesus says, "whatever you bind on earth shall have been bound in heaven, and whatever you loose on earth shall have been loosed in heaven."

The apostles have heard these words before; Jesus had used them in Caesarea Phillipi when he appointed Simon Peter to be the chief steward of the kingdom. Simon still stands as the first among equals, but now Jesus expands the mandate to the rest of the disciples. The keys to the kingdom will be entrusted to the church.

Jesus then identifies the source of his people's power. "Moreover," Jesus says, "I tell you that if two of you on earth agree about anything you ask for, it will be done for you by my Father in heaven. For where two or three are gathered in my name, I am there in the midst of them."

In Judaism, a minimum of ten adult males is required for corporate worship to be valid. Jesus says that in his church, two men or women in agreement is a quorum when they gather under his authority.

The lesson has been about corporate forgiveness, and the disciples understand the process, but they are unclear about personal offenses. Many rabbis, citing the prophet Amos, say that God forgives three times but no more, and His people should do the same.

Simon Peter asks, "Lord, how many times will my brother sin against me, and I still forgive him? As many as seven times?"

Peter wants to frame the question in a way that sounds gracious, so he doubles the number in Amos and adds one more for good measure. Seven is the number of completeness. Peter feels he is being more than generous and is shocked when Jesus replies, "I tell you, not just seven times but as many as seventy-seven times."

Jesus draws on a story from Genesis and contrasts the limitless vengeance threatened by Lamech with the limitless forgiveness God offers. Jesus wants his followers to understand that forgiveness isn't about keeping a tally of wrongs done—forgiveness is an attitude that reflects the heart of God.

"The kingdom of heaven," Jesus says, "may be compared to a king who wanted to settle accounts with his servants. When he began to settle up, one was brought to him who owed him ten thousand talents. The man could not pay the debt, so his master ordered him to be sold, together with his wife and children and all that he had, so that payment could be made.

"The servant fell at his feet, imploring him, 'Be patient with me, and I will repay you everything.' And out of pity for him, the master of that servant released him and forgave him the debt.

"But when that servant went out, he found one of his fellow servants who owed him a hundred denarii. Grabbing him by the throat, he began to choke him, saying, 'Pay me back what you owe me!'

"His fellow servant fell down and pleaded with him, 'Be patient with me, and I will repay you.' But he refused and threw him in prison until he could repay the debt.

"His fellow servants saw what had taken place. They were horrified and reported to their master what they had seen. Then his master summoned him and said to him, 'You wicked servant! All that debt I forgave you because you pleaded with me. Wasn't it your duty to show mercy on your fellow servant, just as I showed mercy on you?' And his master was furious and delivered him to the torturers until he could pay all his debt."

Jesus pauses to be sure his apprentices have understood the story, and then adds, "My heavenly Father will treat every one of you the same way unless you forgive your brother from your heart."

The parable is shocking. In an honor-and-shame-based society such as Israel, revenge is not only acceptable, it is lauded. An eye for an eye is justice. Jesus doesn't disagree but suggests there is an alternative: mercy.

The monetary amounts mentioned in the parable tell the tale. The second debtor owed a hundred denarii—a substantial amount given the average day laborer was paid one denarii. At that rate, it would take about four months to repay the debt. The first debtor, on the other hand, owed ten thousand talents. One talent was the equivalent of six thousand denarii; to repay ten thousand talents would require two hundred thousand years—far too great a debt to ever hope to repay—and this is Jesus's point. God has forgiven each of his children an incalculable debt, and they are obliged to pass that mercy on.

The story reminds the disciples of what Jesus had taught about forgiveness in the sermon on the mountainside. Jesus had looked each of them in the eye and said, "If you forgive others for their offenses, your heavenly Father will forgive you as well, but if you do not forgive others, neither will your Father forgive your offenses."

Forgiveness, Jesus teaches, is reciprocal. When a person experiences God's forgiveness, his eyes are opened, and he can see the immeasurable debt he has been released from. His repentance will bring perspective. He will see how minor the sins committed against him are when compared to the sins he has committed against God. His nature will change—the forgiven will become forgiving.

But those who do not forgive demonstrate they have not changed. Despite God's offer of full forgiveness, they refuse to turn to Him. Instead, like the man in the parable, they demand what is owed them. And that is exactly what they will receive.


WHEN AUTUMN ARRIVES, the nation's attention turns to *Sukkoth*, the Feast of Booths, the country's most popular festival. One day when Jesus is visiting his family, his brothers encourage him to attend the celebration. "Leave here and go to Judea," they tell him, "so that your disciples there may also see the works you are doing. For no one does anything in secret if he seeks to be well known. If you're doing these things, show yourself to the world!"

His brothers' proposal is reasonable; the huge festival crowd could translate into thousands of followers, but Jesus is not interested in pandering to the multitudes. "My time has not yet come," he tells his brothers, "but your time is always here. The world cannot hate you, but it hates me, because I testify about it that its works are evil. You go up to the feast. I am not going up to this feast because my time has not yet fully come."

Jesus tells his brothers that anytime is right for them to travel to the festival; they are causing no trouble, and no one is seeking to harm them. Jesus, on the other hand, has been marked for death. He has intentionally missed this year's entire festival season so far. He will not go to Jerusalem until God instructs him to do so.

Those instructions come just as the celebration is getting started. The Holy Spirit prompts Jesus to go to Sukkoth, but Jerusalem is a three-day walk, and he will not arrive until the festivities are well underway.

The shortest route to the capital is the ridge road through Samaria. Jesus sends a couple of disciples ahead to a Samaritan village to arrange for lodging, but when the villagers learn they are on their way to Jerusalem, they refuse them hospitality.

When the two return with the news, James and John are furious. "Lord!" they shout. "Do you want us to call fire down from heaven to consume them?" The two brothers are inspired by Elijah, who had called fire down on two companies of Samaritan soldiers not far from this very village. Was there not biblical precedence to destroy these Christ rejecters?

Jesus shakes his head and rebukes the aptly nicknamed Sons of Thunder. The villagers weren't rejecting the Messiah—they were rejecting a group of Jews on their way to a religious festival in Jerusalem. Jesus reminds them that there are other villages they can stay in.

As they continue walking, they are joined by a teacher of the Law who tells Jesus, "I will follow you wherever you go."

Few religious scholars have recognized Jesus's true identity, and he would gladly have the scribe as a disciple, but he knows the man's understanding of what it means to follow him is shallow.

"The foxes have holes and birds of the air have roosts," he tells the lawyer, "but the Son of Man has nowhere to lay his head."

The man is being encouraged to count the cost—following Jesus will lead to a cross.

Jesus continues walking south. Along the way, he meets a man and says, "Follow me."

The offer is intriguing, but the man is not willing to risk the condemnation of his family and community. "Lord," he replies, "first let me go and bury my father."

The man's father is not dead or dying. Otherwise, the man would be home attending to his family. His request is motivated by the traditional duty of a son to live at home to care for his mother and father until their death.

The man assumes that Jesus will not tell his disciples to violate the expectations of family and friends, but this is exactly what Jesus demands. "Leave the dead to bury their own dead," he tells the man, "but as for you, go and proclaim the kingdom of God."

As Jesus continues walking toward Jerusalem, he has a third encounter with a man interested in becoming a disciple. "I will follow you, Lord," the man promises, "but first let me take leave of those at my home."

The man expresses a desire to follow Jesus, but his request is insincere. The man is not asking to be allowed time to go home and say good-bye to his family. He's asking if he may "take leave" of his parents. To take leave is not to inform them of his decision but to ask for permission to leave.

Jesus knows the man is more interested in pleasing his parents than in following him and says, "No one who puts his hand to the plow and looks back is fit for the kingdom of God."

Jesus chooses the image of a plowman to stress the primacy of discipleship. A Palestinian plow is very light, and the plowman must perform several operations at the same time. With his left hand, he keeps the tool upright and lifts it over rocks while applying whatever pressure is necessary to make the appropriate furrow depth. In his right hand is a six-foot goad tipped with an iron spike to keep the oxen in line. Then, with both hands full, he must constantly look ahead to keep the furrow straight. It's a job that demands total concentration. Jesus says apprenticeship to him is like that.

Jesus wants those who are interested in following him to know that apprenticeship is not a task to be added to other interests. Discipleship will not only disrupt life's normal rhythms, it will redefine them.

17

# LIGHT OF THE WORLD

OCTOBER, AD 32

*In him was life, and that life was the light of all people. The light shines in the darkness, and the darkness has not mastered it.*

—John 1:4–5

ISRAEL'S YEARLY RELIGIOUS calendar revolves around a cycle of sevens. In the Torah, God commands seven festivals to be held in the first seven months, and each is to be an expression of the nation's most sacred day: the Sabbath. Three of the feasts are considered so important that attendance is obligatory for all Jewish men, yet, as this year's festival season draws to a close with the Feast of Sukkoth, Jesus has attended none of them.

Sukkoth, the Feast of Booths, is held six months after Passover and is the nation's most popular festival. Like the other feasts, it combines thanksgiving for God's provision with a retelling of sacred history. Sukkoth was prescribed by God to remind His people of the lessons they learned in the wilderness and to recall the time when God dwelt in a temporary shelter alongside them.

In the Torah it is written, "All native Israelites shall dwell in booths so that your descendants may know that I made the people of Israel dwell in booths when I brought them out of the land of Egypt—I am the Lord your God."

In obedience to God's Word, dwellings made of green boughs are constructed throughout the land. Temporary shelters surround the city walls and sit in courtyards and atop many roofs, and for eight days the people of Israel live outdoors in the leafy booths and recite the lessons learned during forty years in the wilderness.

Much time is spent recalling the teachings of Moses, but equal time is spent celebrating God's goodness. It's autumn, and the second harvest is in. Grapes are becoming new wine; olives have been pressed to yield their oil; and larders are filled with ripe figs, dates, and pomegranates.

It is a time of abundance, and normally the people are in high spirits, but this year a pall lies over the feast. Jesus is being talked about all over town, and opinions vary. Some say he is a good man, and others are convinced he is a deceiver, but all the discussions take place privately because no one wants to be identified as a follower of Jesus. They have been warned of the consequences.

When Jesus misses the first days of the festival, the Jewish leaders assume he will not attend, and his arrival in the middle of the week is unexpected. They find Jesus on the temple mount preaching to a large crowd. Those in the audience are surprised by his grasp of the Scriptures and his ability to apply them. Several ask, "How does this man have such learning when he has never been taught?"

Jesus overhears the question. "My teaching is not my own," he tells the crowd. "It comes from the One who sent me." Like other rabbis, Jesus claims his authority comes from another, but unlike other rabbis, Jesus says his authority comes directly from God.

"Anyone who chooses to do the will of God will know whether my teaching is from God or whether I am speaking on my own authority."

According to Jesus, recognizing truth doesn't require theological training. Truth is self-authenticating—but only when the one evaluating it is committed to doing God's will. Knowing the truth requires trusting God enough to act on what He says. Then one will be able to discern whether Jesus's words are from God.

But this goes to the heart of his opponents' problem—they do not seek to know God's will. They are more interested in impressing one another.

"The one who speaks on his own authority seeks his own glory," Jesus tells them, "but the one who seeks the glory of the One who sent him is true, and in him there is no unrighteousness."

The Jews are proud of their heritage and how God entrusted them with His Law, but Jesus wants them to realize that there is a big difference between receiving the Law and living it. "Hasn't Moses given you the Law?" he asks the crowd. "Yet none of you keeps the Law. Why are you looking for an opportunity to kill me?"

The indictment shocks his audience. One shouts, "You have a demon!"

Another asks, "Who is trying to kill you?"

Some in the crowd are pilgrims from faraway lands, but most live locally and know exactly what the teacher is talking about. When Jesus was in Jerusalem last year, he incurred the wrath of the Sanhedrin by healing a man on the Sabbath and then claiming God's authority to do so. The desire of the Sanhedrin to silence Jesus is a secret to no one in town.

Jesus knows they are still upset about last year's Sabbath healing. He looks into the angry faces surrounding him and says, "I did one work, and you are all amazed. This is why Moses gave you circumcision—not that it's from Moses, but from the patriarchs—and you circumcise a man on the Sabbath. If a man can receive circumcision on the Sabbath so that the law of Moses may not be broken, are you angry with me because on the Sabbath I made a man's whole body well? Stop judging by mere appearances—judge with right judgment."

Many in the crowd nod in agreement; it is commonly accepted that some of God's commandments override others. Jesus uses a classic example—circumcision. The rite preceded Mosaic Law and was never negated by it. According to the rabbis, the rite makes the boy being circumcised "complete." Thus circumcision has always taken precedence over Sabbath labor restrictions. Jesus's argument is simple—if circumcision, which "completes" one body part, takes precedence over Sabbath law, then how much more so an act that brings wholeness to the entire body?

The crowd begins to wonder. How could this be the man the religious leaders want to silence? What he says makes perfect sense. The people whisper questions to one another. Several who live in Jerusalem ask, "Isn't this the man they're trying to kill? And here he is, speaking publicly, and they say nothing to him!"

Has the Sanhedrin had a change of heart? Some ask, "Can it be the authorities really know that this is the Messiah?"

Others are skeptical and point out, "But we know where this man comes from, and when the Messiah appears, no one will know where he comes from."

The rabbis taught that while the birthplace of the Messiah had been revealed by Micah, the rest of his identity would be shrouded in mystery until he revealed himself. Most in the crowd are convinced there is nothing mysterious about the carpenter from Nazareth.

"You know me, and you know where I am from?" Jesus asks. "I have not come of my own accord, but the One who sent me is true—the One you do not know. I know Him, for I am from Him, and He sent me."

Some in the crowd are ready to make a citizen's arrest. Jesus's words are not only insulting, they are blasphemous. But others in the audience hear Jesus's confession differently and say, "The Messiah, whenever he comes—will he do more signs than this man has done?"

The Pharisees become alarmed when they hear people voicing faith in Jesus and rush to the nearby Hall of Hewn Stones. They report the mood of the audience to the Sanhedrin, and the temple guard is immediately dispatched to arrest Jesus. Within a few minutes the policemen are in the crowd and pushing their way to the front to arrest the teacher, when they hear Jesus say, "I will be with you a little longer, and then I go to the One who sent me. You will seek me but you will not find me, and where I am you cannot come."

Jesus's words halt the soldiers, and they become part of the questioning crowd. "Where does this man intend to go that we will not find him?" they ask.

One in the throng scoffs, "Surely he isn't planning to go to the Diaspora and teach the Greeks?"

Another is confused and asks, "What does he mean by saying, 'You will seek me but you will not find me, and where I am you cannot come'?"

Jesus, aware of the Sanhedrin's plot to arrest him, does not stay to answer questions. While the crowd is debating the meaning of his message, Jesus quietly walks away and is not seen at the temple until the last day of the feast.

MEANWHILE, THE DAILY rituals of the holy week constantly remind the celebrants of how God took care of them for forty years in the wilderness. Two rites in particular capture the heart of the festival.

The most important is the water rite, designed to recall how God saved Israel by bringing water from the rock. It has been a sacred part of the feast for more than two hundred years. Every morning of the festival week, the crowds participate in an elaborate ritual. A holy procession walks south from the temple, singing and making music as they travel the quarter mile to the Pool of Siloam. One of the priests fills a golden pitcher with living water from the Gihon Spring, which feeds the pool. Thousands of pilgrims line the parade route and shout praises as the procession returns to the temple. The water is brought to the altar, and is poured out in conjunction with the morning drink offering while a Levitical choir sings the *Hallel* (Psalms 113–118). When the choir reaches Psalm 118, the pilgrims join in the celebration by holding up their *etrogs* (citron fruit) and waving their *lulavs* (fans made from branches of willow, myrtle, and palm) and shouting, "Give thanks to the Lord!"

On the seventh day of the feast, the entire ritual is repeated seven times. The altar is saturated with water and prayers for rain in the coming year. More importantly, there are prayers for an outpouring of the Holy Spirit. Seven times the people sing the passage in Psalm 118 that affirms, "The stone that the builders rejected has become the cornerstone." Seven times they profess, "Blessed is he who comes in the name of the Lord!" When the closing verse is sung, the temple walls reverberate with the declaration, "Give thanks to the Lord, for He is good—His love endures forever!"

As the final words of the ceremony are spoken, the people in the temple plaza lift their lulavs and shout praises for several minutes.

As their cries of thanksgiving die, another voice is heard. Jesus has reappeared at the temple. "If anyone thirsts," he cries out, "let him come to me and drink. Whoever believes in me, as the Scripture says, 'Rivers of living water will flow from within him.'"

The apostles have heard this offer before; Jesus gave a woman in Samaria a similar invitation.

Some who hear Jesus's words are impressed. Several in the crowd turn to their neighbor and say, "This really is the Prophet."

Others say, "This is the Messiah!"

But some shake their heads and say, "Is the Messiah to come from Galilee? Doesn't the Scripture say that the Messiah will be a descendant of David and will be born in Bethlehem, the village where David lived?"

When the Levites return to the Sanhedrin empty-handed, the council demands an explanation. "Why didn't you bring him?"

The guards have but one defense. "No one ever spoke like this man!"

Annoyed with the excuse and angry that Jesus is not under arrest, the leaders shout, "Have you also been deceived? Have any of the authorities or the Pharisees believed in him? But this crowd that does not know the Law—they are accursed!"

The Levites know better than to respond, but one of the Sanhedrin's own brings up a procedural issue. Nicodemus, one of the council's most illustrious teachers, says, "Surely our law doesn't condemn a man without first giving him a hearing and learning what he is doing?"

The question infuriates the council. Technically, Nicodemus is right, but now is not the time for subtleties of the law—the foundations of the faith are being challenged. "Are you from Galilee as well?" they snarl. "Search the Scriptures, and you will see that no prophet arises from Galilee."

Nicodemus knows as well as they do that important prophets have come from Galilee, but correcting them would serve no good purpose, so he falls silent. His admonition, however, slows their deliberations, and they are unable to agree on a plan before they are forced to suspend the meeting in order to prepare for the closing ceremonies of Sukkoth.

The sun sets, and the city grows dark for the first time in six nights.

The evenings during the festival were devoted to a ritual that offered another reminder from the wilderness—the pillar of fire that ultimately led Israel to the Promised Land.

The rite takes place in the Court of Women. In the courtyard are four pillars. Each rises seventy five feet (fifty cubits), and during the feast they become lamp stands. Each pillar is crowned with four golden bowls that are kept filled with olive oil. Beginning the second evening of the feast, these massive menorahs are lit nightly and are bright enough to illuminate every courtyard in town. Under the glow of the lamps, God's people dance and sing hymns late into the evening.

One of the most prominent features of the nightly ceremony takes place on the fifteen broad steps that go down into the Court of Women. A Levite choir and orchestra are assembled on the top step. As they descend each step, they sing one of the fifteen Psalms of Ascent (120–134), singing the final psalm in the courtyard surrounded by worshipers.

For the past six evenings the candelabra have been lit, and the celebration has gone far into the night, but tonight the menorahs stand unattended. Sunset has ushered in the eighth day of the feast.

As night falls, Jesus is preaching at the treasury adjoining the now-dark Court of Women. "I am the light of the world," he proclaims. "Whoever follows me will not walk in darkness but will have the light of life."

Several Pharisees hear Jesus's claim. They ignore the invitation and focus on a technicality. "You are testifying on your own behalf," they challenge. "Your testimony is not valid."

The Pharisees see Jesus's claim as self-testimony. But because they are only interested in discrediting him, they misunderstand what he is saying and make the same allegations they made last year when he healed a man on the Sabbath. Back then Jesus had provided several witnesses to corroborate his claim, but his opponents had refused to hear them.

Knowing their hearts, Jesus answers, "Even if I testify on my own behalf, my testimony is valid because I know where I came from and where I'm going, but you don't know where I came from or where I'm going. You judge according to human standards—I judge no one. Yet even if I do judge, my judgment is valid, for it is not I alone who judge, but I and the Father who sent me. And even in your Law it is written that the testimony of two people is valid. I am one witness, and the One who sent me is the other—the Father."

The religious leaders confer. They had asked for corroborating testimony, and Jesus is claiming an invisible father as his second witness. "Where is your father?" they demand.

The Pharisees want to cross-examine the alleged witness, but Jesus tells them, "You know neither me nor my Father. If you knew me, you would also know my Father."

Jesus realizes that no amount of discussion will convince the religionists, so he repeats something he said earlier, but this time with a much sharper point. "I am going away, and you will search for me," he tells them, "and you will die in your sin. Where I am going, you cannot come."

The verdict is harsh, but his audience is not listening. One smirks and says, "Will he kill himself, since he says, 'Where I am going, you cannot come'?"

Jesus looks into their cold flat eyes and says, "You are from below; I am from above. You are of this world; I am not of this world. I told you that you would die in your sins, for unless you believe that I am, you will die in your sins."

Jesus explains the cause of the misunderstanding—they are from two different worlds. The Pharisees are from a world where humans have the final word and are the ultimate authority. Jesus is from a kingdom that is submitted and obedient to God, and he admonishes them to turn around or face eternal damnation.

But the Pharisees hear none of that. What they hear is Jesus saying, "Unless you believe that I am . . . ." but not finishing his statement. "I am" what? The teacher makes no sense.

"Who are you?" they ask.

Jesus smiles and says, "Just what I have been telling you from the beginning."

He is offering the Pharisees a simple answer to their question—his words reveal his identity. "I have much to say and to judge concerning you," Jesus continues. "But the One who sent me is true, and what I have heard from Him I declare to the world."

For some in the audience, there is the beginning of comprehension, but most are hopelessly confused. Jesus knows it cannot be otherwise and says, "When you have lifted up the Son of Man, then you will know that I am, and that I do nothing on my own authority, but I speak just as the Father taught me. And the One who sent me is with me. He has not left me alone, for I always do the things that are pleasing to Him."

As Jesus says these things, many in the crowd nod in agreement and profess faith in him. Jesus knows there are many kinds of faith, and he says to those who profess belief, "If you dwell in my word, you are truly my disciples, and you will know the truth, and the truth will set you free."

Many in the audience are deeply offended at Jesus's implication. "We're descendants of Abraham and have never been enslaved to anyone!" they exclaim. "How can you say, 'You will be set free'?"

Jesus knows the crowd's faith is fickle and says, "Truly, truly, I tell you, everyone who practices sin is a slave to sin. The slave doesn't remain in the house forever. The son remains forever. So if the son sets you free, you will be free indeed. I know that you are descendants of Abraham—yet you seek to kill me because my word has no place in you. I speak of what I have seen with my Father, and you, too, do what you have heard from your father."

The people protest, "Abraham is our father."

Jesus shakes his head and says, "If you were children of Abraham, you would be doing the works Abraham did, but now you seek to kill me, a man who has told you the truth that I heard from God. This is not what Abraham did. You are doing the works of your father."

"We were not born of fornication!" they shout. "We have one Father—God!"

"If God were your Father," Jesus says, "you would love me, because I came from God. I did not come on my own—He sent me. Why do you not understand my message? It is because you are not able to hear my word. You are children of your father, the Devil, and you want to carry out your father's desires. He was a murderer from the beginning and does not stand in the truth because there is no truth in him. When he lies, he speaks his native language, for he is a liar and the father of lies. But because I speak the truth, you do not believe me. Who among you can prove me guilty of sin? If I'm telling the truth, why don't you believe me? Whoever is of God hears the words of God. You don't hear them because you are not of God."

Jesus claims the crowd's unbelief stems not from their lack of comprehension but from their spiritual paternity. Like their father, they are unwilling to trust and obey God. That would require submission, and they despise anyone telling them what to do.

"Did we not rightly say that you are a Samaritan and demon-possessed?" they scoff.

Jesus replies softly, "I do not have a demon, but I honor my Father, and you dishonor me. Yet I do not seek my own glory—there is One who seeks and judges. Truly, truly, I tell you, whoever keeps my word will never see death."

This pronouncement infuriates the crowd even more. Surely these are the words of a deceiver or a lunatic. "Now we know that you are demon-possessed!" they exclaim. "Abraham died, as did the prophets, yet you say, 'If anyone keeps my word, he will never taste death.' Are you greater than our father Abraham? He died, and so did the prophets. Who do you think you are?"

Jesus responds to their angry accusations by gently explaining, "If I glorify myself, my glory is nothing. My Father, whom you claim as your God, is the One who glorifies me. You do not know Him, but I know Him. If I were to say that I do not know Him, I would be a liar like you, but I do know Him, and I keep His word. Your father Abraham looked forward to the time when he would see my day. He saw it and was glad."

This comment brings guffaws from the Pharisees. "You're not yet fifty years old, and you've seen Abraham?"

The suggestion is preposterous. Who does this fellow think he is?

Jesus smiles and says, "Truly, truly, I tell you, before Abraham was, I Am."

There is a moment of silence as the listeners process what Jesus has claimed, then everyone is shouting at once. The prophet is declaring the Divine Name is his own.

The Jews have no legal authority to execute lawbreakers, but the mob is so infuriated they are willing to risk Roman reprisal. There are construction projects on the temple mount, and vigilantes start gathering stones to kill the false prophet, but when they look up, Jesus is gone.

A full report is made to the Sanhedrin, and even those who sympathize with Jesus wonder what caused him to make such outrageous statements.

# 18

# PRIDE AND PREJUDICE

OCTOBER–DECEMBER, AD 32

*"Whoever listens to you, listens to me, and whoever rejects you, rejects me, and whoever rejects me, rejects the One who sent me."*

—Luke 10:16

THE FEAST OF Sukkoth is over, and the pilgrims have returned to their homes, but Jesus remains in Jerusalem. He wants to provide the nation's capital every opportunity to hear the gospel, and he knows that despite threats from the Sanhedrin to excommunicate anyone sympathetic to his message, there are souls in Jerusalem ready to turn to God.

One day as he and the apostles walk down the street, they pass a blind beggar. It is the Sabbath, and the twelve are reflecting upon how God works in the world. One gestures toward the beggar and callously asks, "Rabbi, who sinned—this man or his parents—that he was born blind?"

The apostles believe that sin and suffering are always integrally linked. The rabbis teach there is no death without sin (for God said, "The soul who sins will die"), and there is no suffering without guilt (for God said, "If they violate My statutes and do not keep My commandments, I will punish their transgression"). The apostles have been taught since childhood that certain maladies and deformities are divine punishment for particular sins. In their minds, there is no question about the reason for the man's blindness. They are simply curious about the details.

Jesus can only shake his head at the question. His apprentices sound like Job's comforters. Yes, the Scriptures teach infirmities are sometimes the result of personal sin, and certainly there are children born with disorders caused by the destructive lifestyle of a parent, but this does not mean all afflictions are punishments for sin. There is another possibility.

"Neither this man nor his parents sinned," Jesus says, "but this happened so that the works of God might be displayed in him. We must work the works of the One who sent me while it is day. Night is coming when no one can work. As long as I am in the world, I am the light of the world."

The disciples ponder Jesus's words as they watch him squat close to the ground, spit in the dirt, and stir it with his finger to make mud. He takes a small amount and smears it on the man's eyelids. "Go—wash in the pool of Siloam," Jesus instructs him.

The blind man does not understand, but he obeys. He slowly makes his way down the hill to the pool and rinses the mud from his eyes. He blinks, then squints in the bright afternoon sun—the man born blind can now see.

When the healed man returns home, his neighbors are shocked. "Isn't this the man who used to sit and beg?" one asks.

Some nod and say, "Yes, it's him."

Others can't believe it's the same man. "No," they say, "it's not him, but he looks like him."

"I am the man!" the beggar insists.

An unconvinced neighbor asks, "Then how were your eyes opened?"

The one born blind replies, "The man called Jesus made mud and put it on my eyes and told me, 'Go to Siloam and wash.' So I went and washed and received my sight."

This sounds impossible. There must be more to the story. "Where is he?" the neighbors ask.

The man can only shrug and say, "I don't know."

His neighbors are at a loss, but one suggests that since this is obviously a supernatural incident, perhaps the religious experts can explain what has happened. They bring the beggar to the synagogue, and the healed man recounts how he received his sight as simply as he can. "He put mud on my eyes, and I washed, and I see."

The explanation draws raised eyebrows and an immediate response from the Pharisees who are judging his case. "This man is not from God—he doesn't keep the Sabbath." The accusation stems from Jesus's violation of the traditions of the elders by "working" on the Sabbath to make the mud and apply it to the man's eyes.

The Pharisees' hatred will not allow them to believe that the man is telling the truth. In the entire history of the world there has never been a person with the ability to heal congenital blindness. Further, the ability to cure blindness is to be one of the signature abilities of the coming Messiah, which prompts some who are listening to ask, "How can a sinner perform such miraculous signs?"

An argument breaks out, but when it becomes evident that neither side is gaining ground, the Pharisees turn again to the beggar. "What do you say about him?" they ask. "It was your eyes he opened."

The restored one immediately answers, "He's a prophet!"

The Pharisees scoff at the notion. They have heard enough to realize they will not get reliable testimony, but at least they can expose the beggar as a liar. Since he claims he was congenitally blind, they need only question his parents.

His mother and father are located and brought before the judges. "Is this your son, who you say was born blind? How is it that he now sees?"

The healed man's parents are overjoyed that their son can see, but they also fear the Pharisees. "We know that he's our son and that he was born blind," they admit, "but we don't know how he can see or who opened his eyes. Ask him—he's old enough to speak for himself."

The Pharisees shake their heads. More useless testimony. They again summon the man who claims he was healed and admonish him to recant. "Give glory to God!" they demand. "We know this man is a sinner."

But the one who was made well refuses to condemn Jesus. "Whether he is a sinner or not, I don't know. One thing I do know—I was blind, but now I see."

His inquisitors' eyes narrow. "What did he do to you?" they ask. "How did he open your eyes?" They seek specific violations they can use to arrest the prophet.

But the restored man has heard enough. He has given his testimony. Emboldened by his increasing comprehension of what has happened, he wryly suggests, "I've told you already, and you didn't listen. Why do you want to hear it again? You don't want to become his disciples, too, do you?"

The Pharisees turn crimson; one shakes his finger in the beggar's face and rails, "You are this man's disciple—we are disciples of Moses. We know that God spoke to Moses, but as for this fellow, we don't even know where he comes from!"

The formally blind man shakes his head in mock wonder. "Now that's amazing!" he says. "You don't know where he comes from, and yet he opened my eyes. We know that God does not listen to sinners, but He does listen to those who worship Him and do His will. No one has ever heard of opening the eyes of a man born blind. If this man were not from God, he could do nothing."

The enlightened beggar's answer is not theologically airtight, but close enough to send the Pharisees into a rage. "You were born steeped in sin!" they curse. "And you are teaching us?"

The religious leaders have heard enough. The man is immediately thrown out of the synagogue and told not to return.

News of the excommunication travels quickly. Jesus hears what happened and goes in search of the man. When he finds him, he asks, "Do you believe in the Son of Man?"

The reference is cryptic, and the man does not understand. "And who is he, sir? Tell me, so that I may believe in him."

Jesus looks into eyes once blind and says, "You have seen him—he is the one who is speaking to you."

When the man hears this, he falls to his knees and says, "Lord, I believe."

"For judgment I came into this world," Jesus tells him, "so that the blind may see and those who see may become blind."

Some Pharisees overhear Jesus's words. Convinced he could not possibly be talking about them, they ask, "Are we also blind?"

"If you were blind," Jesus replies, "you would have no sin. But since you say, 'We see,' your sin remains.

"Truly, truly, I tell you, he who does not enter the sheepfold through the door but climbs in by another way—that one is a thief and a robber. But the one who enters through the door is the shepherd of the sheep. To him the doorkeeper opens, and the sheep hear his voice, and he calls his own sheep by name and leads them out. When he has brought out all his own, he goes ahead of them, and the sheep follow him because they know his voice. But a stranger they will not follow—they will flee from him because they do not recognize the voice of strangers."

Sheep and shepherds are well known to those listening. Thieves, wolves, and lions roam the countryside, and protective enclosures like sheepfolds are essential. There are different kinds of sheep pens; Jesus describes the more permanent kind often found in villages. Open to the sky and made of stone, its walls rise six feet or more and are covered with thorns to further dissuade predators. A heavy wooden door bars the sheepfold's single entrance. Access is controlled by a gatekeeper who is on duty throughout the night.

Communities can bring hundreds of sheep into the fold without concern about the flocks becoming mixed because every sheep knows the distinctive call of its shepherd and will follow him alone. When the shepherd is ready to move, he simply calls to his own and begins walking. His flock will always follow.

The audience is familiar with shepherds and sheep, but they can't make sense of the word picture. They do not understand that Jesus is responding to the ban on Sabbath healing. Jesus is alluding to Ezekiel's pronouncements when he was commanded to "prophesy against the shepherds of Israel, prophesy and say to them, 'Thus says the Lord God: woe to the shepherds of Israel who only take care of themselves! Should not shepherds take care of the flock?'"

Jesus wants the nation's current leaders to see their spiritual kinship to those who ruled in Ezekiel's day. God's condemnation of those shepherds was searing. "The weak you have not strengthened, the sick you have not healed, the broken you have not bound up, the scattered you have not brought back, the lost you have not sought, but with force and harshness you have dominated them."

The religionists can't see themselves as spiritual descendants of those evil shepherds, so Jesus expands the metaphor. "Truly, truly, I tell you, I am the door for the sheep. All who came before me are thieves and robbers, but the sheep did not listen to them. I am the door. Whoever enters through me will be saved and will go in and out and find pasture."

Jesus is still using the shepherding image, but by referring to himself as the door, he indicates he has shifted the imagery from the village sheepfolds to the makeshift folds erected in the wilderness. When a shepherd is forced to keep his sheep in open country, the pen may be as simple as a circle of thorny brambles piled high. The entrance is left open, and the shepherd himself becomes the door by sleeping in the portal.

Jesus again picks up the thread in Ezekiel. "The thief comes only to steal and kill and destroy," he warns. "I came that they may have life, and have it abundantly. I am the good shepherd. The good shepherd lays down his life for the sheep."

Jesus says that all the messianic pretenders who came before him had false motives. "The hired hand, who is not the shepherd and doesn't own the sheep, sees the wolf coming and abandons the sheep and flees, and the wolf attacks the flock and scatters the sheep. The man runs away because he is a hired hand and cares nothing for the sheep. I am the good shepherd. I know my own, and my own know me, just as the Father knows me and I know the Father, and I lay down my life for the sheep."

Some in the audience nod in agreement, but many have faces of stone. Jesus wants Israel's leaders to see that God's mission goes far beyond the petty traditions they busy themselves with. "I have other sheep that are not of this fold," he tells them. "I must bring them also, and they will listen to my voice, and they will become one flock with one shepherd."

The prophet Jeremiah spoke of a day when the Gentiles would "no longer stubbornly follow their own evil heart" but would turn to the Lord. And in the scrolls of Isaiah, God declared that the Servant of the Lord would not only restore Israel, he would be "a light of the nations so that My salvation may reach to the end of the earth." God promised that one day "My house shall be called a house of prayer for all peoples."

Jesus is announcing the arrival of that day.

The broadening of God's mission to encompass the Gentiles will bring profound changes to God's ancient people, and Jesus knows many in Israel will oppose those changes to the death, but he will not shrink from his mission.

"The Father loves me because I lay down my life so that I might take it up again. No one takes it from me, but I lay it down voluntarily. I have authority to lay it down, and I have authority to take it up again. This charge I have received from my Father."

To some, the claims are absurd. "He has a demon and is insane," they conclude. "Why listen to him?"

But others are not so sure. "These are not the words of one who is possessed by a demon," they say. "Can a demon open the eyes of the blind?"

Opinions are divided, but Jesus knows what the ultimate verdict will be, and he knows it will not be long in coming.


WINTER IS APPROACHING, and Jesus wants to bring his message to the people of Judea one more time before the rains disrupt travel. He chooses seventy-two apprentices from his followers and divides them into thirty-six pairs.

"The harvest is plentiful," he tells them, "but the workers are few. Pray, therefore, to the Lord of the harvest to send out workers into His harvest. Go! Behold, I send you out as lambs in the midst of wolves. Carry neither moneybag nor knapsack nor sandals, and greet no one on the road. Whatever house you enter, first say, 'Peace to this house!' And if a child of peace is there, your peace will rest on that person, but if not, it will return to you. And remain in the same house, eating and drinking what they provide, for the worker deserves to be paid. Don't move around from house to house, and whenever you enter a town and they receive you, eat what is set before you. Heal the sick who are there and tell them, 'The kingdom of God is come upon you.'"

The image Jesus paints of being lambs surrounded by wolves is disturbing, but he tells his apprentices they need not fear; they need only pray. Prayer, Jesus assures them, is their most powerful resource. By staying in constant communication with the Father, they will be taken care of every step of the way. There is no need to encumber themselves with supplies, or even money—their heavenly Father will meet their needs.

They are told that when they enter a town, they are to seek a person of peace—someone who will receive them as God's emissaries. The disciples are to stay with this person and minister to the village, healing the sick and crushing all demonic opposition.

Jesus knows, however, that some communities will be hostile to his message. "But whenever you enter a town and they do not receive you," Jesus tells the seventy-two, "go into its streets and say, 'Even the dust of your town that clings to our feet we wipe off in protest against you. Nevertheless know this—the kingdom of God has come.'"

There will be no neutral territory on this mission. Jesus's message will be either received or rejected. When it is spurned, the disciples are to perform a prophetic act of judgment. They are to announce the arrival of the kingdom and symbolically declare the village unclean by wiping the town's dust from their feet.

They are then to move on to the next town and allow God to deal with those who reject His message. "I tell you," Jesus proclaims, "on that day it will be better for Sodom than for that town.

"Woe to you, Chorazin! Woe to you, Bethsaida! For if the mighty works done in you had been done in Tyre and Sidon, they would have repented long ago, sitting in sackcloth and ashes. It will be better at the judgment for Tyre and Sidon than for you. And you, Capernaum, will you be exalted to heaven? No, you will be brought down into Hades."

The disciples are surprised at the harsh assessment of the towns they have spent so much time in, but Jesus wants them to see beneath the veneer of piety. Ultimately it all comes down to one thing. "Whoever listens to you," Jesus says, "listens to me, and whoever rejects you, rejects me, and whoever rejects me, rejects the One who sent me."

His instructions complete, Jesus blesses the seventy-two and sends them forth.

When they return a few weeks later, they bring news of the mission's success. "Lord," they exclaim, "even the demons submit to us in your name!"

Jesus rejoices with his apprentices, and as they celebrate he tells them, "I saw Satan fall from heaven like a flash of lightning. Behold, I have given you authority to trample on serpents and scorpions and over all the power of the enemy—nothing will hurt you. But don't rejoice that the spirits submit to you; rejoice that your names are written in heaven."

Jesus lifts his eyes and says, "I thank You, Father, Lord of heaven and earth, that You have hidden these things from the wise and the learned and have revealed them to little children. Yes, Father, it pleased You to do it this way."

Jesus's prayer is contrary to the teachings of the rabbis. Conventional wisdom says only the educated elite can know the secrets of God, but Jesus says the elite can't understand God's truth—only little kids can.

"All things have been handed over to me by my Father," Jesus announces. "No one truly knows the Son except the Father, and no one truly knows the Father except the Son and those to whom the Son chooses to reveal Him."

A murmur spreads through the crowd. How can the teacher claim that he alone knows God, and that he alone gets to decide whom to reveal God to?

Jesus offers no evidence to support his claim. Instead, he turns to his disciples and says, "Blessed are the eyes that see what you see, for I tell you that many prophets and kings desired to see the things you see, and did not see them, and to hear the things you hear, and did not hear them."

The disciples are interested in learning more about this secret knowledge, but Jesus is interrupted by a religious scholar who stands and says, "Teacher, what must I do to inherit eternal life?"

The question sounds harmless, but Jesus knows it is a test. There is a question behind this question, and the man is there to challenge him. Jesus deflects the test by sending the scribe to the Scriptures. "What is written in the Law?" Jesus asks. "How do you read it?"

The scholar responds by quoting two key passages from the Torah. "'You shall love the Lord your God with all your heart and with all your soul and with all your strength and with all your mind,' and 'love your neighbor as yourself.'"

"You have answered well," Jesus says. "Do this, and you will live."

The scribe has answered his own query with two excellent texts, but the passages describe one who has devoted body, mind, and soul to loving his neighbor. This troubles the religionist—he knows he is unwilling to love those who are not like him. Seeking to justify his narrow criteria for who qualifies as a neighbor in the text he cited, the scholar asks Jesus, "And who is my neighbor?"

Jesus knows the lawyer's real question and answers with a parable. "A man was going down from Jerusalem to Jericho, and he fell into the hands of robbers who stripped him and beat him and went away, leaving him half dead. Now, a priest happened to be going down the same road, and when he saw the man, he passed by on the other side. Likewise a Levite, when he came to the place and saw him, passed by on the other side. But a Samaritan who was traveling that way came upon the man, and when he saw him, he had compassion and went to him. He poured oil and wine on the man's wounds and bandaged him. Then he put him on his own animal and brought him to an inn and took care of him. The next day he took out two denarii and gave them to the innkeeper, saying, 'Take care of him, and when I return, I'll reimburse you for any extra expense you may have.'"

Jesus pauses to let the story to sink in, then asks, "Which of these do you think became a neighbor to the man who fell into the hands of robbers?"

Jesus's question places the emphasis on what makes someone a neighbor. And as the parable ultimately reveals, it is not race or social standing or even living in the same neighborhood that makes someone a neighbor. A person becomes a neighbor by compassionately caring for those God brings into his life.

The scribe grudgingly recognizes this, but is loathe to admit there is such a thing as a good Samaritan. He can only bring himself to say, "The one who showed him mercy."

Jesus nods and says, "You go and do likewise."

The lawyer is left to ponder his opportunity. Jesus leaves to visit friends in Bethany, a two-mile walk from Jerusalem. Within an hour, he and a few of his disciples arrive in the village and are met by their friends Martha and Mary.

Jesus and his companions are welcomed into their home and provided pillows to rest upon while a meal is prepared. The men recline on the cushions, and Jesus begins teaching. Martha goes to the kitchen, but Mary places herself at Jesus's feet. The disciples are surprised—women never do this—but since Jesus says nothing, they say nothing.

In the kitchen, Martha labors alone and fumes. Her sister is completely inconsiderate. Jesus surely sees this, yet he allows Mary to sit idly while her responsible sibling does all the work. Soon Martha is out of the kitchen and striding across the room. She glares at Mary, then complains to Jesus. "Lord, do you not care that my sister has left me to serve alone? Tell her to help me."

Jesus does care, but Mary is not his current concern. He smiles and says, "Martha, Martha, you are worried and troubled by many things—there is need of only one thing. Mary has chosen the better part, and it will not be taken away from her."

Martha drops her eyes and swallows hard, but she knows Jesus is right. More importantly, she knows he loves her and only wants God's best for her. She returns to the kitchen and soon a wonderful meal is enjoyed by all. It is late by the time the visitors stand to offer their thanks for the gracious hospitality. Good-byes are exchanged, and the company departs for Jerusalem.

WINTER AND THE month of Kislev arrive. Jesus plans to remain in the capital until *Hanukkah*, which begins on the twenty-fifth of the month. He spends many days teaching in and around Jerusalem and many hours in prayer. One day, when Jesus is returning from an extended time of prayer, one of the disciples says, "Lord, teach us to pray, as John taught his disciples."

"When you pray," Jesus tells them, "say 'Father, hallowed be Your name. Your kingdom come. Give us each day our daily bread and forgive us our sins, for we forgive everyone who is indebted to us. And let us not be brought into temptation.'"

The disciples have heard a version of this prayer before. It is the kind of prayer that reflects the heart of one who has been forgiven and indelibly changed.

Meditating on the prayer will help his apprentices understand what they should pray for, but Jesus also wants them to understand how to pray, and he tells them a parable. "Can you imagine one of you has a friend, and you go to him at midnight and say, 'Friend, lend me three loaves; a friend of mine has arrived on a journey, and I have nothing to set before him,' and the one inside answers, 'Don't bother me! The door is already locked, and my children are with me in bed, and I can't get up and give you anything'?"

The question is long and twisted, but Jesus's humor is not lost on the disciples. He is asking them to imagine an impossible scenario—a neighbor refusing to help provide hospitality when an unexpected guest arrives in town. Hospitality is so deeply ingrained in the culture and the fabric of village life that something like this would simply never happen.

Jesus says, "I tell you, even if he will not get up and give the neighbor anything because he is his friend, yet because of the neighbor's bold shamelessness he will get up and give him whatever he needs. So I tell you—ask and it will be given to you, seek and you will find, knock and the door will be opened to you. For everyone who asks receives, and the one who seeks finds, and to the one who knocks, the door will be opened."

Now the point of the parable becomes plain—if the petitioner can go boldly and without shame to request help from a neighbor who may not even like him, how much more boldly can he petition the God who loves him? The key, according to Jesus, is to ask, seek, and knock—pray, pursue God, and be persistent.

"Which father among you whose child asks for a fish will give a snake instead of a fish? Or if the child asks for an egg will give a scorpion? If you, then, who are evil, know how to give good gifts to your children, how much more will your heavenly Father give the Holy Spirit to those who ask Him!"

Jesus's point is simple: loving parents would never give their child something harmful, and if this is true of fallible parents, how much more so of the heavenly Father. And if earthly parents give "good gifts," how does one describe the gift the Father will give?

The analogy makes sense to the apostles, but they do not understand Jesus's reference to the gift of the Holy Spirit. The men are intrigued by the possibilities, but no one asks Jesus to explain, and they will not fully understand this gift until Pentecost.

# 19

# The Gathering Storm

DECEMBER, AD 32

*"Do you think I have come to bring peace to the earth?"*

—Luke 12:51

HANUKKAH APPROACHES, AND Jerusalem prepares for an influx of pilgrims. The winter rains slow preparations but do little to dampen people's spirits. Homes all over town are being readied for the popular eight-day celebration. But while families prepare festive candles to brighten the feast, the most powerful men in the nation sit in dark halls and plot the death of Jesus.

His recent comments likening Israel's religious leaders to the evil shepherds in Ezekiel's day cannot be allowed to stand, but the council must proceed cautiously—Jesus is popular with the rabble. They decide their best approach is to isolate Jesus from the crowds. Not coincidentally, Jesus begins getting invitations to private banquets hosted by the city's elite.

Jesus knows why the doors of Jerusalem's leading citizens are opening to him, and he welcomes the opportunity to discuss the issues that separate them. At a lavish luncheon in the home of a prominent Pharisee, Jesus exchanges greetings with the host, then casually walks past the ceremonial washbasins to an open place at the foot of the table and reclines to eat.

There is a murmur around the table. While ritual hand washing before meals is not commanded in Scripture, it is an important tradition and a common practice. The guests stir restlessly and are unsure how to respond to the slight.

Jesus looks to the head of the table and says, "Now, you Pharisees clean the outside of the cup and dish, but inside you are full of extortion and wickedness. Fools! Didn't the One who made the outside make the inside also? So give for alms those things that are within, and behold, everything will be clean for you. But woe to you Pharisees, for you tithe mint and rue and herbs of all kinds, but you bypass justice and the love of God. These were the things you ought to have done, without neglecting the others."

The Pharisees are surprised at the bold direction the conversation is taking. Their concern was a violation of the hand-washing code, but Jesus's mention of dishes expands the scope of the discussion to include all ritual cleansing.

His complaint is simple: the Pharisees ascribe importance to trivial matters while ignoring what is essential. Jesus says that if they will simply pay attention to building integrity in their hearts and demonstrating the Father's forgiving loving-kindness to others, they will become cleaner than any ritual can make them.

Jesus looks into the obdurate faces surrounding him for any hint of repentance. Seeing none, he continues. "Woe to you Pharisees, for you love the seat of honor in the synagogues and to be greeted with respect in the marketplaces. Woe to you, for you are like unmarked graves that people walk over without knowing it."

The graveyard analogy infuriates those around the table. Walking on a grave, even unknowingly, makes a person ceremonially unclean. According to Jesus, not only are the Pharisees themselves unclean, they are contaminating those they teach.

Some at the table are unwilling to receive the rebuke. A religious scholar says, "Teacher, when you say these things you insult us also."

The lawyer assumes that the charges leveled against the Pharisees do not apply to scribes, but in Jesus's eyes there is little difference between the two.

"Woe to you lawyers also!" Jesus declares. "For you weigh the people down with burdens they can scarcely carry, and you will not lift a finger to help them carry the load. Woe to you, for you build the tombs of the prophets whom your fathers killed. Thus, you are witnesses, and you agree with the deeds of your fathers: they did the killing; you do the building.

"Because of this, the Wisdom of God said, 'I will send them prophets and apostles. Some they will kill and others they will persecute.' As a result, this generation will be held responsible for the blood of all the prophets shed from the foundation of the world—from the blood of Abel to the blood of Zechariah, who perished between the altar and the sanctuary. Yes, I tell you, it will be charged against this generation."

The allegation is clear. The scribes, like the Pharisees, preach trivia. Further, the spirit that motivated the ancient Israelites to reject and kill God's prophets is alive and well in the hearts of those gathered around the table. They build elaborate monuments to the prophets, but they ignore their teachings. Worse, they block others from hearing the message.

"Woe to you lawyers!" Jesus says. "For you have taken away the key of knowledge—you did not enter yourselves, and you hindered those who were entering."

The wide-ranging condemnation of the religious system creates chaos at the table. Jesus stands and walks out the door, but several scribes and Pharisees follow him into the street, peppering him with malicious questions. They receive no response.

JESUS CONTINUES TO preach daily to large crowds on the temple mount. One day as he is teaching, a man in the audience calls out to him, "Teacher, tell my brother to divide the family inheritance with me."

The request is not unusual; rabbis are often called upon to resolve such disputes because inheritance laws are in the Scriptures, and rabbis are tasked with interpreting and applying Scripture. But the man's question betrays his true intent. He is not seeking justice; he simply wants the teacher to take his side against his brother.

Jesus shakes his head and says, "Man, who made me a judge or arbitrator over you?"

"Watch out!" Jesus warns the crowd. "Be on your guard against all forms of greed, for a man's life does not consist in the abundance of his possessions."

Jesus shares a parable to help them remember the warning. "The land of a certain rich man was very productive, and he thought to himself, 'What shall I do? I have no place to store my crops.' Then he said, 'This is what I'll do—I'll tear down my barns and build larger ones, and there I will store all my grain and my goods. And I'll say to my soul, "Soul, you have stored up enough good things to last you for many years. Relax! Eat, drink, be merry."' But God said to him, 'Fool! This night your soul is required of you. And the things you've prepared, whose will they be?'"

Jesus pauses a few moments to let the story seep in, and says, "This is how it will be for anyone who accumulates treasure for himself and is not rich toward God."

Jesus is not condemning wealth; he's making an observation about how easily it can become a god. "Be on guard. Keep awake," he warns. "Let your loins be girded and keep your lamps burning."

Jesus knows how easy it is to be lulled into a false sense of security and urges his apprentices to be watchful—they are to have their loins girded and their lamps burning. Both images picture readiness. When men wanted to be ready to move quickly, they would gird their loins by lifting their long garments and binding them around their hips.

God had told His people during the first exodus to gird their loins and be ready to move quickly. Jesus repeats the admonition for those who will follow him in the second.

"Be like servants who were put in charge," Jesus says. "Each with their work and watching for their master to return home from the wedding banquet, so that when he comes and knocks, they can immediately open the door for him. Blessed are those servants whom the master finds keeping watch when he comes. I tell you truly, he will gird himself for service and have them recline at the table, and he will come and serve them. Therefore be alert, for you do not know when the master of the house will come—in the evening or at midnight or when the rooster crows or in the morning—lest he come suddenly and find you asleep.

"And what I say to you, I say to everyone. Watch! But know this—if the master of the house had known what hour the thief was coming, he would have stayed awake and not let his house be broken into. Therefore, you also must be ready, for the Son of Man is coming at an unexpected hour."

The message to followers of Jesus is simple: be ready at all times for anything. There is no way of knowing or predicting the future. The disciples understand the basic message, but they are unclear about whom Jesus is warning. Peter asks, "Lord, are you telling this parable to us or to everyone?"

Jesus smiles and says, "Who then is the faithful and wise steward, whom the master will put in charge of his household, to give them their food allowance at the proper time? Blessed is that servant if his master finds him doing this when he returns! I tell you truly, the master will put him in charge of all he owns. But if that servant says in his heart, 'My master is gone for a long time,' and he begins to beat the menservants and maids, and to eat and drink and get drunk, the master of that wicked servant will come on a day when he does not expect him and at an hour he does not know, and will cut him in pieces and assign him a place with the unfaithful. And the servant who knows his master's will but doesn't get ready or carry out his master's wishes will be beaten with many blows. But the one who does not know and does things that deserve punishment will be beaten with few blows. From everyone to whom much has been given, much will be required, and from the one to whom much has been entrusted, even more will be demanded."

The answer to Simon Peter's question is clear: the parable is for everyone. All will be held accountable for the gifts and abilities given them. But Jesus wants his disciples to understand that this judgment does not take place only in the future; it is happening even now.

"I came to cast fire on the earth," Jesus tells them, "and how I wish it were already kindled! I have a baptism to be baptized with, and how great is my distress until it is completed! Do you think I have come to bring peace to the earth? No, I tell you, but rather division. For from now on in one house there will be five divided, three against two and two against three. Father will be divided against son and son against father, mother against daughter and daughter against mother, mother-in-law against her daughter-in-law and daughter-in-law against mother-in-law."

Borrowing and strengthening the words of the prophet Micah, Jesus emphasizes that the judgment has already begun—it begins the moment a decision is made about Jesus.

"When you see a cloud rising in the west," Jesus observes, "you immediately say, 'It's going to rain,' and it does. And when you see the south wind blowing, you say, 'There will be scorching heat,' and there is. Hypocrites! You know how to interpret the appearance of earth and sky—why do you not know how to interpret the present time?

"And why do you not judge for yourselves what is right? As you go with your accuser before the magistrate, make every effort on the way to settle with him, lest he drag you to the judge, and the judge hands you over to the officer, and the officer throws you in prison. I tell you, you won't get out until you have paid the very last lepton."

The disciples have heard Jesus use this image before, but then he was speaking about relationships with others. Now he speaks about a relationship with God. The "debts" in the parable are sins. Jesus's counsel is simple: seek reconciliation with the One you have sinned against as soon as possible, while you are "on the way" to Judgment Day. Otherwise, the entire debt must be worked off, and not even eternity can afford that much time.

The talk about judgment makes the crowd uncomfortable. They want to feel better about their standing with God, so when someone mentions a group of Galileans who were recently executed by Pilate, others in the audience join in. They assume Jesus will be sympathetic with the plight of the worshippers who were unjustly killed, but Jesus redirects the conversation back to their own culpability.

"Do you think that these Galileans were worse sinners than all the other Galileans because they suffered these things?" Jesus asks. "No, I tell you, but unless you repent, you will all likewise perish. Or those eighteen who were killed when the tower in Siloam fell and killed them—do you think that they were worse offenders than all others living in Jerusalem? No, I tell you, but unless you repent, you will all likewise perish."

The crowd begins grumbling. They have been taught to take comfort in the fact that bad things only happen to bad people.

Jesus, mindful of the nation's indifference to God's mercy, offers a warning veiled in a parable. "A man had a fig tree planted in his vineyard," Jesus says, "and he came looking for fruit on it and found none. So he said to the vinedresser, 'Look, for three years now I've come looking for fruit on this fig tree, and still I find none. Cut it down. Why waste the soil?' But the vinedresser replied, 'Master, leave it alone for one more year until I dig around it and put fertilizer on it. Then if it bears fruit next year, well and good; but if not, you can cut it down.'"

The parable offers hope, but insists Israel's destiny is in her hands. The Owner of the tree is patient—He will withhold judgment for another season, but not forever.

One Sabbath Jesus is preaching in the synagogue, and a woman who suffers from a severe back condition is present. Her affliction has fused her spine into a perpetual arch, and for eighteen years her only view of the world has been from knee height. Jesus invites her to come to him. All eyes follow the woman as she laboriously shuffles to the front of the synagogue.

When she reaches Jesus, he lays his hands on her back and says, "Woman, you are freed from your infirmity." As he speaks, the woman feels her spine strengthen, and for the first time in nearly two decades she stands eye-to-eye with her neighbors.

She begins babbling praises to God, but an angry voice silences her. "There are six days on which work should be done!" the voice booms. "Come on those days and be healed—not on the Sabbath day!"

The invective comes from the ruler of the synagogue. He is convinced Jesus has violated the Sabbath, and his rebuke is a public challenge. By affirming the traditions of the elders, he asserts his authority to interpret the Scriptures and condemns the healer's lawlessness.

The traditions are widely respected, and several in the congregation nod in agreement, but Jesus shakes his head and says, "Hypocrites!

Does not each of you on the Sabbath untie his ox or take his donkey from the manger and lead it out to give it water? And ought not this woman—a daughter of Abraham whom Satan bound for eighteen years—be set free from this bondage on the Sabbath day?"

The congregation erupts in praise. The red-faced synagogue ruler can only stare at the ground.

A FEW DAYS later, Hanukkah begins. It is not one of the feasts decreed in the Torah but a festival commemorating the rededication of the temple in the days of the Maccabees. One hundred and fifty years ago the Jews ousted the Syrian King, Antiochus Epiphanes, after he defiled the temple by sacrificing pigs on the altar and erecting a statue of Zeus in the Holy of Holies. Each year on the twenty-fifth day of Kislev, the eight-day festival commemorates Israel's short-lived religious and national independence.

Because Hanukkah does not demand a trip to the temple and the feast can be observed in homes, Jerusalem is only a fraction of the size it had been a few weeks earlier when the temporary shelters of Sukkoth blanketed the hills. Nevertheless, thousands are in town to celebrate what is affectionately known as the Festival of Lights.

On one of the feast days, Jesus is teaching in Solomon's Colonnade, a covered porch that stretches two hundred yards along the eastern side of the temple, so named because it is believed the foundation of the first temple lies beneath it.

Jesus's message hasn't changed in three years, and his opponents are becoming increasingly frustrated with his unwillingness to identify himself as the Christ. "How long will you keep us in suspense?" they grumble. "If you're the Messiah, tell us plainly."

Jesus shrugs and says, "I did tell you, and you don't believe. The works I do in my Father's name speak for me, but you don't believe because you are not my sheep. My sheep hear my voice, and I know them, and they follow me. I give them eternal life, and they will never perish, and no one will wrest them out of my hand. My Father, who has given them to me, is greater than all, and no one can wrest them out of the Father's hand. I and the Father are one."

When the audience hears Jesus claim to be one with God, there is a loud murmur, and some of the men stoop to the ground for rocks.

"I have shown you many good works from the Father," Jesus shouts above the din. "For which of these works are you going to stone me?"

A man holding a large rock responds angrily, "It's not for a good work that we're going to stone you, but for blasphemy, because you, a mere man, make yourself out to be God."

Jesus nods and says, "Is it not written in your Law, 'I said, "you are gods"?' If He called them gods to whom the Word of God came—and Scripture cannot be annulled—what about the one whom the Father set apart and sent into the world? Why do you accuse me of blasphemy because I said, 'I am God's son'? If I'm not doing the works of my Father, then don't believe me. But if I do them, believe the works even if you don't believe me, so that you may know and understand that the Father is in me, and I am in the Father."

The crowd knows the Torah identifies Israel as "God's firstborn," and they have all read how Moses "became a god" to Pharaoh.

Jesus cites Psalm 82, which calls humans "gods." The passage is understood by many rabbis to identify Israel at the time the Law was given, and the Jews are comfortable being called God's children, yet they are ready to stone Jesus for claiming to be God's son.

Jesus determines it is time to leave Judea. He walks east from Jerusalem on the Jericho road. When he comes to the Jordan, he turns north and follows the river to Batanea, the isolated region where he began his ministry three years earlier. His plan is to use the remaining few months before Passover to prepare his disciples for his death, but despite the remote location, thousands find him.

Jesus teaches daily in the towns and along the river. He encourages people to put their faith in God rather than rely on their Jewish heritage. One day someone asks, "Lord, will those who are saved be few?"

The teacher smiles; the one who asks the question has been listening. "Strive to enter through the narrow door," Jesus says, "for many, I tell you, will try to enter and will not be able to. Once the master of the house has gotten up and shut the door, you will stand outside and knock on the door, saying, 'Lord, open to us.' And he will answer you,

'I do not know where you come from.' Then you will say, 'We ate and drank with you, and you taught in our streets.' But he will reply, 'I tell you, I do not know where you come from. Depart from me, all you workers of unrighteousness!' There will be weeping and gnashing of teeth when you see Abraham and Isaac and Jacob and all the prophets in the kingdom of God, but you will be thrown out. And people will come from east and west and from north and south and recline at the table in the kingdom of God. And behold, the last shall become first, and the first shall become last."

Jesus never answers the question about how many will be saved. Instead, he explains how salvation works. He likens it to a door that opens only from the inside. Once God opens the way to salvation, anyone can go in, yet the opening is narrow and requires one to turn in order to enter. But Jesus says the invitation will one day expire, and the narrow door will become a closed door. Today is the day to turn and enter.

The crowd is not surprised to hear the plea for an immediate response; prophets have long stressed urgency. What startles them is Jesus's revelation that Gentiles will have prominent places in the kingdom while many children of Abraham will be refused admittance.

The notion that heathens will become God's chosen people is incomprehensible to the audience, yet Jesus is teaching directly from the Scriptures. Isaiah spoke of an eschatological banquet in Jerusalem that would be held not just for the Jews but "for all peoples."

The Isaiah passage is familiar to Jesus's audience, but their deeply rooted racism has blinded them. Some rabbis even teach that the "invitation" Gentiles will receive to the banquet will be an invitation to be judged by the Messiah. Other rabbis are more lenient, allowing that Gentiles may attend if they become Jewish proselytes, but Jesus has distorted the teaching beyond recognition. There is no way that God would invite the children of Cain to the feast but leave Abraham's children locked outside.

As the crowd grapples with Jesus's pronouncement, a group of Pharisees approaches him and says, "Get away from here—Herod wants to kill you."

Jesus nods and says, "Go tell that fox, 'Behold, I cast out demons and perform cures today and tomorrow, and on the third day I complete my task. In any case, today, tomorrow, and the next day I must be on my way—it is impossible for a prophet to be killed outside of Jerusalem.'"

# 20

# KINGDOM IN THE MIDST

DECEMBER, AD 32–FEBRUARY, AD 33

*"Behold, the kingdom of God is in the midst of you."*

—Luke 17:21

THE RAINY SEASON is waning. Snow still covers the higher elevations, but the Jordan Valley where Jesus is wintering is subtropical and experiencing torrential downpours. Between storms Jesus and his disciples travel between the villages along the river. There is little public ministry; most of their time is devoted to training.

Jesus continues to receive requests to attend banquets hosted by religious leaders hoping to discredit him. One Sabbath he accepts an invitation to lunch at the home of an influential Pharisee, and as soon as he enters he knows a trap has been laid.

The trap is in the form of a guest who was invited under false pretenses. The man's bloated limbs make it obvious that he is afflicted with dropsy. Jesus knows the man is out of place at this luncheon because it is widely believed that this condition is a punishment for sin. Yet, here he sits in the home of a Pharisee, awkwardly trying to fit in.

A large number of scribes and Pharisees are reclined around the table enjoying casual conversation and ignoring the dropsical man.

Jesus asks, "Is it lawful to heal on the Sabbath or not?"

Everyone at the table has a ready answer, but all remain silent. Jesus knows why they won't respond and refuses to subject the man with edema to their evil games. He heals the man and sends him home.

Jesus then turns to his tablemates and asks, "If one of you has a son or an ox that falls into a well on a Sabbath day, will you not rush to pull him out?"

Again the Pharisees do not respond, but this time for a different reason—they have no way of answering without incriminating themselves. But Jesus isn't interested in winning a debate; he wants them to see how their desire for status is blocking their entrance into the kingdom of God.

"When you're invited by someone to a wedding banquet," he tells his fellow guests, "don't sit in a place of honor, for someone more distinguished than you may have been invited by your host. Then the host, who invited both of you, may come to you and say, 'Give this person your place.' Then in humiliation you will head to the lowest place. Instead, when you're invited, go and sit in the lowest place, so that when your host comes he may say to you, 'Friend, move up higher.' Then you will be honored in the presence of all who sit at the table with you. For everyone who exalts himself will be humbled, and the one who humbles himself will be exalted."

Jesus's counsel is based on the familiar but often ignored wisdom of Solomon. In a culture that values personal honor above all else, being forced to move to a lower seat with everyone watching is an excruciating experience, but Jesus wants them to understand that there is no need to seek the higher places—their identity is not defined by where they sit at the table.

He then turns to the host with similar counsel: "When you give a luncheon or dinner, don't invite your friends or your brothers or your relatives or your rich neighbors, lest they also invite you in return and you are repaid. But when you give a feast, invite the poor, the crippled, the lame, and the blind—you will be blessed because they cannot repay you, for you will be repaid at the resurrection of the righteous."

By the time Jesus is finished, his tablemates are shaking their heads in disbelief. If a system like this were to be implemented, the very fabric of society would unravel. Like the rest of the Roman Empire, Jewish culture operates according to the quid pro quo ethics of reciprocity.

Gifts are never given freely; unwritten laws dictate that when someone gives something to another or helps them in any way, the recipient is obligated to return the favor. If there cannot be reciprocity in kind, which is often the case when the gift is from a wealthy person to one who is impoverished, the recipient is morally bound to be loyal and of service to his patron. This web of obligation weaves the empire together. Without the hierarchical order the patronage system brings, society could not function.

Jesus disagrees. He views the gift-and-obligation system as harmful, and he is provided an opportunity to explain why when one of the guests responds to his remark about the resurrection of the righteous.

"Blessed is the one who will eat bread in the kingdom of God!" a man exclaims.

The declaration is made in the hope of drawing a comment from the teacher about the highly anticipated messianic banquet. Jesus accommodates the request with a parable.

"A man prepared a great banquet and invited many guests," Jesus says. "When the time for the banquet came, he sent his servant to tell those who had been invited, 'Come, for everything is now ready.'

"But they all began to make excuses. The first said to him, 'I've bought a piece of cropland, and I must go see it. Please accept my regrets.' Another said, 'I've bought five yoke of oxen, and I'm on my way to try them out. Please accept my regrets.' Another said, 'I've married, so I can't come.'

"The servant returned and reported these things to his master. The master of the house became angry and told his servant, 'Go at once into the streets and lanes of the city and bring in the poor and crippled and blind and lame.'

"After the servant had done this, he said, 'Master, what you commanded has been done, and there is still room.'

"So the master told the servant, 'Go out into the highways and hedges and urge people to come in so that my house may be filled.'"

The parable makes it plain that there is a broad conspiracy to insult the host of the banquet. All the guests had earlier confirmed they would attend, but on the day of the feast, when the table is overflowing with food, and the host sends word to his guests that the celebration is beginning, one by one they refuse to come. Three refusals are alluded to, but these are only representative. All those invited—enough people to fill a banquet hall—renege on their promise.

One asks to be excused because he has bought some farmland sight unseen, and he is off to see his purchase. The alibi is absurd—no one would buy a piece of cropland until they had inspected every inch of it and knew everything from the soil's arability to how much sun the field would receive in the winter.

Another sends his regrets because he's on his way to try out five pair of oxen he recently purchased. This is another preposterous excuse. Given the cost of these prized farm animals and the many considerations involved in evaluating them, a farmer would not even bid on a yoke of oxen until conducting a careful physical examination and seeing the pair work together.

Another guest doesn't even bother to ask to be excused; he simply informs the host he will not attend because he recently married and will be busy with his wife. This is another blatant fabrication; the banquet is not being held during the man's honeymoon, otherwise he would never have accepted the invitation in the first place. His intent is to dishonor the host. And so it goes with all who had originally accepted the invitation.

The host is angry, but the food has been prepared, and the banquet will go forward. The servant is sent out again with invitations, and when there is still room at the table, he is sent a third time. The master will force no one to attend, but he wants a full banquet hall and will go to great lengths to persuade people to come to his feast.

The scribes and Pharisees are confounded by how the parable ends. It is widely held that a person afflicted with a disease like dropsy is accursed and will not have a seat at the Lord's table or a place in the kingdom. Jesus says that not only will the blind and maimed have a place at the table, for some it will be a seat of honor.

The pious Pharisees will not accept the idea that they are the outsiders described in the story, so Jesus personalizes the parable. He looks into the eyes of those reclined around the table and says, "I tell you, none of those men who were invited will taste my banquet."

The banquet Jesus refers to is the messianic banquet—a metaphor for eternal life. The scribes and Pharisees perceive they are being likened to those who dishonor the Host and reject His salvation. They're right about that, but Jesus is not condemning them; he's inviting them to change. Jesus is urging them to realize that it is not bodily defects or diseases that bar one from heaven but an unwillingness to participate in the life God offers. Everyone who accepts the Host's invitation will be at the banquet.

When it becomes evident to Jesus that the influential Pharisee and his guests are not interested in accepting his invitation, Jesus thanks the man for his hospitality and leaves. He and his followers walk to the next town. Jesus spends his days teaching his apprentices about what it means to be his disciple. Using the hyperbole common in Jewish preaching, he is blunt about the cost: "Whoever comes to me and does not hate father and mother and wife and children and brothers and sisters, yes, and even life itself, cannot be my disciple. Whoever does not carry his cross and come after me cannot be my disciple."

Jesus uses two powerful images to explain the priorities of those who follow him, and both portray apprenticeship as allegiance. The startling analogies are offered to help the crowd realize that the preeminence of God is at the heart of Jesus's gospel.

The call to hate one's self is not a call to self-loathing; Jesus has taught his followers to love others as they love themselves. Nor is the command to hate family to be taken literally. The audience understands the hyperbole—Jesus is saying one's love for God should be so deep that, by comparison, the love of anything else is hate.

The ultimatum about cross bearing is even more daunting. The only time a cross is borne is when a convicted criminal is carrying it to the place of his crucifixion. Jesus says his followers will live like one who is condemned and on his way to execution—a person obviously not interested in amassing wealth or status.

All the talk about crucifixion and hate makes it clear that discipleship has a price. Jesus offers two metaphors to encourage potential apprentices to count the cost.

"Suppose one of you wants to build a tower," Jesus says. "Will he not first sit down and estimate the cost to see if he has enough money to complete it? Otherwise, when he has laid a foundation and isn't able to finish, all who see it will ridicule him, saying, 'This fellow began to build and was not able to finish.'

"Or suppose a king is going out to engage another king in war. Will he not first sit down and consider whether he is strong enough with ten thousand men to oppose the one who comes against him with twenty thousand? And if he can't, he will send an emissary to discuss the terms of peace while the enemy is still a long way off.

"In the same way, any of you who does not renounce all that he has cannot be my apprentice. Salt is good, but if the salt has lost its taste, how can its saltiness be restored? Flavorless salt is fit neither for the soil nor the manure pile—it is thrown away. He who has ears to hear, let him hear."

The Pharisees who are in the audience frown and shake their heads. Why would they want to follow Jesus? They whisper to one another, "This fellow welcomes sinners and eats with them."

Jesus knows what motivates their complaint and tells three parables to describe how far this kind of grumbling is from the heart of God.

"Suppose one of you has a hundred sheep and loses one of them. Won't he leave the ninety-nine in the open country and go after the one that is lost until he finds it? And when he finds it, he joyfully puts it on his shoulders and goes home. He calls together his friends and neighbors and tells them, 'Rejoice with me—I've found my lost sheep!'"

Jesus pauses to allow the scribes and Pharisees to absorb the story, and then says, "I tell you that, in the same way, there will be more joy in heaven over one sinner who repents than over ninety-nine righteous persons who have no need of repentance.

"Or suppose a woman has ten silver coins and loses one of them. Won't she light a lamp and sweep the house and carefully search until she finds it? And when she finds it, she calls her friends and neighbors and says, 'Rejoice with me—I've found my lost coin!' In the same way, I tell you, there is joy in the presence of the angels of God over one sinner who repents."

The scribes and Pharisees look at one another and shrug. Why are they being told these stories?

Jesus shares a third parable that will make his point clear. "There was a man who had two sons. The younger son said to his father, 'Father, give me the portion of property that is coming to me.' So the father divided his estate between them. A few days later, the younger son gathered all he had and traveled to a distant land, and there he squandered his wealth in wild living.

"When he had spent everything, a severe famine arose in that country and he began to be in need, so he hired himself out to one of the citizens of that region, who sent him to his farm to feed pigs. He longed to fill himself with the pods the pigs ate, but no one gave him anything.

"He came to his senses and said, 'How many of my father's hired hands have more than enough bread, but here I am dying of hunger! I will get up and go to my father and say, "Father, I have sinned against heaven and before you. I am no longer worthy to be called your son. Treat me like one of your hired hands."'

"So he set off and went to his father. But while he was still a long way off, his father saw him and was filled with compassion and ran and embraced him and kissed him. Then the son said to him, 'Father, I have sinned against heaven and before you; I am no longer worthy to be called your son.'

"But the father said to his servants, 'Quick! Bring the finest robe and put it on him. Give him a ring for his hand and sandals for his feet. And get the fattened calf and kill it. Let's have a feast and celebrate, for my son was dead and now he lives; he was lost, but now is found!' And they began to celebrate."

The scribes and Pharisees assume the lesson is over. Jesus has told three parables, and all make the same point—God cares inordinately for the lost. But Jesus is not done with the parable. There is another message, this one directed toward those who grumble about the way he welcomes sinners. Jesus continues the story by announcing the arrival of the prodigal's brother.

"Now his older son was in the field, and when he returned and drew near to the house, he heard music and dancing. He called one of the servants and asked what was going on, and the servant replied, 'Your brother is back, and your father has killed the fattened calf because he has returned safe and sound.'

"The older brother became angry and refused to go in. His father came out and pleaded with him, but he said to his father, 'Listen! These many years I've slaved for you, and I never disobeyed your orders, yet you've never given me even a young goat so that I might celebrate with my friends. But when this son of yours came back after squandering your money on prostitutes, you killed the fattened calf for him!'

"And his father said to him, 'My son, you are always with me, and all that is mine is yours. But it was fitting to celebrate and be glad, for your brother was dead and is now alive—he was lost and has been found.'"

By the time Jesus completes the parable, the frowns on the faces of the Pharisees and scribes have turned to scowls. They walk away cursing Jesus under their breath and brood on how they can silence him.

PASSOVER IS ONLY a few weeks away, and Jesus still has much to teach his fledgling church. Soon these men and women will be the sole stewards of the Christian faith, and they cannot naively wander into the future.

One day Jesus tells them a strange parable he hopes will spur a more active faith. "There was a rich man who had an estate manager, and charges were brought to him that this man was squandering his possessions. So he summoned the estate manager and said, 'What is this I hear about you? Turn in a complete account of your handling of my property, for you can no longer be manager.'

"The estate manager said to himself, 'What shall I do now? My master is taking the management position away from me. I'm not strong enough to dig, and I'm ashamed to beg. I've decided what I can do so that when I'm dismissed from my position people will welcome me into their homes.'

"The manager invited each person who owed money to his master to come in and discuss their debt. He asked the first, 'How much do you owe my master?'

"The man said, 'Eight hundred gallons of olive oil.'

"The estate manager said to him, 'Take your bill, sit down, and quickly write four hundred.'

"Then he asked another, 'And how much do you owe?'

"'A thousand bushels of wheat.'

"The estate manager said to him, 'Take your bill and write eight hundred.'

"The master commended the dishonest manager because he acted shrewdly."

The parable ends with a surprising twist; the conniving steward is praised for his cleverness and foresight. Then Jesus makes the application: "For the children of this world are more shrewd in dealing with their own kind than are the children of light. I tell you, use worldly wealth to make friends for yourselves, so that when it's gone, you will be welcomed into the eternal dwellings."

Jesus loves to populate his parables with colorful characters, and the estate manager is a memorable one. He is clearly a scoundrel and is identified as dishonest from the outset, yet Jesus says this child of the world has a lesson for the children of light—he used the wealth he had oversight of to make friends with those who would help him in his time of need. Jesus says his followers should do likewise. They should use their money to make friends who will help when they are in need. But the "friends" Jesus mentions are not other people—these are friends who can "receive you into the eternal dwellings." These friends are God and His angels.

Jesus would have his audience understand that, in a sense, everyone is like the manager in the story. Each person is given someone else's stuff to take care of. Those who are God's friends trust Him to take care of them in all circumstances. They will invest God's resources in God's causes. Good stewardship, Jesus says, is about integrity, and is thus intimately related to devotion.

"Whoever is faithful in little is also faithful in much," Jesus says, "and whoever is dishonest in little is also dishonest in much. So if you haven't been trustworthy in handling unrighteous mammon, who will entrust to you the true riches? And if you haven't been trustworthy with someone else's property, who will give you property of your own?

"No servant can serve two masters, for either he will hate the one and love the other, or he will be devoted to the one and despise the other. You cannot serve God and Mammon."

Some Pharisees are listening in, and when they hear Jesus disparage the love of money, they ridicule him.

Jesus turns to them and says, "You're the ones who justify yourselves in the sight of others, but God knows your hearts—that which is prized by men is an abomination in the sight of God.

"There was a rich man who was clothed in purple and fine linen and who ate sumptuously every day. At his gate lay a poor man named Lazarus, covered with sores, who longed to be fed with what fell from the rich man's table. Even the dogs would come and lick his sores.

"The time came when the poor man died and was carried by the angels to be with Abraham. The rich man also died and was buried. In Hades, where he was being tormented, he lifted up his eyes and saw Abraham in the far distance and Lazarus at his side. He called out, 'Father Abraham, have mercy on me and send Lazarus to dip the tip of his finger in water and cool my tongue, for I am in agony in these flames.'

"But Abraham said, 'Child, remember that during your lifetime you received your good things, while Lazarus received bad things, but now he is comforted here, and you are in anguish. And besides all this, between us and you a great chasm has been fixed, so that those who might wish to pass from here to you cannot do so, and none may cross from there to us.'

"The rich man said, 'Then, Father Abraham, I beg you to send him to my father's house, for I have five brothers. Let him warn them, so they don't end up in this place of torment.'

"But Abraham said, 'They have Moses and the prophets—let them hear them.'

"And the rich man said, 'No, Father Abraham! If someone goes to them from the dead, they will repent.'

"But Abraham said to him, 'If they won't hear Moses and the prophets, neither will they be convinced even if someone rises from the dead.'"

The parable is not directed toward the rich but toward those who make wealth their god and turn their backs on the beggar at their gate. The Pharisees, frustrated with the false prophet who only speaks in parables, shake their heads in disgust and walk away.

THE WINTER RAINS subside, and the hills blossom with new life. Jesus continues to train the apostles for the intense persecution ahead. To underline how important faithfulness will be, he one day says to the twelve, "Who among you who has a servant plowing or tending sheep says to him when he has come in from the field, 'Come immediately and take your place at the table'? Will he not rather say to him, 'Prepare supper for me—get yourself ready and serve me while I eat and drink, and afterward you will eat and drink'? Does he thank the servant because he did what was commanded?"

Jesus pauses, then says, "So you also, when you have done all that you were commanded, say, 'We are worthless servants—we have only done what we were obligated to do.'"

Jesus uses the concept of servitude to describe the ideal attitude of his apprentices—when they do all they are commanded to do and complete their assigned tasks, they understand that they have only done their duty. Slaves do not seek status—they seek to do the will of their master.

One day as Jesus and his followers enter a village, he is met by ten lepers who cry out, "Jesus, Master! Have mercy on us!"

Jesus walks over to the ten, greets them, and simply says, "Go and show yourselves to the priests."

An official examination by a priest is required in order for a leper to be reinstated into society, but this, of course, is always done after the healing, not before. To obey Jesus will require faith, but the ten want to be healed, so they walk away together in search of a priest. As they are walking to the synagogue, their leprosy vanishes. As the sores dry up and disappear, the ten become aware of what has happened. Nine of the healed lepers continue toward the synagogue. One runs back and falls on his face at Jesus's feet.

The disciples are shocked—the only one who expressed gratitude was a Samaritan.

"Were not ten cleansed?" Jesus asks. "Where are the other nine? Has no one returned to give glory to God except this foreigner?"

The healer helps the man to his feet. "Get up and go your way. Your faith has saved you."

This is a powerful lesson for the disciples. God's grace goes out to all, but many never receive its ultimate benefit. Faith is more than accepting God's kindness—it is turning back to the Lord.

The lesson is lost on the Pharisees. They want to know when God's kingdom will come. They are convinced that spectacular signs will herald the Messiah's establishment of the kingdom, but Jesus warns the sign seekers they are looking in the wrong direction.

"The kingdom of God is not coming in ways that can be observed," Jesus tells them, "nor will they say, 'Look, here it is!' or 'There it is!' for behold, the kingdom of God is in the midst of you."

The religionists seek a sign in the heavens, yet God's greatest sign is standing before them. If they want to see and experience the kingdom of heaven, there is no need to look for signs announcing its address. It is here now—present in the person and promises of Jesus.

The religious leaders see none of this and sneer at Jesus's asinine claim that the kingdom is in their midst. Everyone knows that the kingdom of God will not appear on earth until the Messiah comes.

# DEATHLESS

FEBRUARY–MARCH, AD 33

*"Do not be surprised at this—the time is coming when the dead will hear his voice and come out of their graves."*

—John 5:28–29

SPRING HAS COME to Israel. The winter rains have left the grass tall and green, and the hills are speckled with wildflowers. The trees blossom, leaf, and bear tiny fruit. The winter barley is beginning to ripen, and the wheat will soon follow. The grain harvest is but a few weeks away, around the time of Passover.

Jesus is in Galilee, near the border of Samaria, preparing his followers for what awaits him in Jerusalem. There is much to be done and little time, but before Jesus can continue the apostles' training, he must address their fears. He tells them a story about an unrighteous judge.

"There was a judge in a certain city who neither feared God nor respected people, and there was a widow in that city who kept coming to him and saying, 'Grant me justice against my adversary.'

"For a while the judge refused, but later he said to himself, 'Though I neither fear God nor respect people, yet because this widow keeps bothering me, I will grant her justice so that she will not wear me out by her continual coming.'"

Jesus pauses to let his apprentices reflect on the story, and then adds,

"Hear what the unrighteous judge says. And will not God grant justice to His chosen ones who cry out to Him day and night? Will He delay long in helping them? I tell you, He will vindicate them speedily. Nevertheless, when the Son of Man comes, will he find faith on earth?"

The disciples draw two lessons from the parable. First, if an unjust judge can be persuaded to administer justice for someone he doesn't care about, how much more can God be trusted to vindicate those He dearly loves?

The second lesson is intrinsically related—those who follow Jesus must learn to trust God's timing. Jesus encourages his apprentices to emulate the widow's perseverance in prayer. There will be trials and hardships and times when they will wonder if God is even listening. Jesus says that when those days inevitably come, continue to cry out to God to grant justice—God will bring vindication in due season. Meanwhile, pray and persevere and know that God has good reasons for allowing things to unfold as they do. He will not be late in fulfilling His promise.

There are some in the audience who can't imagine this teaching is addressed to them. After all, they are not like the rabble. Jesus challenges them to look in the mirror.

"Two men went up to the temple to pray," Jesus says, "one a Pharisee and the other a tax collector. The Pharisee, standing by himself, prayed, 'God, I thank you that I am not like other people—extortioners, rogues, adulterers, or even like this tax collector. I fast twice a week; I give a tenth of all my income.' But the tax collector, standing far off, would not even lift his eyes to heaven, but beat his breast, saying, 'O God, be merciful to me, a sinner!'

Jesus pauses, then says, "I tell you, this man returned home justified, rather than the other. For everyone who exalts himself will be humbled, but the one who humbles himself will be exalted."

Jesus says a reversal is coming. The self-righteous need to rethink their inclination to believe they are better than others. God is not interested in relative righteousness.

THE TRAINING OF the twelve continues. They travel east of the Jordan to a more sparsely populated region, but Jesus cannot escape the tests and traps laid by the nation's religious leaders. One day a group of Pharisees asks, "Is it lawful for a man to divorce his wife for any reason he wants?"

Few subjects are more volatile than a man's rights regarding divorce, and Israel's religious scholars are not in agreement concerning what the Scriptures teach about ending a marriage. To determine under what circumstances divorce is permissible, they invariably go to the passage in Deuteronomy and point out that Moses said a husband can end the marriage if he finds "any matter of indecency" in his wife.

The scribes debate how to apply this passage. The rabbinic school of Shammai focuses on the word *indecency* and defines it very narrowly; little outside of sexual immorality is viable grounds for divorce. The Hillel school gives more weight to the *any matter* clause and broadens the definition of what constitutes indecency—in effect, Hillel's interpretation gives the husband the right to divorce his wife for almost any reason. Not surprisingly, this is the favored interpretation among men. Women have few marriage rights, and even those are often ignored.

"What did Moses command you?" Jesus asks.

"Moses allowed a man to write a certificate of divorce and send her away," they reply.

Jesus shakes his head. He had asked them what Moses commanded; they responded by telling him what Moses permitted. To find what Moses *commanded*, they must go to the first book he wrote, which is where Jesus takes them.

"Have you not read that from the beginning that the Creator 'made them male and female,' and said, 'For this reason a man will leave his father and mother and be joined to his wife, and the two will become one flesh'? As a result, they are no longer two, but one flesh. Therefore, what God has joined together, let no one separate."

Jesus goes back to the days before humanity's fall to remind them of God's original purpose for marriage, but the Pharisees protest. "So why did Moses give the commandment to 'give her a divorce certificate and send her away'?"

The counterquestion makes it obvious that the religionists are not listening. Jesus says, "Moses, in response to your hardness of heart, permitted you to divorce your wives, but it was not this way at the beginning."

Jesus points out that Moses provided a concession, not a commandment. He would have them see that marriage is more than a legal bond. Genesis says the man and woman become one flesh. A blood relationship is formed that is only to be dissolved by death. If the Pharisees want to know the divine perspective on divorce, it is readily available in the writings of the prophet Malachi. But the hard glares of the Pharisees tell Jesus that these men are not interested in hearing what God has to say.

Later that evening the disciples ask for a fuller explanation, and Jesus devotes significant time to teaching them about God's will concerning marriage. He stresses that the union must never be devalued, because the marriage covenant is not based on what is comfortable and convenient—it is sourced in God's very purpose for creation. Marriage reflects the Lord's covenant relationship with His people. Thus, it is to be held inviolate.

"Whoever divorces his wife, except for sexual immorality, and marries another, commits adultery against her," Jesus says. "And if she divorces her husband and marries another, she commits adultery. And he who marries a woman divorced from her husband commits adultery."

The twelve know Jesus's narrow view on divorce and are not surprised by his blunt statements, but they are again reminded how much this interpretation restricts a man's options. One jokingly remarks, "If that's the way it is for a man with his wife, it's better not to marry."

The disciples chuckle at the humorous notion—no man would choose celibacy over even the worst wife. Not that it's an option; marriage and fatherhood are considered religious obligations in Israel, but Jesus uses the humorous comment to make a serious point about celibacy.

"Not everyone can accept this saying," Jesus tells his apprentices, "but only those who have been given the ability, for there are eunuchs who were born that way from their mother's womb, and there are eunuchs who have been made eunuchs by men, and there are eunuchs who have made themselves eunuchs for the sake of the kingdom of heaven. Whoever is able to accept this, let him accept it."

Jesus's teaching about celibacy goes against the traditions of the elders.

In Judaism, marriage is a duty. The celibate life is never recommended, yet Jesus says God gives some the gift of celibacy in order to further kingdom goals. His metaphor of castration is shocking but assures the lesson will be remembered. There is also a word of encouragement for those who are physically impotent or have been castrated—while others may forbid them to participate at the temple, they are welcome in the kingdom of God.

JESUS DAILY OFFERS God's salvation to the people of the Jordan River Valley, and his message of grace and mercy is popular with the poor and downtrodden. Children are especially attracted to the gentle teacher and often sit at his feet listening to his stories. Parents also continuously bring infants and toddlers to be blessed and healed. In a land where six out of ten children never reach their sixteenth birthday, Jesus has looked into the fear-filled eyes of many mothers and fathers, and he never tires of blessing and caressing children.

The disciples, however, grow increasingly concerned about the noisy little distractions running around the camp. The teacher is an important man. He has better things to do than bless babies and play with kids. One day when the children are particularly exuberant, a disciple begins rebuking one of the parents.

Jesus overhears his frustrated apprentice and interrupts him. "Permit the children to come to me—do not hinder them, for to such as these belongs the kingdom of God. I tell you truly, anyone who will not receive the kingdom of God like a child will never enter it."

Jesus says that to receive the kingdom, one's attitude toward God must be like that of a toddler toward her parents. It is a relationship of innate trust. Those who behave as autonomous "adults" toward God will not be able to enter because the kingdom is made up of the childlike. While his followers ponder the lesson on discipleship, Jesus takes several children into his arms and blesses them.

Later, when Jesus is preparing to leave, a well-dressed young man steps from the crowd, kneels before him, and asks, "Good teacher, what must I do to inherit eternal life?"

The man is sincere, but his use of flattery indicates he has learned nothing from Jesus's message. Moments earlier he heard Jesus teach that eternal life is a gift to be received—now he asks Jesus how he can earn it. The wealthy man is trapped in the same status-seeking system his peers are—a compliment requires one in return. The rich man honored Jesus with a respectful title; he expects a proper response.

But Jesus will not participate. "Why do you call me good?" Jesus asks. "No one is good except God alone."

Jesus is willing to discuss eternal life, but he will first establish the criteria. The man views himself and others like him as generally good, but Jesus wants him to know that relative goodness is not under discussion when it comes to eternal life. The good is God alone. It is obvious to Jesus that the rich man's spirit is troubled. Otherwise, he would be content to obey the Torah.

"You know the commandments," Jesus reminds him. "'Do not murder,' 'Do not commit adultery,' 'Do not steal,' 'Do not bear false witness,' 'Do not defraud,' 'Honor your father and mother,' and, 'You shall love your neighbor as yourself.'"

Jesus provides a representative list that includes five of the ten commandments. He does not mention the first four (which deal with one's relationship with God), or the tenth, which concerns covetousness. Instead, he focuses the wealthy ruler's attention on the commandments that deal with personal relationships.

The young man hastily answers, "Teacher, all these I have kept from my youth. Where do I still fall short?"

The man is convinced that he has faithfully observed God's commandments, but he is concerned that this won't be enough to qualify him for eternal life.

Jesus knows what is haunting the ruler and keeping him in denial and pushing him to inquire what more he can do.

"You lack one thing," Jesus says. "If you want to be complete, go, sell all that you have and distribute the money to the poor, and you will have treasure in heaven. Then come follow me."

The audience is stunned by Jesus's counsel, and the young man is appalled. Jesus has exposed what the man has been struggling with for years—the tenth commandment against covetousness. But this is only part of it, because by violating the tenth commandment, he also violates the first. God views covetousness as worship of the god Mammon.

Given the young man's heart, Jesus's prescription is that he renounce his status and become like a little child. He is to donate his wealth to the poor and become part of Jesus's entourage.

The young man's thoughts are jumbled. The teacher suggests something that, in theory, could be done, but the remedy is imprudent. What would happen to the family name? If he were to give everything away to join this ragtag band, his family would become the laughingstock of the community. No, the man decides, the counsel is foolhardy and must be ignored. He walks away in despair.

Jesus is saddened by the young man's response. As he watches him leave, he says, "How difficult it will be for those who have wealth to enter the kingdom of God!"

The apostles are amazed. They have been taught their entire life that earthly prosperity signifies heaven's approval.

Jesus sees the astonishment in their faces and says, "Children, how difficult it is to enter the kingdom of God. It's easier for a camel to go through the eye of a needle than for a rich person to enter the kingdom of God."

The apostles shake their heads in disbelief. "Then who can be saved?"

The proverb Jesus shared with them says it is impossible to earn eternal life, even for the affluent. The disciples cannot fathom how this could be. Is it not the wealthy who fund God's projects? Without the beneficence of the rich, who would provide alms for the poor? Who would build and endow the synagogues and schools? Who would fund the orphanages?

Jesus knows the source of his apprentices' confusion. His declaration that eternal life is impossible to earn has undermined their understanding of salvation. His followers ascribe much of the good in society to the patronage system. If the wealthy who do so much good in the world won't be saved, who will?

This is the conclusion Jesus hoped they would reach, and he assures them, "For humans this is impossible, but not for God—all things are possible with God."

The disciples appreciate the encouraging words but are still concerned. "Look," Simon Peter says, "we've left everything and followed you. What then will there be for us?"

"I tell you truly," Jesus assures them, "at the renewal of all things, when the Son of Man sits on his glorious throne, you who have followed me will also sit on twelve thrones, judging the twelve tribes of Israel. And everyone who has left house or wife or brothers or sisters or mother or father or children or lands for my sake and for the sake of the kingdom of God will receive a hundred times as much in this age—houses and brothers and sisters and mothers and children and lands, with persecutions—and in the coming age, eternal life. But many who are first will be last, and the last first."

Jesus alludes to Daniel's prophecy to describe the enthronement of the Son of Man at the end of days. On that day there will be great rewards for those who abandoned status-seeking to follow Jesus. In addition to eternal life and manifold wealth, they will be awarded positions of leadership. But the rewards are not limited to the twelve—Jesus says everyone who makes the kingdom their top priority will be compensated a hundredfold in both this world and the next.

Jesus's praise is sincere, but it doesn't apply to everything Simon Peter said. The apostle's words were only partly right, for Peter is trapped in the same status consciousness as the young ruler who walked away—there is a sense of entitlement and a desire for preeminence. Jesus shares a parable to help his followers see things from God's perspective.

"The kingdom of heaven is like a landowner who went out early in the morning to hire laborers for his vineyard. After agreeing with the laborers on a denarius for the day, he sent them into his vineyard. When he went out about nine o'clock he saw others standing idle in the marketplace and said to them, 'You also go into the vineyard, and I will pay you whatever is right.' And off they went. Going out again about noon and at three in the afternoon, he did the same. At about five o'clock, he went out and found others standing around and said to them, 'Why do you stand here idle all day?' 'Because no one has hired us,' they replied. He said to them, 'Off you go, too, into the vineyard.'

"And when evening came, the owner of the vineyard said to his foreman, 'Call the laborers and pay them their wages, beginning with the last to the first.'

"When those hired about five o'clock came, each of them received a denarius, so when those hired first came, they assumed they would receive more, but each of them also received a denarius. On receiving it, they began to grumble against the landowner, saying, 'Those men who were hired last worked only one hour, and you've made them equal with us who have endured a whole day's work in the scorching heat.'

"'Friend,' the landowner replied to one of them, 'I haven't cheated you. Didn't you agree with me on one denarius? Take your pay and go. I want to give the one who was hired last the same as I gave to you. Am I not allowed to do what I wish with what belongs to me? Or are you envious because I am generous?'

"So the last will be first, and the first last."

The disciples are bewildered by the parable. They can't detach themselves from their culture's meritocracy, so what Jesus describes sounds unfair. Rewards should be proportional to work done.

Jesus disagrees. He says the kingdom of heaven does not operate like earthly realms, and some who come into the kingdom late will surpass some who came in early.

The implications for the disciples' entitlement notions are profound. Jesus says that no one is superior to anyone else in God's kingdom. This is as true for individuals as it is for nations. Distinctions like Jew and Gentile and male and female and master and slave do not exist in the kingdom. A spirit of unity transcends those descriptors. There are different roles, but everyone shares an equal and incomprehensibly glorious treasure—eternal life and the opportunity to participate in God's endless adventures.

The teaching about God's unbounded generosity has multiple applications, and the apprentices want to hear more about the kingdom of heaven, but further explanation will have to wait. A messenger arrives from Bethany with urgent news. Jesus's dear friend, Lazarus, brother of Martha and Mary, is near death.

The plea from the sisters is terse. "Lord, the one you love is ill."

Jesus nods and says, "This illness will not end in death. It is for the glory of God, so that the Son of God may be glorified through it."

Jesus knows he cannot get to Bethany before Lazarus's death, so he awaits the Father's instructions. Two days later Lazarus dies, and Jesus says, "Let us go to Judea again."

Worried looks cloud the faces of his followers. Bethany is a suburb of Jerusalem. "Rabbi, a short while ago the Jews were seeking to stone you, and you're going back there again?"

Only a few weeks have passed since the debacle at the Feast of Dedication, and the venomous threats of the Jerusalemites still haunt the disciples. To return now would be unwise.

"Are there not twelve hours in the day?" Jesus asks. "If anyone walks in the day, he does not stumble because he sees the light of this world. But if anyone walks around at night, he stumbles because the light is not in him."

Jesus then tells them the reason for the trip. "Our friend Lazarus has fallen asleep, but I go to wake him."

The disciples don't understand that Jesus is speaking figuratively, and they use the news as an excuse not to go. "Lord, if he has fallen asleep, he will be all right."

Jesus shakes his head and says, "Lazarus has just died, and I am glad for your sake I was not there—so that you may believe. But let us go to him."

The twelve nod gloomily and begin to pack. They are convinced no good can come of this. Thomas, like the rest of the apostles, believes that returning to Bethany is a mistake, but this afternoon he is ready to follow Jesus anywhere. "Let us go as well," Thomas says, "so that we may die with him."

The apostle's courage is admirable but misguided.

When Jesus and his followers arrive in Bethany, the town is enduring a spring cleaning in anticipation of the many thousands who will pass nearby on their way to the temple for the Passover celebration. It has been four days since Lazarus died, and the fourth day of grieving is particularly sad. The rabbis teach that the spirit of one who has died lingers around the body for three days looking for a way to reenter, but after that, the body's physical deterioration will block the spirit from ever returning. Thus, traditionally, there are three days of weeping. Then, on the fourth day, when all hope of recovery is abandoned, heavy mourning begins.

On the afternoon of the fourth day, Martha gets word that Jesus has arrived and is at the outskirts of the village. She runs to him and says, "Lord, if you had been here, my brother would not have died. But even now I know that whatever you ask from God, God will give you."

Martha is confident that if Jesus had been there in time he would have healed her brother, and she wants him to know she has not lost her faith in him. Jesus smiles and says, "Your brother will rise again."

Martha bites her lip; she has heard these words dozens of times over the past few days. Like most Jews, she believes that one day God's people will be restored to bodily life, but on this first day of heavy mourning, those words are cold comfort.

"I know that he will rise again in the resurrection on the last day."

Jesus looks into Martha's eyes and says, "I am the resurrection and the life. Whoever believes in me will live even though he dies, and whoever lives and believes in me will never die. Do you believe this?"

Martha returns his gaze and says, "Yes, Lord. I believe that you are the Christ, the Son of God, who has come into the world."

Her faith is personal, and her confidence is complete—Jesus is the Messiah, and his words have given her hope that will sustain her despite the loss of her brother.

Jesus knows his promise was not fully heard, but Martha will hear it soon enough. She returns home to tell her sister about her conversation with Jesus. When Mary hears that Jesus requested she come see him, she quickly rises and runs in the direction Martha points, tears streaming down her cheeks. Many neighbors and friends see her hasty departure and assume she is going to the tomb. They follow to console her.

When she reaches Jesus, she falls at his feet and sobs, "Lord, if you had been here, my brother would not have died."

"Where have you laid him?" Jesus asks.

Mary wipes the tears from her cheeks and says, "Lord, come and see."

As they walk to the tomb, Jesus weeps. Some say, "See how he loved Lazarus!"

But others are confused and ask, "Could not he who opened the eyes of the blind man also have prevented this man from dying?"

When they arrive at the tomb, instead of mourning, Jesus gives an abrupt command. "Roll away the stone!"

Martha is horrified. "Lord," she whispers, "by this time, there will be an odor—he has been dead four days."

Jesus turns and solemnly reminds her, "Did I not tell you that if you believed you would see the glory of God?"

Martha bows her head and steps back, her mind racing to understand Jesus's words.

The stone is large, but several men are able to roll it aside. The spectators grow quiet; many shake their heads in disbelief and brace themselves for the stench.

Jesus lifts his eyes toward the heavens, and his voice rings over the graveyard. "Father, thank You for hearing me. I know that You always hear me, but I said this for the benefit of the crowd standing here, so that they may believe that You sent me."

Jesus then turns to the open tomb and commands, "Lazarus, come out!"

A low murmur arises; now all are shaking their heads. The man has been dead four days. His spirit is in Hades, and his body is in corruption. Even a fool should know that Lazarus is beyond hope.

But just then a tiny, almost imperceptible sound escapes the tomb. A hush falls over the gathering. Did they imagine it? No. There it is again, a shuffling sound, and it's growing louder.

The crowd gasps when a shadow appears in the doorway. A man staggers from the tomb wrapped head to foot in burial linen. He steps outside and halts, his face still covered by the kerchief placed there on the day of his death. For several long moments, there is a stunned silence. Then Jesus turns to the two sisters, smiles, and says, "Unbind him and let him go."

# The Passover Plot

MARCH, AD 33

*"What are we going to do? . . . . If we let him go on like this, everyone will believe in him, and the Romans will come and take away both our place and our nation!"*

—John 11:47–48

THE FIRST MAJOR festival of the year is less than two weeks away, and Jerusalem is preparing for crowds that will increase the population five-fold. The lights burn late in the Hall of Hewn Stones, but the Sanhedrin's deliberations have nothing to do with the upcoming holy days. Israel's ruling council is consumed with a report just in from Bethany—Jesus is back and has raised a man who had been dead four days. There appears to be no end to the powers of the Galilean sorcerer. Every step they have taken to silence him has failed.

"What are we going to do?" a frustrated councilman asks. "This man is performing many miraculous signs. If we let him go on like this, everyone will believe in him, and the Romans will come and take away both our place and our nation!"

The complaint reveals the Sanhedrin's true concern—their status and security. Their eye is toward Rome. They fear a messianic movement forming behind Jesus that could cost Israel both their quasi-autonomy and temple privileges. It has happened before, and the religious rulers dread a recurrence.

A loud voice pierces the confusion; the men turn and look into the reddened face of the high priest, Joseph Caiaphas. Appointed by the Roman prefect, Valerius Gratus, twelve years earlier, he now has a strong bond with Gratus's successor, Pontius Pilate. Caiaphas is rude and ill-tempered, but he is also influential, and his words have weight.

"You know nothing at all!" he tells the Sanhedrin. "You don't realize that it is better for you that one man die for the people than the whole nation perish."

The councilmen, impressed, nod and whisper to one another. The high priest has spoken God's truth. By the end of deliberations that evening no official action has been taken, but a decision has been made. All that remains is arranging the Nazarene's demise in a way that will create the least disturbance.

Jesus is in Bethany when he learns of the Sanhedrin's unofficial verdict. He knows he will confront Caiaphas, but now is not the time. He tells his followers to pack. They will be leaving immediately.

Jesus and his disciples walk northeast to the village of Ephraim. Here on the frontier of the wilderness Jesus prays and prepares for the maelstrom ahead.

After resting a few days in Ephraim, he leads his followers to the Jordan, and they turn south toward Jericho. The road is already crowded with pilgrims. Many are Galileans who are going to the city early in order to be ritually purified before the Passover.

Anticipation of what might happen in Jerusalem is higher than usual this year. It has been widely reported that Jesus publicly blasphemed God during Hanukkah and came near to being stoned on the temple mount. Many wonder if the Nazarene will show himself again so soon.

Jesus is aware of the speculation swirling around him as he joins the throngs headed to the festival. The revelers are boisterous and in good spirits. They laugh and sing the Psalms of Ascent as they walk. The apostles, on the other hand, are somber and say little. The teacher has given them much to think about, most of it disturbing, and with every step toward the capital, their sense of foreboding grows.

Jesus compounds their apprehension later that morning when he calls the twelve aside and says, "Look, we're going up to Jerusalem, and all the predictions of the prophets about the Son of Man will be fulfilled. He will be betrayed to the chief priests and scribes, and they will condemn him to death and deliver him over to the Gentiles to be mocked and spit on and flogged and crucified and killed, and after three days he will rise."

The apostles shake their heads and look at one another. The one they have identified as the Messiah is saying he must die. The twelve assume that Jesus is telling them some kind of parable. He can't be speaking literally.

Later that morning when they stop to rest, the two sons of Zebedee approach Jesus with their mother at their side. They have brought her because older women can make requests that would be inappropriate coming from anyone else. When she steps forward, Jesus smiles and says, "What do you wish?"

She gestures toward James and John and says, "Declare that these two sons of mine are to sit one on your right and one on your left in your kingdom."

Jesus looks at the two brothers who instigated the request. James and John are religiously studying their sandals.

"You don't know what you are asking," he tells them. "Can you drink the cup that I am about to drink or to be baptized with the baptism I am about to be baptized with?"

The two look up with hope in their eyes and answer in unison, "We can!"

The brothers have no idea that Jesus is speaking about being immersed into death, and Jesus knows that when he undergoes that brutal baptism next week, his disciples will be hiding in fear. But he also knows that faith is a process, and a day will come when they will be ready to suffer and die with him.

"You will indeed drink my cup and be baptized with the baptism I am baptized with," Jesus says. "But to sit on my right and left is not mine to grant. These places belong to those for whom they have been prepared by my Father."

The sons of Zebedee nod and quietly retreat. When the other apostles hear what happened, they become angry. They, too, have an interest in status. Jesus again calls the twelve aside for instruction, this time on a well-worn topic.

"You know that the rulers of the Gentiles lord it over them, and their great men impose their authority on them—it is not to be like that among you. Whoever among you who wants to become great is to be your servant, and whoever would be first is to be the slave of all, just as the Son of Man came not to be served but to serve and to give his life as a ransom for many."

The apprentices struggle with Jesus's summary of the fifty-third chapter of Isaiah, a passage he has adopted as his own. The prophecy speaks of a righteous servant who will be "an offering for sin" and die as a ransom for his people, but what does that have to do with the glorious destiny of the Messiah?

THEY COME TO the ancient oasis of Jericho. The old city on the hill whose walls fell long ago now lies in ruins. Jesus walks past the rubble and south toward the new city in the valley. New Jericho sprang up as a suburb around an opulent residence built by the Hasmonean dynasty. The home was later expanded into three palaces by Herod the Great to serve as his winter residence. No expense was spared to build the extravagant escape. In addition to ornate Roman pools and bath houses, Herod built a gymnasium, a theater, and a track for horse-and-chariot races, all surrounded by lush tropical gardens.

After Herod's death, this portion of his kingdom was given to his son, Archelaus. He developed the winter palace even further, enveloping it in a large grove of palms, but more than twenty years have passed since Archelaus was deposed for incompetence and exiled to Gaul. The palaces are now under Roman jurisdiction and are used less frequently, but the city has continued to grow because of its strategic location. With Passover a week away, the town is filled with people on their way to Jerusalem.

Jesus enters Jericho, and a growing number of people recognize him. Soon he is at the center of a noisy crowd walking down the road.

A blind beggar who is simply known as bar Timaeus (son of Timaeus) is sitting on the side of the road with a another blind mendicant. Bartimaeus and his companion hear the commotion and ask what is happening. When they are told Jesus of Nazareth is passing by, they begin shouting, "Lord, have mercy on us! Son of David!" Again and again they plead, "Jesus, have mercy on us! Son of David!" When the crowd commands them to be silent, the two men cry out even louder, "Lord, have mercy on us! Son of David!"

Jesus stops and requests the two be brought to him. Several run and tell the beggars, "Take heart! Get up. He's calling you!"

When Bartimaeus hears the invitation, he struggles to his feet, throws off his cloak, and walks on wobbly legs toward what sounds like the center of the crowd, his partner close behind. Soon the two blind men are standing before Jesus.

"What do you want me to do for you?" Jesus asks.

"Lord, we want our eyes to be opened—we want to see!"

Jesus smiles and touches the men's eyes saying, "Receive your sight; your faith has saved you."

The two men instantly regain their sight and begin praising God.

A few minutes later, the band of disciples is once again moving toward Jerusalem, their number now increased by two. All are in a celebratory mood, Jesus's prophecy of impending crucifixion a distant memory.

As they walk toward the outskirts of town, Jesus stops under a sycamore tree and looks up at a small man perched in the branches. Jesus smiles and extends his arm. "Zacchaeus, hurry and come down, for I must stay at your house today."

Jesus is addressing one of the wealthiest and most despised men in Jericho. Zacchaeus is small in stature, but he has great power and vast estates. He is the region's chief tax collector and has a dark reputation. Zacchaeus hurries down from his perch and says he would be honored to have Jesus in his home.

Many in the crowd grumble, "He has gone to be the guest of a sinful man."

The tax magnate has no illusions about his past; he knows he has leveraged his position to extort money, and he is ready to make restitution. "Behold, half of my possessions, Lord, I will give to the poor, and if I have defrauded anyone of anything, I am going to pay back four times as much."

Jesus smiles and says, "Today salvation has come to this house, for he, too, is a son of Abraham. For the Son of Man came to seek and to save the lost."

When Jesus says, "today salvation has come," the crowd's thoughts turn to one of their favorite subjects—God's timetable for the coming of the Messiah. The gift of sight given the two beggars heightens expectations. Healing the blind is a signature ability of the Christ. Many believe the long-awaited kingdom of God is about to appear. They have been taught since childhood that the Messiah will appear dramatically, and what better time for the unveiling of the Messiah than Passover?

Jesus tells them a parable to help them understand that the kingdom will unfold in two stages and not all at once as they expect.

"A man of noble birth traveled to a faraway country to receive for himself a kingdom and then return. Summoning ten of his servants, he gave them ten minas and said to them, 'Do business with these until I come back.'

"But his citizens hated him and sent a delegation after him, saying, 'We don't want this man to rule over us.'

"When he received his kingdom and returned, he ordered the servants to whom he had given the money to be summoned so that he might find out what they had gained by doing business.

"The first came before him, saying, 'Lord, your mina has made ten minas more.'

"And he said to him, 'Well done, good servant! Because you have been faithful with the little I entrusted to you, you shall have authority over ten cities.'

"And the second came, saying, 'Lord, your mina has made five minas.'

"And he said to him, 'And you are to be over five cities.'

"Then another came, saying, 'Lord, here is your mina. I have kept it stored in a handkerchief because I was afraid of you—you are a severe man. You take what you did not deposit and reap what you did not sow.'

"The nobleman said to him, 'I will condemn you from your own mouth, evil servant! You knew, did you, that I was a severe man, taking what I did not deposit and reaping what I did not sow? Why then did you not put my money in the bank? Then when I returned I could have collected it with interest.'

"And he said to those who stood by, 'Take the mina from him and give it to the one who has the ten minas.'

"And they said to him, 'Lord, he has ten minas!'

"The king replied, 'I tell you that to everyone who has, more will be given, but from the one who has not, even what he has will be taken away. But as for these enemies of mine who did not want me to reign over them—bring them here and slaughter them before me.'"

When Jesus finishes the story, his audience begins whispering questions to one another. The parable is complex, and they struggle to decipher the different characters and how any of it relates to the messianic kingdom.

In essence, it's the story of a nobleman who entrusts a portion of his estate to his servants while he goes away to secure a vassal kingship. On his return there is a reckoning. The amount the servants were given was small (a mina was equivalent to about four months wages for a laborer). The assignment was a test of their faithfulness.

As the story unfolds, it becomes evident that the third servant does not know his master. To justify his inaction, he misrepresents the king as harsh and impossible to please, but the monarch's treatment of the other servants proves that accusation false. Justice can sometimes be interpreted as sternness, but in truth, this lord is generous and merciful. The wicked servant cannot see this. As the eighteenth psalm says: to those who are merciful, blameless, and pure, God shows Himself merciful, blameless, and pure. But to the crooked, God appears to be twisted.

The evil servant could have simply put the money in the bank and the king would have been satisfied, but it turns out the servant is no different from the country's citizens who refused to be ruled, and his end will be the same. Ultimately, all who oppose the king will get their wish—they will be placed outside his kingdom.

Jesus finishes his teaching and then spends the rest of the evening visiting with Zacchaeus. He rises early the next morning to make the arduous sixteen-mile ascent to the Mount of Olives. The cool spring air is bracing, the sun is at their back, and the mountain passes are not yet crowded. They arrive in Bethany by early afternoon and make their way to the home of Lazarus, Martha, and Mary.

Sunset ushers in the Sabbath, a simple meal with friends, and rest. Jesus is told a banquet is being held in his honor the following evening. The dinner will be hosted by Martha and Mary in the home of Simon the Leper.

AS THE SUN sets on Sabbath the next day, many in the village gather at the home of Simon to fete Jesus. While the guests are talking, Mary inconspicuously walks behind Jesus carrying a large alabaster flask. With a twist of her wrist, she snaps off the flask's slender neck. The room is filled with the exotic aroma of Indian nard, the fragrance of choice for the well-to-do. All eyes are drawn to the woman with the flask. They watch her lavishly pour the rare liquid over Jesus's head. Jesus remains still as the costly oil runs through his hair, onto his shoulders, and down his back. The dinner guests watch speechlessly as Mary then moves to his feet and anoints them with the remaining nard. The guests grow even more alarmed when she shamelessly lets down her long hair and begins to wipe Jesus's feet.

A murmur springs up around the table, but Mary is oblivious to the stares and whispers. Minutes pass, and the apostles have time to think about the cost of the oil Mary used to anoint Jesus. They exchange looks and whisper, "Why such waste?"

Judas, who carries the money box, verbalizes the thoughts of the others. "Why wasn't this perfume sold for three hundred denarii and given to the poor?"

Jesus, rather than exposing Judas's motive for asking the question, honors Mary's devotion. "Leave her alone. Why do you trouble the woman? She has done a good thing for me. You will always have the poor with you, and you can help them whenever you want, but you will not always have me. She has done what she could. She has anointed my body ahead of time to prepare it for burial, and I tell you truly, wherever this good news is proclaimed in the whole world, what this woman has done will be told in memory of her."

The disciples and dinner guests are surprised at Jesus's response. The value of the perfume was significant, the amount one would have to work an entire year to earn. How could pouring it on someone in a moment of spontaneous extravagance ever be acceptable? A respectable young man was recently told he must give all his wealth to the poor, yet this woman, it seems, is praised for her wastefulness.

Jesus, however, did not honor Mary because she flattered him. He honored her to make a statement. His apprentices underestimate the hatred of the religious leaders. The recent miracle in Bethany and resultant popularity of Lazarus has galvanized the Sanhedrin. They believe their worst fears are about to be realized—a sorcerer with the power to raise the dead is going to bring Israel to ruin.

The necessity of killing Jesus is a given, but now it appears more drastic action is required. The chief priests meet and decide that Lazarus must also die. He is a walking testimony to the power of the Nazarene. So long as Lazarus is alive, people will be favorably inclined toward Jesus. But the nation's religious leaders have a plan, and soon everyone will know the truth about the Galilean.

# 23

# On a Donkey's Colt

MARCH, AD 33

*Shout in triumph, O people of Jerusalem! Behold, your king is coming to you.*

—Zechariah 9:9

THE TEMPLE IN Jerusalem is the highest point in the Holy City, but to the east, across the Kidron Valley, is a round ridge that was a place of worship long before the temple was built. Samuel, the last of the judges, worshiped on this mountain, as did King David. In Ezekiel's day, when the glory of the Lord departed the temple, it moved to this ridge. Zechariah prophesied the Messiah would reveal himself to the world from this mountain. Everyone in Israel is aware of the significance of the Mount of Olives, and it is not by coincidence that Jesus makes the mount his final earthly residence.

He is staying with his friends Lazarus, Martha, and Mary in the village of Bethany on the mount's eastern slope. For several days, Jesus has been within two miles of Jerusalem, but he has not yet entered the city. He is awaiting a specific day on the Jewish calendar: the tenth of Nisan—the day each year when the lambs to be sacrificed on Passover are brought into Jerusalem.

When the day arrives, Jesus tells his disciples they will be going to the city that afternoon for the presentation of the lambs. Walking west from Bethany, they are soon at the summit and approaching the town of Bethphage. Jesus tells two of his apprentices, "Go into the village ahead. Upon entering, you will find a donkey tied there with her colt. Untie them and bring them to me. If anyone says anything to you, you are to say, 'The Lord needs them,' and he will release them at once."

The two hurry into the village and find the mother and foal where Jesus said they would be. When the disciples begin untying the donkeys, the animals' owner walks over and questions them.

The two men smile and repeat Jesus's words. The donkeys' owner nods and allows them to take the animals.

The two donkeys are brought to Jesus, and he tells his followers he will ride the foal into the city. His disciples do not understand why their master is so particular about how he enters the city, but they prepare the animals, and soon Jesus is riding the colt down the mountainside.

The road is filled with people coming from Jericho. Many are Galileans, and they recognize Jesus as he rides above the throng. Spiritual fervor is high, and some believe Jesus will be crowned king of the Jews in Jerusalem.

Jesus would have them recognize him as a king, but his choice of mount should alert them to the kind of king he is. The donkey symbolizes two things to the Jews: humility and peace. In olden days, a king went into battle astride a warhorse, but he rode a donkey when he came in peace.

Long ago the prophet Zechariah predicted Zion's king would be gentle and come riding into Jerusalem on a donkey's colt, but he also prophesied that the future king's realm would extend "to the ends of the earth."

The implications of Zechariah's prophecy are lost on the crowd, but they sense something extraordinary is happening and want to honor Jesus. Several remove their cloaks and spread them across the road. Others throw down palm branches and shout, "Hosanna!" (*Give salvation now!*).

The procession nears the city gates, and they are met by another large crowd coming out of Jerusalem. They, too, are waving palm branches and crying out, "Hosanna! Blessed is he who comes in the name of the Lord, even the king of Israel!"

The two groups merge, shouting, "Hosanna to the Son of David!" and "Blessed is the coming kingdom of our father, David!"

The noisy crowd draws the attention of the priests who oversee the shops on the western slope of the Mount of Olives, the traditional marketplace for animal merchants. Because it is Nisan 10, the day the sacrificial animals must be presented, the valley is filled with bleating lambs and worshippers seeking an acceptable substitute.

The priests and Pharisees hear the commotion and see the multitudes turning to Jesus. They shake their heads and say, "It's useless. Look—the world has gone after him."

The religionists had planned to keep quiet and bide their time, but when the crowd becomes effusive in their praise, they fear momentum is building to proclaim Jesus as Messiah. One of the Pharisees says, "Teacher, rebuke your disciples."

Jesus smiles and says, "I tell you, if they were silent, the stones would start shouting."

The procession nears the massive city walls. The hosannas continue, but Jesus grows melancholy and tears stream down his face. "If only you had recognized on this day the things that lead to peace!" he laments. "But now it is hidden from your eyes. Indeed, the days will come upon you when your enemies will set up a barricade around you and surround you and hem you in on every side. They will dash you and your children within you to the ground, and they will not leave within you one stone upon another, because you did not recognize the time of your visitation."

Jesus is not prophesying a disaster to come in the distant future—in less than forty years, Jerusalem will lie in ruins.

Jesus enters the city, and the crowds around him merge with the thousands of visitors filling the streets. His entry goes unnoticed at the busy gate, and the significance of his arrival atop the colt is understood by no one. Jesus dismounts the foal and walks up the temple steps. His apprentices follow tentatively. Death threats forced them to leave the city in haste a few months ago, and nothing has changed.

The disciples are relieved when the journey ends anticlimactically. Jesus walks around the plaza, surveys the activities, and leaves. He and his followers are soon out of the city and walking back up the hill to spend a quiet evening with Lazarus and his sisters.

THE NEXT MORNING Jesus rises early. After a time of prayer, he gathers the apostles and walks toward Jerusalem. As they near the summit of the Mount of Olives, Jesus sees a fig tree in full foliage a short distance from the road. He knows the unripe figs won't be palatable this time of year, but he's hungry and walks over to pluck a few of the *paggim* to eat on his way to Jerusalem. He is surprised to find the tree has no fruit but realizes the tree's deceptive barrenness can serve as a parable.

He says to the tree, "May no one ever eat fruit from you again."

Fig trees are symbols of peace and prosperity and have long been associated with God's people. The prophets used the fig tree to report Israel's standing with God—Hosea, Joel, and Micah all pleaded with the people to repent of their spiritual barrenness, but they refused time and again, leading God to pronounce through the prophet Jeremiah, "There are no grapes on the vine, nor figs on the fig tree."

For Jesus, the words of the prophets are not a condemnation of Israel's people but an indictment against her leaders. They honor God with their words, but their hearts are far from Him.

Within an hour, Jesus is in the city and on the temple mount; he goes directly to the marketplace that has been set up beneath the Royal Stoa in the Court of the Gentiles. At the first Passover of his public ministry, Jesus lodged a loud, symbolic protest. He has not disrupted the temple's commerce since then because he knows the next protest will set in motion events that will put him on a cross, but the waiting is past.

The Passover is only two days away, and thousands are gathered in the temple plaza. Jesus strides through the marketplace. Tables are tossed, sheep pens are opened, and coins and animals scatter in all directions. Several of the merchants and money changers saw this happen three years ago and do not wait for Jesus to get to them; they fold up shop and melt into the crowd.

Jesus turns to the priests who are overseeing the commerce and says, "Is it not written, 'My house shall be called a house of prayer for all the nations'? But you have made it a den of thieves!"

When Jesus describes them as thieves, he is not accusing them of stealing from others—it is God they rob. The Lord's temple is to be a place of worship and prayer, not a bazaar and not a bank.

Jesus's rebuke is an invitation to repent, but the leaders aren't listening. The crowd at the temple, however, is taking in every word. His miracles amaze the audience, as does his knowledge of the Scriptures. The children who are present run through the crowd laughing and singing, "Hosanna to the Son of David!"

The chief priests and scribes are watching everything unfold, and when they hear the children singing messianic praises, their faces redden. They glare at Jesus and say, "Do you hear what the children are saying?"

Jesus smiles and says, "Yes, and have you never read, 'Out of the mouth of infants and nursing babies you have prepared praise'?"

The eighth psalm says God's glory is expressed in the cooing of babies; Jesus says this makes the children's praise appropriate. But the religious leaders cannot make the connection—the psalm Jesus quoted from is a psalm of praise to God.

In the crowd that morning is a group of Gentiles. They were born and raised in a culture that has many gods but few morals, and the monotheistic worship and ethics of Judaism are appealing. The Jews refer to this kind of Gentile as a *God-fearer*. They are often referred to as "half-proselytes" by the devout because while they appreciate much that Judaism offers, they are unwilling to be circumcised and submit to the dietary laws and other restrictions.

They have heard Jesus teach and would like to meet him but are afraid to approach. They bring their request to one of his apostles. "Sir," they say to Philip, "we wish to see Jesus."

This creates a dilemma for Philip; he has heard the master say his mission is to the lost sheep of the house of Israel, and he is not sure if bringing the Gentiles to Jesus would be appropriate. He goes to his fellow apostle, Andrew, for counsel. Andrew, too, knows about Jesus's mission to the Jews, but he has also heard Jesus say he will turn away no one who comes to him. For Andrew, it's an easy decision because he loves introducing people to Jesus.

Philip and Andrew bring the Gentiles' entreaty to their master, but Jesus hears more than an appeal in their words.

"The hour has come for the Son of Man to be glorified," Jesus replies. "Truly, truly, I tell you, unless a grain of wheat falls into the ground and dies, it remains alone, but if it dies, it bears much fruit."

Jesus uses the planting metaphor to explain why he is about to be glorified in a most unexpected way. Those listening struggle to understand. Rather than explain the metaphor, Jesus applies it to anyone interested in becoming his apprentice.

"Whoever loves his life will lose it," Jesus says. "Yet whoever hates his life in this world will keep it for eternal life. If anyone serves me, let him follow me, and where I am, there my servant will be as well. If anyone serves me, the Father will honor him."

The promise of God's favor is welcomed, but the crowd has also heard Jesus speak of a cross. The teacher wants them to know their apprenticeship will ultimately result in blessings; meanwhile, there will be crosses.

Jesus's own cross will soon be a physical reality, and as the time draws near, the horror of what lies ahead is on his mind. "Now is my soul troubled," he confesses. "And what shall I say? Father, save me from this hour! But for this purpose I have come to this hour. Father—glorify Your name!"

The heavens begin to rumble. Some believe it is thunder and others think they have heard an angel, but it is the voice of the Father answering Jesus's prayer that His name be glorified.

"I have glorified it," the Voice proclaims, "and I will glorify it again."

Jesus realizes that those who do not know God cannot recognize his voice, but they should at least recognize the preternatural rumbling as God's affirmation of Jesus's prayer.

"This voice has come not for my benefit but for yours," Jesus tells the crowd. "Now is the judgment of this world; now the ruler of this world will be cast out. And I, when I am lifted up from the earth, will draw all people to myself."

Jesus says two things are about to happen simultaneously—he will draw all people to himself, and Satan will be dealt a death blow. Both will be accomplished, Jesus says, when he is "lifted up."

This term confuses the crowd; they understand it to be a metaphor for death on a cross, and this does not fit their perception of the Messiah. "We heard from the Law that the Christ remains forever," a man says. "So how can you say the Son of Man must be lifted up? Who is this Son of Man?"

They want to hear more about the identity of the Son of Man. He can't be the Christ, because the Christ will not die, so what kind of being is this Son of Man?

Jesus does not answer their question. Instead, he says, "The light is among you for a little while longer. Walk while you have the light, so that darkness will not overtake you. The one who walks in the darkness does not know where he is going. While you have the light, believe in the light, so that you may become children of light."

Those who turn toward the light, Jesus says, will inherit the identity of the light. His message convinces some he is the Messiah, but they say nothing; they have leadership positions they would lose if they confessed their faith.

Jesus invites them to move from the shadows. "Whoever believes in me, believes not in me but in the One who sent me. And whoever sees me sees the One who sent me. I have come into the world as light, so that whoever believes in me will not remain in darkness.

"If anyone hears my words and does not keep them, I do not condemn him, for I did not come to judge the world but to save the world. Whoever rejects me and does not receive my words has a judge: the word I have spoken will be his judge on the last day. For I have not spoken on my own authority, but the Father who sent me has Himself given me a commandment—what to say and what to speak. And I know that His commandment is eternal life. Whatever I say, therefore, is just what the Father has told me to say."

Jesus says he is God's Word because he only speaks what the Father tells him to speak.

The crowd hears his claim, but most shake their heads and walk away.

The hour is late, and it has been a long day; Jesus and the apostles retire to Bethany.

THE NEXT MORNING they rise early and walk back down the Mount of Olives. They pass the fig tree Jesus had cursed the day before, and the apostles are shocked to see the large tree has withered. "Rabbi, look!" Peter says. "The fig tree you cursed has withered."

Jesus looks into the faces of his apprentices and says, "Have faith in God. I tell you truly, if you have faith and do not doubt, you will not only do what has been done to the fig tree, but even if you say to this mountain, 'Be taken up and thrown into the sea,' and you do not doubt in your heart but believe what you say will come to pass, it will be done for you. Therefore I tell you, whatever you ask in prayer, believe that you have received it, and it will be yours. And when you stand praying, forgive anything you have against anyone so that your Father in heaven will also forgive you your failings."

The disciples ponder Jesus's words as they walk to the city and climb the steps to the temple mount. The hour is early, but thousands of pilgrims are milling about the plaza.

Jesus goes into one of the stoas in the Court of the Gentiles and begins teaching. A short while later he is interrupted by the sounds of angry voices. He stands and sees several men dragging a half-dressed woman. She is thrown to the pavement before him. Jesus glances at the sobbing woman who lies shivering at his feet, and then looks into the eyes of the men who brought her, and waits.

"Teacher," the Pharisees say, "this woman has been caught in the act of adultery. The Law of Moses commands us to stone such women. So what do you say?"

Jesus shakes his head as they set their trap. He knows the only way they could have caught this woman in the physical act was by lying in wait. Instead of answering their question, Jesus bends to the ground and begins writing in the dust. The scribes and Pharisees press for an answer, but Jesus ignores them and continues to write on the ground.

After a few minutes, Jesus stands and addresses the woman's accusers. He agrees that she should be executed—so long as it is done according to the Scriptures.

"Let him who is without sin among you be the first to throw a stone at her."

Jesus then bends down and resumes writing in the dust. The prerequisite he calls for is not an attempt to make it impossible to execute her; it is the Law of Moses. When the lawgiver outlined the steps necessary to convict someone of an offense, a key stipulation was that those who make the accusation have no culpability in the offense. Jesus is not saying the first stone must be thrown by a sinless person; he is reminding them that the Law of Moses says the accusers cannot be guilty of twisting the truth in order to get a conviction.

The words have a profound effect on the woman's accusers. No one speaks, and no stones are picked up; the men all know they entrapped the woman. The Holy Spirit convinces each of his guilt, and one by one, starting with the eldest, the men who brought the charges slither into the crowd and disappear.

When her accusers are gone, Jesus asks the adulteress to stand. "Woman, where are they?" he asks. "Has no one condemned you?"

The woman for the first time lifts her eyes. She examines the faces surrounding her and says, "No one, sir."

"Neither do I condemn you," Jesus says. "Go, and from now on, sin no more."

The woman has not sought forgiveness or shown any sign of repentance. Nevertheless, like many before her, she is a recipient of God's grace—she is given an opportunity to change, no strings attached. What she does with that opportunity is up to her.

# 24

# CONFRONTATION

MARCH, AD 33

*"Woe to you, scribes and Pharisees. Hypocrites! You shut the kingdom*
*of heaven in people's faces—you won't go in yourselves, and you won't*
*let anyone else in either. . . . You snakes, you brood of vipers, how can*
*you escape being condemned to hell?"*

—Matthew 23:13, 33

THE DIFFERENT SECTS that make up the Sanhedrin squabble about
even the smallest matters, but the priests, Pharisees, and elders are of
one mind about Jesus. He must be silenced. A plan is devised, and a
cadre of scholars and priests is assembled. The quasi-official delegation
finds Jesus in the plaza teaching.

"By what authority are you doing these things?" they demand. "And
who gave you this authority?"

"I will ask you one question," Jesus says. "Answer me, and I will tell
you by what authority I do these things. The baptism of John—where
did it come from? Was it from heaven or from humans? Answer me."

Jesus is using the standard rabbinic technique of answering a question with a counterquestion that, if answered correctly, will provide the
answer to the original question. If the inquisitors can identify the source
of John's authority, they will have identified the source of Jesus's authority
as well.

The priests and scholars, however, are not interested in determining truth; they have come to destroy a threat. They huddle and discuss how to respond, but can't agree. "If we say, 'From heaven,' he will say, 'Then why didn't you believe him?' But if we say, 'From man,' all the people will stone us, for they are convinced John was a prophet."

The delegation from the Sanhedrin can't come up with a safe answer, so they feign ignorance. "We do not know," they say.

"Then neither will I tell you by what authority I do these things," Jesus says. "But what do you think? A man had two sons. He went to the first and said, 'Son, go and work in the vineyard today.' The son answered, 'I don't want to,' but later he changed his mind and went. The man went to his other son and said the same thing. 'I will, sir,' he answered, but he didn't go."

Jesus pauses, then asks, "Which of the two obeyed his father?"

The faces of the priests and scholars grow tight. "The first," they answer warily.

Jesus nods and says, "I tell you truly, the tax collectors and the prostitutes will go into the kingdom of God before you. For John came and showed you the way of righteousness, and you didn't believe him, but the tax collectors and the prostitutes believed him. And even when you saw this, you refused to change your minds and believe him."

The lesson about the identity of the Baptist has come full circle. John had spent many months in Judea, and the chief priests and prominent citizens Jesus is addressing are very familiar with John's message.

"Hear another parable," Jesus says. "There was a landowner who planted a vineyard. He put a fence around it, dug a winepress in it, and built a watchtower. He then leased it to tenant farmers and traveled away. At harvesttime he sent a servant to the tenants to get some of the fruit of the vineyard, but the farmers beat him and sent him away empty-handed. He sent them another servant; they beat him on the head and treated him shamefully and sent him away empty-handed. He sent a third servant. They wounded and threw this one out also. He sent another, and him they killed. And so it went with many others—some they beat and some they killed. Then the owner of the vineyard said, 'What shall I do? I will send my beloved son. Perhaps they will respect him.' But when the tenants saw the son, they said to one another, 'This is the heir. Come, let us kill him, and the inheritance will be ours.' And they took him and threw him out of the vineyard and killed him."

Jesus ends the parable abruptly and asks, "When the owner of the vineyard comes, what will he do to those farmers?"

The priests and scholars confer briefly and answer, "He will bring those evildoers to an evil end and lease the vineyard to other farmers who will give him his share of the fruit at harvesttime."

Jesus nods and says, "He will come and destroy those farmers and give the vineyard to others."

The crowd listening to the story is shocked by the behavior of the murderous tenants and several exclaim, "May this never be!"

Jesus looks into the faces surrounding him. Within forty-eight hours these same people will not only witness the death of the son, most in the crowd will vindicate the evil tenants who kill him.

The parable is the history of Israel in story form and is sourced in Isaiah's song of the unfruitful vineyard. Centuries earlier, God had prompted the prophet to write lyrics lamenting Israel's barrenness. "My beloved had a vineyard on a very fertile hillside. He dug it and cleared it of stones and planted it with choice vines. He built a watchtower and dug out a winepress. He looked for it to yield grapes, but it yielded wild grapes. And now, O inhabitants of Jerusalem and men of Judah, judge between me and my vineyard—what more was there to do for my vineyard that I have not done?"

The promise Israel once possessed is likened to a vineyard that God richly provided for. It would be expected that a vineyard so well taken care of would yield much fruit, but the nation and her leaders have a long history of murdering the messengers of the vineyard owner.

Jesus looks the lawyers in the eye and challenges them. "Have you never read in the Scriptures, 'The stone that the builders rejected has become the cornerstone; this was the Lord's doing, and it is wonderful to see'? Therefore I tell you, the kingdom of God will be taken away from you and given to a people producing its fruits."

Jesus quotes the famous Hallel psalm but gives it a different application. When Psalm 118 was written, the rejected stone represented Israel.

Jesus applies the image to himself. He wants them to realize that a change is taking place in the vineyard. The wicked tenants—the corrupt priesthood and elders who lead the nation—will be removed, but Jesus does not say they will be replaced by another group of leaders. He says the kingdom will be given to a nation identified by Daniel as "the people of the saints of the Most High." This new nation will be neither Jew nor Gentile but a community of all who follow Jesus. These will produce godly fruit and become the new vineyard.

All this, says the psalmist, is the Lord's doing.

Jesus shares another reference to the stone, this time from the prophet Isaiah. "The one who falls on this stone will be broken to pieces, and when it falls on anyone, it will crush him."

The Jewish leaders bristle but say nothing, and Jesus tells them another story. "The kingdom of heaven is like a king who prepared a wedding banquet for his son. He sent his servants to summon those who had been invited to the banquet, but they refused to come. So he sent other servants and said, 'Tell those who have been invited, "Look, I have the meal ready. My oxen and fattened calves have been butchered, and everything is ready. Come to the wedding banquet."' But they made light of it and went their way, one to his farm, another to his business, while the rest of them seized the king's servants and abused and killed them.

"The king was furious. He sent out his troops and destroyed those murderers and burned their city. Then he said to his servants, 'The wedding banquet is ready, but those who were invited were not worthy. Go out to the street corners and invite everyone you find to the wedding.' So the servants went out into the streets and brought in everyone they could find, good and bad alike, and the wedding hall was filled with guests. But when the king came in to inspect the guests, he noticed a man who was not wearing wedding clothes and said to him, 'Friend, how did you get in here without wedding clothes?' The man was speechless. Then the king told the servants, 'Bind him hand and foot and throw him into the outer darkness, where there will be weeping and gnashing of teeth.' For many are called but few are chosen."

The scribes, chief priests, and elders realize they have been bested by the quick-witted Galilean and withdraw.

WHEN WORD OF the defeat gets back to the ruling council, some Pharisees offer an ingenious plan to ensnare Jesus, but they are unwilling to initiate it. They still sting from their last attempt to trap him, so they enlist several men skilled in rhetoric to present the question as their own.

The sophists find Jesus in the temple plaza and approach obsequiously. "Teacher, we know that you have integrity and teach the way of God accurately, and you do not care about anyone's opinion, for you are not swayed by status. Tell us, then, what you think—is it lawful to pay the poll tax to Caesar or not?"

The hirelings are confident they can damage the reputation of Jesus regardless of his answer. If he says the yearly tax to Rome should be paid, he can be discredited with the Jews, and if he says God's people are under no obligation to pay, he can be turned over to Pilate on the charge of sedition.

Jesus ignores the flattery and says, "Why are you trying to trap me? Hypocrites! Show me the coin that is used for paying the poll tax."

When one of the elders reaches into his pocket and pulls out a denarius, Jesus asks the crowd, "Whose likeness and inscription is this?"

Many in the audience shout, "Caesar's."

Jesus smiles and says, "Then render to Caesar the things that are Caesar's, and to God the things that are God's."

The wordsmiths who brought the question concede and withdraw.


THE SADDUCEES HEAR of the Pharisees' failure and are impressed with Jesus's political savvy. They will take a different approach; they will expose the lay preacher's theological naiveté. The priests find Jesus in the plaza and have their servants make a path for them through the crowd. Soon they have pushed and shoved their way to the front.

One of the Sadducees smirks and says, "Teacher, Moses said, 'If a man dies having no children, his brother is to marry the widow and raise up offspring for his brother.' Now there were seven brothers. The first married and died, and since he had no offspring, he left his wife to his brother. The same thing happened with the second and third, down to the seventh. Then last of all, the woman died. So when they rise again, whose wife will she be? All seven were married to her."

The hypothetical dilemma they propose is based on the Sadducees' belief that there will not be a bodily resurrection; they are convinced their question uncovers the absurdity of the doctrine.

Jesus shakes his head and says, "You are wrong, because you know neither the Scriptures nor the power of God. The people of this age marry and are given in marriage, but in the age to come, those considered worthy of being raised from the dead will neither marry nor be given in marriage. Indeed, they can no longer die, because they are like angels and are children of God, being children of the resurrection.

"And as for the dead being raised, have you not read in the book of Moses, in the story about the bush, how Moses himself showed that the dead rise—for God spoke to him, saying, 'I *am* the God of Abraham, and the God of Isaac, and the God of Jacob'? He is not the God of the dead but of the living, for all live to him. You are very wrong."

The priests are infuriated but can say nothing to refute Jesus's point. His simple grammar lesson has negated their entire argument.

Others from the Sanhedrin see the exchange and grudgingly admit, "Teacher, you have spoken well."


WHEN THE PRIESTS' failure becomes known, the Pharisees again take the initiative. Their ruse with the coin didn't work; perhaps a more theological approach will fare better. A small group of lawyers approach Jesus. A learned scholar presents the test question. "Teacher," the scribe asks respectfully, "what is the most important commandment in the Law?"

The question issues from the rabbinic belief that the Law of Moses contains six hundred and thirteen commandments, and while all are important, some are more significant than others. The rabbis debate which commandments carry more weight and how these can be prioritized. The religious scholar is hoping Jesus will cite a commandment he can refute with a weightier one.

Jesus, however, goes to the essence of the Law. "The most important one is, 'Hear, O Israel: The Lord our God, the Lord is one. And you shall love the Lord your God with all your heart and with all your soul and with all your mind and with all your strength.' This is the great and first commandment, and the second is like it: 'You shall love your neighbor as yourself.' All the Law and the writings of the prophets hang on these two commandments. No other commandment is greater than these."

The scribe shakes his head in appreciation and amazement. "Well said, Teacher. You are right in saying He is one, and there is no other besides Him. To love Him with all your heart, and with all your understanding, and with all your strength, and to love your neighbor as yourself is more important than all the burnt offerings and sacrifices."

Jesus smiles and says, "You are not far from the kingdom of God."

The lawyer blushes and looks to the ground, his spirit in turmoil.

His peers from the Sanhedrin can't rescue him. They, too, are frustrated.

Jesus knows they are at their collective wit's end and wants to encourage them to move beyond their superficial understanding of the Messiah. "Why do the scribes say that the Messiah is the Son of David?" Jesus asks. "What do you think about the Messiah? Whose son is he?"

"The son of David," they reply warily.

Jesus nods and asks, "Then how is it that David, inspired by the Spirit, calls him Lord? For David himself says in the Book of Psalms, 'The Lord said to my Lord, "Sit at my right hand until I make your enemies your footstool."' David himself calls him Lord, so how is the Messiah his son?"

Jesus is not challenging the fact that the Messiah would be a descendant of David; he is explaining the unique relationship between the two. The term *Son of David* is accurate in one sense. Jesus is David's physical progeny. But ultimately it is an inadequate title. The Jews have yet to understand that the Messiah is not only David's descendant—he is also David's Lord.

The religious scholars can't explain why David would address his son as Lord, and Jesus turns to the audience. "Beware of the scribes and the Pharisees who sit on Moses's seat," he warns. "Do and observe whatever they tell you, but don't do as they do, because they preach but don't practice. They tie up heavy, cumbersome burdens and put them on other people's shoulders, but they are not willing to lift a finger to move them. Everything they do is for show—they make their phylacteries broad and their fringes long, and they like to walk around in long robes. They love the place of honor at banquets and the best seats in the synagogues and greetings in the marketplaces and being called rabbi by others. They devour widows' houses and then make a show of saying long prayers. They will receive harsher condemnation."

The warning is blunt: honor the position the religious leaders hold as spokespersons for God and honor the teachings of Moses they expound, but be discerning and do not imitate their lifestyle—the teachers have no integrity and don't practice what they preach.

Many in the crowd nod in agreement. Jesus's assessment of the religious leaders is harsh but accurate. The people have seen how the rabbis relish celebrity status.

Jesus admonishes his followers to avoid honorific titles. "You are not to be called 'Rabbi,' for you have one teacher, and you are all classmates. And call no one on earth 'Father,' for you have one Father, who is in heaven. Nor are you to be called 'Master,' for you have one master—the Messiah. The greatest among you is to be your servant. Whoever lifts himself up will be brought low, and whoever lowers himself will be lifted up."

Jesus is addressing a challenge he knows his church will battle throughout history—status seeking—the desire to be "lifted up." Jesus mentions three honorific titles of his day—rabbi, father, and master—to make a point about all titles: they are part of the world's system and have no value in God's kingdom.

Jesus turns again to Israel's religious rulers and tells them how God sees them. "Woe to you, scribes and Pharisees. Hypocrites! You shut the door to the kingdom of heaven in people's faces. You won't go in yourselves, and you won't let anyone else in either.

"Woe to you, scribes and Pharisees. Hypocrites! You travel across land and sea to recruit a single proselyte, and then you make the new convert into twice the child of hell you yourselves are.

"Woe to you, blind guides! You say, 'If anyone swears by the temple, it means nothing, but if anyone swears by the gold in the temple, he is bound by his oath.' You blind fools! Which is greater—the gold or the temple that makes the gold sacred? You also say, 'If anyone swears by the altar, it means nothing, but if anyone swears by the offering that is on the altar, he is bound by his oath.' How blind you are! Which is greater—the offering, or the altar that makes the offering sacred? So whoever swears by the altar swears by it and by everything placed on it, and whoever swears by the temple swears by it and by the One who dwells in it. And whoever swears by heaven swears by the throne of God and by the One who sits on it.

"Woe to you, scribes and Pharisees. Hypocrites! You tithe your mint and dill and cumin, but you have neglected the weightier matters of the law: justice and mercy and faithfulness. These you ought to have done while not neglecting the others. You blind guides—you strain out a gnat but swallow a camel!

"Woe to you, scribes and Pharisees. Hypocrites! You clean the outside of the cup and the plate, but inside they are full of greed and self-indulgence. Blind Pharisee! First clean the inside of the cup so that its outside may be clean as well.

"Woe to you, scribes and Pharisees. Hypocrites! You are like whitewashed tombs that appear beautiful from the outside, but inside they are full of the bones of the dead and all kinds of uncleanness. It's like that with you—outwardly you give people the impression that you're righteous, but inside you are full of hypocrisy and lawlessness.

"Woe to you, scribes and Pharisees. Hypocrites! You build the tombs of the prophets and decorate the graves of the righteous, and you say, 'If we had lived in the time of our ancestors, we wouldn't have taken part with them in shedding the blood of the prophets.' Thus you testify against yourselves that you are the descendants of those who murdered the prophets. Fill up, then, the measure of your ancestors!

"You snakes, you brood of vipers, how can you escape being condemned to hell? Look, that is why I send you prophets and wise men and scribes. Some you will kill and crucify, and some you will flog in your synagogues and persecute in one town after another, so that you may bear responsibility for all the righteous blood that is being shed on earth, from the blood of righteous Abel to the blood of Zechariah the son of Barachiah, whom you murdered between the sanctuary and the altar. I tell you truly, all these things will come upon this generation."

The audience is accustomed to hearing scathing pronouncements; in the Scriptures the prophets often rebuked those who did evil. The crowd is not shocked by the strong invective, but they are surprised by the breadth of the charges. Jesus describes a system that is hopelessly opposed to God and tells the religious leaders to "fill up the measure" of their ancestors—to go ahead and complete what their forefathers started.

The conversation is painful; Jesus loves these people, even those who oppose him, and he laments the future they have chosen for themselves. "Jerusalem, Jerusalem, who kills the prophets and stones those who are sent to her, how often have I wanted to gather your children together as a hen gathers her chicks under her wings, and you were not willing. Behold, your house is left to you desolate. For I tell you, you will not see me again until you say, 'Blessed is he who comes in the name of the Lord.'"

Jesus says God's judgment on the temple is irrevocable—God has abandoned it for another. But those who are listening hear a note of hope for Israel. In the psalm that Jesus quoted, God expresses time and again a "steadfast love that endures forever" for His people.

Judgment is coming, Jesus warns, but it is not too late to turn. The priests and people still have time to say with the psalmist, "Save us, we pray, O Lord! Blessed is he who comes in the name of the Lord!"

When Jesus sees no remorse in the faces of the religious leaders, he walks across the broad plaza and climbs the steps to the Court of the Women, where the temple treasury is located. In the courtyard stand thirteen shofar-shaped chests that collect the people's freewill offerings. Beyond are the rooms where designated offerings are accepted. The courtyard is filled with people bringing money to the temple. Jesus sits on a bench across from the collection trumpets. A number of wealthy men parade by, their gifts announced with pomp and gravity by the priests overseeing the treasury.

Into the bustling throng walks a destitute widow. She slowly makes her way to one of the receptacles and drops in two lepta, the smallest coins in circulation. Sixty-four lepta equal one denarius, which is the average daily wage, so the woman's offering is equivalent to fifteen minutes of work, as small a sum as the priests have seen all day.

Jesus has a different perspective. He turns to his disciples and says, "I tell you truly, this poor widow put more into the treasury than all the others. They all contributed out of their surplus, but she, out of her poverty, has put in everything she had—all she had to live on."

Jesus views the widow's mites as a greater contribution to the treasury than the large sums being cast into the collection boxes because God takes the motivation of the giver into account when assessing an offering's value. And this woman's gift, Jesus says, is priceless.

# 25

# *A* SECOND COMING

APRIL, AD 33

*On that day his feet shall stand on the Mount of Olives to the east of*
*Jerusalem, and the Mount of Olives will be split in two.*

—Zechariah 14:4

FORTY MONTHS HAVE passed since Jesus was baptized in the Jordan.
Few are convinced he is the Messiah; he does the works foretold of the
Anointed One, but his words are those of the Suffering Servant. Even
his most devoted followers do not understand the man they call Lord.

The nation's religious leaders, on the other hand, know all they need
to know about Jesus—he is a threat to the nation. If he is proclaimed
Messiah by the large crowds during the Passover, there will be riots in
Jerusalem and harsh repercussions from Rome.

The priests and Pharisees have no need to worry. Jesus has preached
his last message on the temple mount. He gathers the twelve and walks
toward the Eastern Gate. As he and the apostles cross the courtyard, one
of the men gestures toward the temple and says, "Look, Teacher, what
impressive stones and what magnificent buildings!"

Jesus stops and glances up—the afternoon sun reflecting off the
white marble walls and gold adornments gives the temple the appearance of a mountain afire.

"Do you see these great buildings?" Jesus asks. "I tell you truly, the days will come when not one stone will be left upon another—it will all be demolished."

The disciples are shocked by the prediction and remain silent as they walk from the temple down into the Kidron Valley and up the Jericho Road.

As they near the summit of the Mount of Olives, Jesus leads the twelve off the road. They walk a short distance, and he invites the apostles to sit and rest a few minutes. From this height they can see the entire temple plaza, and because the entrance to the Holy Place faces east, they can look directly into the darkness that cloaks the Holy of Holies.

As the twelve look at the temple, they reflect on what Jesus said earlier. They cannot imagine life without the temple and assume its destruction will initiate the revealing of the Messiah. Peter, Andrew, James, and John walk over to where Jesus is resting and sit down beside him. "Teacher, tell us, when will these things happen, and what will be the sign of your coming and the completion of the age?"

Jesus sees the confusion in their hearts and says, "Watch out. Don't let anyone mislead you, for many will come in my name saying, 'I am the Messiah!' and 'The time is near!' They will lead many astray—do not follow them.

"And when you hear of wars and rumors of war and revolutions, do not be alarmed, for these things must take place first, but the end will not follow immediately. For nation will rise against nation and kingdom against kingdom, and there will be famines and plagues and earthquakes in various places, and there will be terrors and great signs from heaven."

Jesus speaks of natural disasters, social turmoil, and political upheavals that will take a long time to germinate, develop, and come to fruition. He tells his apprentices that there will be a span of years before the destruction of the temple, and another span of years before the consummation of the age. Key events must happen before each can take place—events the faithful must be prepared for and participate in.

Jesus explains: "Before all this occurs, they will seize you and persecute you, but these are just the beginning of the birth pains. Be on your guard, for you will be handed over to the local councils, and you will be beaten in synagogues and prisons, and you will be brought before governors and kings—all on account of my name.

"This will turn out to be an opportunity to tell them about me, so when they arrest you and bring you to trial, settle it in your minds not to worry or prepare your defense in advance. Just say whatever is given you at that time, for it is not you who speaks but the Holy Spirit. I will give you words and a wisdom that none of your adversaries will be able to withstand or contradict.

"Then they will deliver you to be persecuted and put to death, and you will be hated by all nations because of my name. At that time many will be ensnared and betray one another and hate one another, and many false prophets will appear and deceive many. You will be betrayed even by parents and relatives and friends, and some of you they will put to death. But not a hair of your head will perish.

"Because of rampant lawlessness, the love of many will grow cold, but the person who remains faithful to the end will be saved. And this good news of the kingdom must be proclaimed all over the world as a testimony to all the nations—then the end will come."

Jesus explains the role his followers play in a much larger story—the redemption of all creation. Jesus warns them that the way will not be trouble-free. Persecution lies ahead, and the mission, which until now has been limited to Palestine, must be expanded to the entire world before the end will come.

The apostles cannot grasp the scope of the assignment. While the twelve have never traveled beyond their homeland, they know the earth is vast and filled with people of many tribes and languages. With a mission this large, there is no way to know how long it will take, but they know the end will not happen immediately, and it will not come gently.

To prepare his followers for the future, Jesus speaks of two occurrences: the destruction of the temple and the consummation of the age. He wants them to see the first event as a pattern and portent of the second.

"When you see Jerusalem surrounded by armies," Jesus says, "then know that its desolation has come near. When you see what Daniel the prophet spoke about—the abomination of desolation standing in the holy place—then those in Judea must flee to the mountains. Those who are in the city must leave, and those in the country must not return to the city. The one on the housetop must not go down into the house to pack, and the one who is in the field must not return even to get his cloak, for these are days of vengeance, to fulfill all that is written.

"How dreadful it will be for pregnant women and nursing mothers in those days, for there will be great distress upon the land and wrath upon this people. They will fall by the edge of the sword and be taken away as captives into all nations, and Jerusalem will be trampled underfoot by the Gentiles until the times of the Gentiles are fulfilled.

"Pray that you won't have to escape in winter or on the Sabbath, for in those days there will be tribulation greater than at any time since the world began. There will never be anything like it again, and if those days had not been cut short, no one at all would be saved, but for the sake of God's chosen ones, those days will be cut short.

"Then if anyone tells you, 'Look, here is the Messiah!' or 'Look, there he is!' do not believe it," Jesus says. "For false messiahs and false prophets will appear and perform great signs and wonders to deceive, if possible, even the elect.

"Behold—I have forewarned you. So, if they tell you, 'Look, he is in the wilderness,' don't go out there. If they say, 'Look, he is in the inner rooms,' don't believe it. For as lightning flashes across the sky from east to west, so will be the coming of the Son of Man."

Jesus's words bewilder the apostles. He quotes the prophet Daniel's prediction about the abomination of desolation and tells his disciples to see this desecration of the temple as a sign that it is time to flee the city. Jerusalem is about to experience divine judgment. Both the city and the temple will be destroyed.

Jesus wants his followers to see the near-term destruction of Jerusalem as an omen. His reference to the coming of the Son of Man is a fulfillment of Daniel's prophecy and refers to the end of the age, the time when God will set up "the kingdom that will never be destroyed."

It is to the establishment of this kingdom Jesus now turns his attention: "But immediately after the tribulation of those days there will be signs in sun and moon and stars—the sun will be darkened, and the moon will not give its light, and the stars will fall from heaven—and here on earth the nations will be in turmoil, perplexed by the roaring seas and waves. People will faint from fear and foreboding of what is coming upon the world, for the powers of the heavens will be shaken.

"Then will appear in heaven the sign of the Son of Man, and all the tribes of the earth will mourn as they see the Son of Man coming on the clouds of heaven with power and great glory. He will send out his angels with a loud trumpet blast, and they will gather his chosen people from the four winds—from the ends of the earth to the ends of heaven.

"Now, when these things begin to take place, straighten up and raise your heads because your redemption is drawing near."

The apostles listen with increasing amazement. Jesus predicts a day when evil will run rampant and many Christ-followers will fall away. The prophecies from the scrolls of Isaiah, Ezekiel, and Joel are familiar, but the disciples do not know if Jesus is speaking literally or figuratively.

The prophets used these images figuratively to point to political and spiritual disturbances, and God's wrath being visited on those who oppose him, but Jesus also speaks of disturbances in the physical heavens. He says his arrival will be like lightning, that he will come on the clouds, and that amid trumpet blasts he will summon the redeemed of all the ages to join him in the air as he descends to the earth.

This is not the description of a future the apostles have ever heard or even imagined. Yet Jesus assures them that the cataclysmic events he predicted will come to pass.

"Now learn this lesson from the fig tree and all trees," Jesus says. "When their tender shoots come out and the leaves appear, you know that summer is near. In the same way, when you see these things taking place, know that the kingdom of God is near—right at the door. I tell you truly, this generation will not pass away until all these things happen. Heaven and earth will pass away, but my words will not pass away."

Jesus says that all the travails must take place before the end, but it is not clear to the apostles whether he is talking about the end of the temple, the end of the world, or both.

"But concerning that day and hour," Jesus says, "no one knows, not even the angels of heaven, nor the Son, but only the Father. Be on guard so that your hearts are not weighed down with debauchery and drunkenness and the worries of this life. Otherwise, that day will come upon you suddenly, like a trap, for it will come upon all who dwell on the face of the earth. Be always on the watch, and pray that you might have the strength to escape all that is about to happen and to stand before the Son of Man."

Jesus says God's people must be watchful and faithful; his coming will find many unprepared. "Just as it was in the days of Noah, so will it be at the coming of the Son of Man. The people knew nothing about what would happen. They were eating and drinking and marrying and being given in marriage—until the day Noah entered the ark and the flood came and destroyed them all. That's the way the coming of the Son of Man will be.

"It was the same in the days of Lot. People were eating and drinking, buying and selling, planting and building—but on the day Lot left Sodom, fire and sulfur rained from heaven and destroyed them all. So will it be on the day when the Son of Man is revealed.

"On that day, anyone on the housetop who has belongings in the house must not go down to get them, and anyone who is in the field must not return home. Remember Lot's wife.

"I tell you, in that night there will be two in one bed. One will be taken, the other left. Then two men will be in the field; one will be taken and one left. Two women will be grinding at the mill; one will be taken and the other left. So stay awake, for you don't know what day your Lord is coming."

The apostles are confused; they want to participate in the conversation but can think of only one question: "Where, Lord?"

Out of curiosity, they ask where this judgment will take place, but in Jesus's mind the question has no relevance. He knows that when the time comes, the scavengers will reveal the location. "Where the carcass is," Jesus says, "there the vultures will gather."

According to Jesus it will be a time of great joy for those who are ready, but a day of untold horrors for those who are not. Jesus tells three parables to emphasize the importance of being prepared.

"At that time the kingdom of heaven will be like ten bridesmaids who took their lamps and went to meet the bridegroom. Five were foolish and five were wise. When the foolish girls took their lamps, they took no oil with them, but the wise bridesmaids took flasks of oil with their lamps.

"When the bridegroom was delayed, they all became drowsy and fell asleep, but at midnight there was a shout: 'Look! Here comes the bridegroom! Go out to meet him.'

"Then all the bridesmaids woke up and got their lamps ready, and the foolish said to the wise, 'Give us some of your oil. Our lamps are going out.'

"But the wise answered, 'No. We don't have enough for all of us. Go to the store and buy some for yourselves.'

"But while they went to buy it, the bridegroom came, and those who were ready went with him to the wedding celebration and the door was shut.

"Later the other bridesmaids came saying, 'Lord, lord, open up for us!'

"But he answered, 'I tell you truly, I do not know you.'"

Jesus pauses, looks into the faces of his followers, and says, "So stay awake, for you know neither the day nor the hour."

Jesus is teaching about personal accountability, and like many of his stories, it has a twist at the end. At a normal wedding, the doors would not be locked, and tardy bridesmaids would not be refused entrance by the groom. But this is not simply a story about a wedding—it is an explanation of the consummation of the age.

Further, the parable implies the bridegroom's return will be delayed. In the interim, people are to ready themselves for his arrival. The foolish bridesmaids did not take their relationship with the bridegroom seriously, and despite being afforded every opportunity, they chose to ignore the one they claimed to be waiting for.

Jesus says that many offer God only lip service; they claim to be followers, but they will not repent and prepare, and spiritual readiness is not something that can be borrowed. All souls must prepare to meet their God.

Jesus says, "It will be like a man going on a journey who summoned his servants and entrusted his possessions to them. To one he gave five talents, to another two, to another one—to each according to his ability. Then he went away. The servant who had received five talents went at once and traded with them and made five more. In the same way, the servant who was given two made another two. But the one who received one talent went off, dug a hole in the ground, and buried his master's money.

"A long time later the master of those servants returned and settled accounts with them. The one who had received five talents came bringing five talents more, saying, 'Master, you entrusted me with five talents. Look, I gained another five talents.'

"His master said to him, 'Well done, good and faithful servant. You were trustworthy with a few things; I will put you in charge of many things. Enter into the joy of your master.'

"And the one who had the two talents also came forward, saying, 'Master, you entrusted me with two talents. Look, I gained another two talents.'

"His master said to him, 'Well done, good and faithful servant. You were trustworthy with a few things; I will put you in charge of many things. Enter into the joy of your master.'

"Then the servant who had received the one talent approached saying, 'Master, I knew you to be a hard man, reaping where you did not sow and gathering where you did not scatter seed, so I was afraid, and I went and hid your talent in the ground. Look, here is what belongs to you!'

"But his master answered him, 'You wicked and slothful servant! So you knew that I reap where I have not sown and gather where I have not scattered seed? Then you should have invested my money with the bankers; then at my coming I would have gotten it back with interest.

"'So take the talent from him and give it to the one who has the ten talents, for to everyone who has, more will be given, and he will have an abundance. But from the one who has not, even what he has will be taken away. And throw the worthless servant into the outer darkness. There will be weeping and gnashing of teeth.'"

The disciples are familiar with this parable; Jesus has told it before in a slightly different form. Jesus wants his followers to realize that everything they possess ultimately belongs to God: wealth, health, intelligence, abilities, even life itself. Each person is given a portion of God's abundance, and one day there will be a reckoning. Those who make excuses and do nothing with their God-given gifts demonstrate they have no interest in living in God's kingdom.

Jesus tells his apprentices a third story to underline the urgency of responding to his invitation. "When the Son of Man comes in his glory, and all the angels with him, he will sit on his glorious throne. All the nations will be assembled in front of him, and he will separate people one from another as a shepherd separates the sheep from the goats.

"He will put the sheep on his right and the goats on his left. Then the King will say to those on his right, 'Come, you who are blessed by my Father, inherit the kingdom prepared for you from the foundation of the world. For I was hungry and you gave me something to eat; I was thirsty and you gave me something to drink; I was a stranger and you made me your guest; I needed clothes and you clothed me; I was sick and you visited me; I was in prison and you came to me.'

"Then the righteous will answer him, saying, 'Lord, when did we see you hungry and feed you, or thirsty and give you a drink? And when did we see you as a stranger and invite you in, or needing clothes and clothed you? And when did we see you sick or in prison and go to visit you?'

"And the King will reply, 'I tell you truly, whatever you did for one of the least of these brothers and sisters of mine, you did for me.'

"Then he will say to those on his left, 'Depart from me, accursed ones, into the eternal fire prepared for the Devil and his angels. For I was hungry and you gave me nothing to eat; I was thirsty and you gave me nothing to drink; I was a stranger and you did not make me your guest; I needed clothes and you did not clothe me; I was sick and in prison and you did not visit me.'

"Then they, too, will answer, 'Lord, when did we see you hungry or thirsty or a stranger or needing clothes or sick or in prison and not help you?'

"Then he will answer them, 'I tell you truly, whatever you did not do for one of the least of these, you did not do for me.'

"And these people will go away into eternal punishment, but the righteous into eternal life."

The apostles struggle to understand the point of the story. Jesus describes a final judgment when there will be only two kinds of people present—those who received God's messengers and those who rejected them. Both groups will be surprised by how closely Jesus identifies with his disciples. According to Jesus, eternal destinies will be determined on the basis of how a person treats his followers. This is not a new teaching. Jesus is reaffirming a lesson he taught when the twelve and seventy-two were sent out: to reject the messenger is to reject the message, and to reject the message is to reject the One who sent it.

His apprentices are still trying to grasp Jesus's pronouncements when he says, "As you know, in two days it will be the Passover, and the Son of Man will be handed over to be crucified."

This prediction confuses his disciples even more. Jesus says he will soon be dead, yet he seems perfectly content with how things are unfolding. Why? How can the Messiah's death accomplish anything?

WHILE THE APOSTLES sit on the Mount of Olives listening to the prophecy, Caiaphas is at his home in Jerusalem consulting with a group of priests and elders about how to silence the Galilean. Some advocate an immediate arrest; others fear the crowds and counsel prudence. "Not during the festival," they say. "The people may riot."

What the ruling council needs is an insider who can provide them with information they can use to arrest Jesus away from the crowds.

Later that evening their prayers are answered. When Judas Iscariot appears at the high priest's door, the religious leaders can hardly believe their good fortune.

The apostle gets right to the point. "How much will you give me if I hand Jesus over to you?"

They briefly haggle price, but the betrayer's demands are modest; he simply wants to be done with Jesus. They settle on thirty pieces of silver, the value of a slave in Moses's day.

Judas instructs the priests to have the temple guard ready to move quickly. He then goes out into the night and back up the Mount of Olives to join Jesus and his friends. As he climbs the hill, he contemplates his decision to betray the man he pledged allegiance to and wonders how it will all end.

# 26

# THE LORD'S SUPPER

APRIL 2, AD 33

*"I will bring you out . . . . I will deliver you . . . . I will redeem you . . . .*
*I will take you as My own."*

—Exodus 6:6–7

THURSDAY MORNING FINDS Jesus and the twelve in Bethany. Last night's teaching went late, and the apostles are looking forward to a day of rest. Because the Jewish day is reckoned from sunset to sunset, this evening is technically the start of *Hag ha Pesah,* but the significant activities of the Passover won't begin until tomorrow, when the sacrificial lambs are slaughtered.

The Torah dictates that the lambs are to be sacrificed in the last hours of Nisan 14. The lamb is then flayed and roasted whole. The other foods are prepared while the lamb cooks, and the meal is eaten that evening after the date changes to Nisan 15, the first day of *Hag ha Matzot,* the festival of Unleavened Bread.

The apostles assume they will be going to Jerusalem early tomorrow to make arrangements for the Seder, but shortly after sundown Jesus tells Peter and John, "Go and prepare for us to eat the Passover."

The request mystifies the two apostles. The Seder could be prepared this evening, but where would they get the lamb, the centerpiece of the entire meal? It will be impossible to offer a sacrifice at the temple until tomorrow afternoon. Why does the master want to celebrate the Passover a day early and without the lamb?

Peter and John have questions, but all they ask is, "Where will you have us prepare it?"

"As you enter the city," Jesus replies, "a man carrying a jar of water will meet you. Follow him into the house he enters and say to the master of the house, 'The Teacher says to tell you, "My time is at hand. Where is the guest room where I may eat the Passover with my disciples?"' He will show you a large, furnished upper room; prepare it there."

Peter and John again exchange inquiring glances. Apparently the master has everything arranged except the food preparation. The two men are soon on their way to Jerusalem. They enter the city gates and see an unusual sight—a man carrying a water jar. The two apostles follow the man into a home. They repeat Jesus's words to the homeowner and are immediately taken to a spacious upper room that is fully furnished for a banquet.

The apostles thank the man for his kindness and walk to the market to purchase fruits, vegetables, wine, bread, salt, and herbs. They take the food back to the upper room and prepare the meal. The bitter herbs are chopped, the wine is mixed with the right amount of water, the fruits for the *charoseth* are stewed, the bread is wrapped in a napkin, dipping sauces are made, and the table is set.

It is well after dark when Jesus and the other apostles enter Jerusalem and make their way to the upper room.

At formal banquets, dinner guests do not sit in chairs at tables; they recline on pillows around a low, U-shaped banquet table, propping themselves on their left elbow. This leaves only one hand free to eat with, so meals traditionally consist of bread, dipping sauces, and bite-size finger foods.

Jesus sits at the head of the table, but no other seats are assigned. The apostles may sit where they choose. There is room for one on either side of Jesus. John bar Zebedee takes one of those places, Judas Iscariot the other.

When everyone is settled in, Jesus says, "I have eagerly desired to eat this Passover with you before I suffer. For I tell you, I will not eat this meal again until it finds fulfillment in the kingdom of God."

The twelve shift uncomfortably and look at one another. No one wants to ask Jesus to explain the cryptic comment, and Jesus is content to begin the Seder by pouring the first of the four cups of wine to be shared during the meal. He offers a prayer of thanksgiving for God's provision and passes the cup to the apostles saying, "Take this and divide it among yourselves, for I tell you that I will not drink again of the fruit of the vine until the kingdom of God comes."

The apostles share the cup and ponder Jesus's ominous words, but say nothing.

Jesus stands and removes his outer garments. The twelve have no idea why their master is disrobing. They watch incredulously as he strips to his loincloth, wraps a long towel around his waist, pours a basin of water, and begins washing the apostles' feet.

The men are red-faced and speechless. Jesus is performing one of the most demeaning jobs imaginable. When he comes to Simon Peter, the exasperated apostle says, "Lord, are *you* going to wash *my* feet?"

Jesus nods and says, "You don't understand now what I'm doing, but after these things you will understand."

There is much that will not become clear until later, and Jesus counsels patience. Simon isn't listening. "No," he says. "You will never wash my feet."

All Peter can see is the social inappropriateness of the act. Jesus should be doing works that befit his royal status, not performing the menial chores of a slave. But the chief apostle is misinterpreting his master's actions.

Jesus looks into Peter's eyes and says, "Unless I wash you, you have no share with me."

Peter is chastened but continues to misunderstand. "Lord," he says, "then wash not only my feet but my hands and my head as well!"

"A person who has had a bath is completely clean," Jesus replies. "He only needs to wash his feet."

Jesus looks around the table and adds, "And you are clean, but not every one of you."

Judas tenses, but Jesus says no more. Jesus finishes his work, removes the towel, dresses, and resumes his place at the table. He looks into twelve bewildered faces and says, "Do you understand what I've done for you? You call me 'Teacher' and 'Lord,' and you are right, for this is what I am. So if I, your Lord and Teacher, have washed your feet, you also ought to wash one another's feet. I have given you a pattern—what I've done, you do. Truly, truly I tell you, a servant is not greater than his master, nor is a messenger greater than the one who sent him. Now that you know these things, you will be blessed if you do them.

"I am not speaking about all of you; I know the ones I have chosen. But this is to fulfill the Scripture, 'The one who eats my bread has lifted his heel against me.'

"I am telling you this now, before it happens, so that when it does happen you will believe that I am he. Truly, truly I tell you, whoever receives the one I send receives me, and whoever receives me receives the One who sent me."

The twelve look at one another; eleven of the apostles are convinced there has been a mistake, but Jesus is unswerving. "Truly, truly I tell you, one of you will betray me—one who is eating with me. The Son of Man goes as it is written of him, but woe to the one who betrays him! It would have been better for that man if he had not been born."

Eleven of the men have no idea who Jesus is referring to and are plunged into sorrow. They begin asking one another who would do such a thing. Several turn to Jesus, eyes wide, voices hushed. "Is it I, Lord?"

Jesus won't identify his betrayer, and Simon Peter grows frustrated; he motions to John to ask for more information.

John turns to Jesus and whispers, "Lord, who is it?"

Jesus picks up a piece of matzoh and says, "It's the one I'll give this morsel of bread to when I have dipped it."

He leans forward, sops the bread in the sauce, and gives it to the apostle on his right. Judas Iscariot is writhing inside but maintains a calm demeanor. He smiles and accepts the morsel, but feels obligated to say something, so he asks the question everyone else has asked, "Is it I, Rabbi?"

Jesus looks into the eyes of his betrayer and nods. "You have said so. What you are going to do, do quickly."

Without a word, Judas gets up and leaves the room. The eleven overhear Jesus's instructions and assume that because Judas is in charge of the money box he is being sent to purchase supplies or give alms; at Passover the temple courts are kept open all night and are filled with helpless people seeking aid.

Jesus says nothing about Judas's sudden departure, but he knows where Judas is going because Judas didn't leave the room alone—his benefactor went with him.

Jesus became aware of the presence of Satan as soon as he entered the room. The evil angel has been waiting a long time for this night. Jesus may have bettered him in the wilderness, but tonight things will be different. The arch-demon has carefully laid a trap that is sure to end with Jesus dead. And when Judas takes the bread and squanders his last chance to repent, Satan gleefully enters the apostle. And it is to both Judas and his benefactor Jesus issues the command: "What you are going to do, do quickly."

WITH THE TWO now unwittingly on their way to fulfill God's plan, Jesus turns to the eleven. He picks up a new loaf of unleavened bread, prays for the Father's blessing, and breaks it. Each disciple is given a piece. "Take, eat," Jesus says. "This is my body, which is given for you. Do this in remembrance of me."

The eleven eat the bread and reflect on the new significance Jesus is giving it. They have been instructed to eat his broken body. The disciples know he is using figurative speech, but even so, using such terms to describe faith is shocking.

Jesus, however, did not use the image to offend them; he used it to provide an analogy. Just as the Jews eat unleavened bread to remind them of their deliverance from Egypt, followers of Jesus are to associate his death with their deliverance from sin.

The meal continues, but when they come to the third traditional cup, the cup of blessing, Jesus again gives the rite a new significance. He blesses the wine and says, "Take this, and divide it among yourselves. This cup is the new covenant in my blood that is poured out for many for the forgiveness of sins. Do this, as often as you drink it, in remembrance of me."

Another shocking image. Drinking blood of any kind is forbidden. But Jesus chose this image carefully. His allusion is to a passage in Exodus. "Moses took the blood and threw it on the people and said, 'Behold the blood of the covenant that the Lord has made with you in accordance with all these words.'"

Jesus is reminding the eleven that the ancient covenant God made with His people had to be ratified with blood—the same is true of the new covenant spoken of by Jeremiah. "The days are coming, declares the Lord, when I will make a new covenant with the house of Israel and the house of Judah, not like the covenant I made with their fathers on the day I took them by the hand to bring them out of the land of Egypt— My covenant that they broke, though I was their husband, declares the Lord. This is the covenant I will make with the house of Israel after those days, declares the Lord: I will put my law within them, and I will write it on their hearts. And I will be their God, and they shall be My people."

Everyone in Israel looks forward to the inauguration of the new covenant. Jesus links the shedding of his blood to its fulfillment.

Jesus also alludes to the prophet Isaiah's words about the Servant of the Lord who "poured out his soul to death and was numbered with the transgressors, yet he bore the sin of many and makes intercession for the transgressors."

As the eleven reflect on Jesus's teaching, they realize he is bringing together all the images he has used during his ministry. In his few statements over the bread and wine, he has referred to the Son of Man, the Messiah, the Son of David, and the Suffering Servant—yet he used none of those titles.

Jesus knows that one day his followers will understand the significance of what he has said and done at the table, but today the eleven are only partially listening. As Jesus was explaining the new covenant and its blessings, the apostles were coveting rewards of another kind and squabbling about who will be the greatest in the kingdom.

"The kings of the Gentiles lord it over them, and those who exercise authority over them call themselves benefactors," Jesus says. "But you are not to be that way. Rather, let the greatest among you become like the youngest, and the leader like one who serves. For who is greater—the one who reclines at the table or the one who serves? Is it not the one who reclines at the table? But I am among you as one who serves."

The subject Jesus addresses is not a new one; they earlier saw a powerful demonstration of these words when their master picked up the basin and towel. But none of it seems right to the apostles; they all grew up in a world where striving to become great is a good and God-honoring pursuit. The world defines greatness in terms of power and authority, but Jesus says that service is the hallmark of greatness. He seeks leaders who will give and share and serve—not those who want to control others. Jesus's counsel is to follow his example.

The apostles still have a lot of room for improvement, but Jesus knows they have remained constant and have teachable hearts. He wants them to know that God has noticed.

"You are those who have stayed with me in my trials," Jesus says, "and I assign to you the authority my Father assigned to me, so that you might eat and drink at my table in my kingdom and sit on thrones judging the twelve tribes of Israel.

"Now is the Son of Man glorified, and God is glorified in him. If God is glorified in the Son, God will also glorify the Son in Himself, and He will glorify him very soon."

The glorification Jesus speaks of is his death and resurrection. The glory of both Father and Son will be revealed at the cross, and Jesus must prepare his followers for a future without his physical presence. He looks into the faces of his followers and says, "Dear children, I am with you only a little longer. I say to you what I said to the Jewish authorities: 'Where I am going, you cannot come.'

"A new commandment I give to you—love one another. Just as I have loved you, you are to love one another. By this everyone will know that you are my apprentices—if you have love for one another."

Jesus is teaching them how to live in his absence, but Peter is struggling with the comment about leaving. "Lord, where are you going?"

"Where I'm going now, you can't follow," Jesus says. "But you will follow me later."

Peter doesn't fully understand what Jesus is talking about, but he realizes it has something to do with death. "Lord, why can't I follow you now? I will lay down my life for you."

Jesus looks into Simon's eyes. "Will you lay down your life for me?"

The room becomes still. Jesus does not want his next words to be misunderstood. "Tonight you will all fall away because of me, for it is written, 'I will strike the shepherd, and the sheep of the flock will be scattered.' But after I have been raised, I will go ahead of you into Galilee."

Simon Peter says what they are all thinking. "Even if everyone else falls away because of you, I never will."

"Simon, Simon," Jesus says, "Listen! Satan demanded to sift all of you like wheat, but I have prayed for you—that your faith may not fail. And when you have turned again, strengthen your brothers."

Peter disagrees. "Lord, I'm ready to follow you both to prison and to death!"

Peter's intentions are good, but he overestimates himself and underestimates the forces aligned against them.

Jesus makes a grim prediction. "I tell you, Peter, before the rooster crows twice today, you will deny three times that you know me."

Peter grimaces and shakes his head. This is preposterous. "Even if I must die with you," he promises, "I will not deny you!"

The others agree, and for the next few minutes the air is filled with oaths of loyalty and vows of faithfulness.

Jesus does not pursue the point; he continues giving final instructions to prepare the eleven for the changes that are about to take place. He asks, "When I sent you out without moneybag, knapsack, or sandals, did you lack anything?"

"Nothing," the apostles reply.

The men are being asked to recall how they were provided for when the twelve and later the seventy-two were sent out and told to rely on the "people of peace" they would meet along the way to provide food and shelter. This worked well when the gospel message was new and people were willing to listen, but for the most part people were unwilling to change, and the cumulative response of the nation was rejection. A new strategy must be implemented.

"But now," Jesus says, "let the one who has a moneybag take it, and likewise a knapsack. And let the one who has no sword sell his cloak and buy one. For I tell you that this Scripture must be fulfilled in me: 'And he was numbered with the transgressors.' And indeed, what is written about me is being fulfilled."

Jesus uses the words of Isaiah to explain why the changes must happen: the people of Israel are even now numbering him with the transgressors—they are determining he is a false prophet.

Jesus uses the metaphor of a sword to teach his apprentices that they need to prepare spiritually and mentally for resistance. The apostles think Jesus is speaking literally and do a weapons inventory.

"Look, Lord, here are two swords."

Jesus sighs and says, "That's enough." The eleven are seriously misinterpreting his teaching, but all is not lost. There are other resources. God knew his new community of faith would need more guidance than Jesus would be able to provide in his time on earth. It is to this important topic Jesus now turns.

"Let not your hearts be troubled," Jesus says. "Believe in God; believe also in me. In my Father's house are many dwelling places. If this were not so, would I have told you that I am going to prepare a place for you? And if I go and prepare a place for you, I will come again and take you with me, so that where I am, you will also be. And you know the way to where I am going."

The eleven do not understand that it is on the cross that Jesus will secure a place for them in heaven, and Thomas says, "Lord, we don't know where you're going. How can we know the way?"

Thomas wants a map, but Jesus says, "I am the way and the truth and the life—no one comes to the Father except through me. If you know me, you will know my Father as well, and you do know Him and have seen Him."

The apostle Philip, like the others, does not yet realize what he knows and wants supernatural confirmation. "Lord," he says, "show us the Father, and we'll be satisfied."

Philip wants visible proof. He wants to see God with his own eyes. "Have I been with you all this time, Philip, and you still don't know me?

Whoever has seen me has seen the Father. How can you say, 'Show us the Father'? Do you not believe that I am in the Father and the Father is in me? The words that I speak to you I do not speak on my own authority, but the Father who dwells in me—He does His works through me. Believe me when I say that I am in the Father, and the Father is in me; otherwise, have faith in me because of the works themselves.

"Truly, truly I tell you, the one who has faith in me will do the same works that I am doing, and he will do even greater works than these because I am going to the Father. I will do whatever you ask in my name so that the Son may bring glory to the Father."

Jesus is explaining that before the new covenant is initiated, he will be restricted physically, but after his death and resurrection he will be able to work through all his disciples simultaneously. The important lesson for his followers is that fruitfulness depends on a vibrant prayer life. Requests offered in Jesus's name will be answered—not because there is magic in prayer but because praying in Jesus's name means praying in alignment with God's will.

"If you love me, you will keep my commandments. And I will ask the Father, and He will give you another *Paraclete* who will be with you forever. He is the Spirit of truth, whom the world cannot receive because it neither sees Him nor knows Him. You know Him, for He dwells with you and will be in you.

"I will not leave you orphaned—I'm coming to you. In a little while, the world will no longer see me, but you will see me. Because I live, you also will live. On that day, you will know that I am in my Father, and you are in me, and I am in you. Those who accept my commandments and keep them are the ones who love me, and those who love me will be loved by my Father. I, too, will love them and reveal myself to them."

Jesus describes the work he has been doing as that of a *paraclete*. Broadly defined, a paraclete is "one who is called alongside." The term is used in court to refer to legal counselors and advocates, but this is just one application. It is also commonly used to refer to someone who comes alongside another to strengthen and encourage.

Jesus has been his apprentices' counselor and strengthener and encourager for more than three years. Tonight all that will change.

Jesus knows that at the cross the eleven will feel abandoned, and he assures them that despite the way things look, his death will not orphan them. Jesus promises not only to send another paraclete who will never leave them, soon he will return also. People who are wrapped up in the world won't see him, he says, but his disciples will.

This prompts a question from Thaddaeus. "Lord, why are you going to reveal yourself only to us and not to the world?"

Thaddaeus does not understand that those who reject God are deaf and blind. Worldly people would not see God even if he were to appear before them in the flesh.

Jesus smiles and says, "Those who love me will keep my word, and my Father will love them, and we will go to them and make our home with them. Anyone who does not love me will not keep my words, and the word you hear is not mine—it's from the Father who sent me.

"I've told you these things while I am still with you, but the Paraclete—the Holy Spirit, whom the Father will send in my name—will teach you all things and remind you of all the things I told you.

"Peace I leave with you; my peace I give to you. I do not give you the kind of peace the world gives. Don't let your hearts be troubled and don't be afraid. You heard me say, 'I am going away, and I will come back to you.' If you loved me, you would rejoice that I am going to the Father, for the Father is greater than I. Now I've told you this before it happens, so that when it comes to pass you will believe.

"I will not be talking with you much longer like this, because the ruler of this world is coming. He has no power over me, but I do as the Father has commanded me so that the world will know that I love the Father."

Jesus pauses and looks into the faces of the apostles. There is more to say, but the hour is late. The lesson can continue as they walk. "Come," Jesus says. "Let's be going."

The men stand and prepare to leave, but there is one more element in the Seder—they must sing the portion of Psalm 118 that completes the Hallel. As they walk out of the upper room, the walls reverberate with words that have never had more meaning than they have tonight.

*I will praise You—You answered my prayer and have become my*
    *salvation.*
*The stone the builders rejected has become the chief cornerstone.*
*This is the Lord's doing, and it is amazing to see.*
*This is the day that the Lord has made;*
*Let us rejoice and be glad in it.*
*Save us, we pray, O Lord! O Lord, we pray, give us success!*
*Blessed is the one who comes in the name of the Lord!*
*We bless you from the house of the Lord.*
*The Lord is God, and He has given us light.*
*Bind the festival sacrifice with cords to the horns of the altar!*
*You are my God and I praise You. You are my God and I exalt You.*
*O give thanks to the Lord, for He is good—His steadfast love endures*
    *forever!*

# Betrayed

APRIL 2–3, AD 33

*"The one I kiss is the one you want."*

—Matthew 26:48

THE HOUR IS late when Jesus and the eleven make their way down the stairway from the upper room. The streets are still busy, but it has been a long day, and most are hurriedly making their way to their lodgings. Jesus and eleven apostles are walking to a garden on the Mount of Olives, where he likes to pray.

The men travel the back streets, and Jesus teaches as they walk. During the Seder, he had spoken of a mutual indwelling. He said that he would be in his apprentices, and his apprentices would be in him. Jesus expands and deepens the lesson by reinterpreting a well-known metaphor.

"I am the true vine, and my Father is the gardener. He removes every branch in me that does not bear fruit, and every branch that does bear fruit He prunes so that it may bear more fruit.

"You are already clean because of the message I have spoken to you. Remain in me, and I will remain in you. Just as a branch can't bear fruit unless it remains in the vine, neither can you bear fruit unless you remain in me.

"I am the vine; you are the branches. Those who remain in me and I in them will bear much fruit, for apart from me you can do nothing.

Anyone who does not remain in me is like a branch that is thrown away and withers. These branches are picked up and thrown into the fire and burned.

"If you remain in me and my words remain in you, you may ask for whatever you wish, and it will be done for you. By this my Father is glorified: that you bear much fruit and so prove yourselves to be my apprentices."

The apostles partially understand. They are familiar with God being portrayed as a gardener, but in the Scriptures the vine represents Israel and is often described as unfruitful. Time and again the nation was warned that if they remained unfaithful, the divine gardener would one day replant the vineyard.

Jesus says the wild vine that produced sour grapes has been replaced with a new vine, and those who are organically connected to the new vine will yield fruit that glorifies God.

Jesus explains the union. "As the Father has loved me, so have I loved you. Remain in my love. If you keep my commandments, you will remain in my love, just as I have kept my Father's commandments and remain in His love. I've told you these things so that my joy may be in you, and that your joy may be complete.

"This is my commandment, that you love one another as I have loved you. Greater love has no one than this: that he lay down his life for his friends. You are my friends if you do what I command. I no longer call you servants, because the servant doesn't know what his master is doing. Instead, I've called you friends because I've told you everything that I heard from my Father.

"You did not choose me, but I chose you and appointed you to go and bear fruit—fruit that will last—so that the Father will give you whatever you ask for in my name. I am giving you these commands so that you will love one another."

Jesus describes a community that will be identified by their allegiance to God and their love for one another, but he warns his disciples that living this way will put them on a collision course with the spiritual rebels who populate the world.

"If the world hates you, know that it hated me before it hated you.

If you belonged to the world, the world would love you as its own, but you don't belong to the world. I chose you out of the world, so the world hates you.

"Remember what I told you: a servant is not greater than his master. If they persecuted me, they will also persecute you. If they obeyed my teaching, they will obey yours also.

"But they will do all these things to you because of my name, for they do not know the One who sent me. If I had not come and spoken to them, they would have no sin, but now they have no pretense for their sin.

"Whoever hates me also hates my Father. If I had not done among them the works that no one else has done, they would not be guilty of sin, but now they have seen and hated both me and my Father. But this happened so that the word written in their Law might be fulfilled: 'They hated me without a cause.'

"But when the Paraclete comes, whom I will send to you from the Father—the Spirit of truth who comes from the Father—He will testify about me. And you also must testify, for you have been with me from the beginning."

Jesus prescribes a twofold approach toward a world violently opposed to his message: the witness of the Spirit and the testimony of his disciples. Jesus tells them that God will make sure the gospel is spread, but His messengers must prepare for persecution, or they will see their faith swept away.

Until now, Jesus has taken the brunt of the abuse, but he knows that after he's gone the wrath now directed at him will be turned on his apprentices.

"I have told you these things to keep you from stumbling. They will expel you from the synagogues; in fact, the time will come when whoever kills you will think he is serving God. They will do these things because they know neither the Father nor me. I've told you these things so that when they happen, you will remember I told you about them.

"I didn't tell you these things earlier because I was with you, but now I'm going to the One who sent me, yet none of you asks me, 'Where are you going?' Instead, you grieve because of what I told you.

But I tell you the truth—it's better for you that I go away, because if I don't go away, the Paraclete won't come to you. But if I go, I will send Him to you. When He comes, He will convict the world of sin and righteousness and judgment. Of sin, because they do not believe in me; of righteousness, because I go to the Father, and you will see me no longer; of judgment, because the ruler of this world has been condemned."

The apostles hear little after Jesus announces that he is leaving them, and what they do hear makes little sense. How could life be better without Jesus to guide them?

Jesus knows his disciples' understanding of these things will have to wait. "I still have many things to tell you," Jesus says, "but you cannot bear them now. When the Spirit of truth comes, He will guide you in all the truth, for He will not speak on His own. He will speak only what He hears, and He will tell you the things that are to come.

"He will bring me glory because He will tell you whatever He receives from me. All that belongs to the Father is mine—that's why I said the Spirit will tell you whatever He receives from me.

"In a little while you won't see me anymore, but a little while after that you will see me."

Jesus is speaking of his death and resurrection. The apostles don't make the connection. They turn to one another and whisper, "What's this he's telling us? 'In a little while you won't see me, but a little while after that you will see me' and 'because I go to the Father'? What does he mean by 'a little while'? We don't know what he's talking about."

Jesus overhears them and asks, "Are you trying to find out from one another what I meant when I said, 'In a little while you won't see me anymore, but a little while after that you will see me'? Truly, truly I tell you, you will weep and mourn, but the world will rejoice. You will grieve, but your grief will turn into joy.

"A woman who is giving birth is in anguish because her time has come, but when she has given birth to the baby, she forgets her anguish because of her joy—a child has been born into the world.

"So also you have grief now, but I will see you again, and your hearts will rejoice, and no one will take your joy away from you. In that day you will ask nothing of me. Truly, truly I tell you, whatever you ask of the Father in my name, He will give you. So far you have asked for nothing in my name. Ask, and you will receive so that your joy may be full.

"I have said these things to you in figures of speech. The time will come when I will no longer speak to you figuratively but will tell you about the Father in plain language. In that day you will ask in my name—and I am not saying that I will ask the Father on your behalf, for the Father himself loves you because you have loved me and have believed that I came from God. I came from the Father and have come into the world; now I am leaving the world and going back to the Father."

When Jesus finishes his teaching, the eleven nod enthusiastically and say, "Now you are speaking in plain terms and not using figurative speech! Now we can see that you know all things, and there is no need to question you. Now we believe that you came from God."

Jesus can only shake his head. The apostles' zeal is admirable but misinformed. They believe the day Jesus spoke of earlier has already come. They don't realize that these things cannot happen until after the resurrection.

"Now you believe?" Jesus asks.

No one answers. The tone of Jesus's voice suggests that he questions their understanding, and his next words confirm it. "Listen," Jesus says, "a time is coming—indeed it has already come—when you will be scattered, each to his own, and you will leave me alone. Yet I am not alone, for the Father is with me. I have told you these things so that in me you may have peace. In the world you will have anguish, but take heart—I have overcome the world."

The apostles don't understand why Jesus is proclaiming victory but ask no questions. Jesus and the eleven walk out the city gate, cross the trickling Brook Kidron, and begin climbing the Mount of Olives. It is near midnight, but the paschal moon illuminates the entire valley.

THEY WALK A short distance up the hillside, and Jesus stops and begins to pray. "Father, the hour has come. Glorify Your Son so that the Son may glorify You, just as You have given him authority over all people so that he may give eternal life to all those You have given him. And this is eternal life, that they know You, the only true God, and the one You have sent—Jesus Christ. I brought glory to You on earth by accomplishing the work You gave me to do. So now, Father, bring me into the glory we shared before the world existed.

"I have made You known to the people You gave me from the world. They were Yours, and You gave them to me, and they have kept Your Word. Now they know that everything You have given me comes from You because I gave them the words You gave me. They accepted Your words and have come to know with certainty that I came from You, and they believe that You sent me.

"I ask on their behalf. I am not praying for the world but for the ones You have given me, for they are Yours. All that is mine is Yours, and all that is Yours is mine, and my glory is shown through them. I am coming to You. I will remain in the world no longer, but they are still in the world. Holy Father, protect them by the power of Your name—the name You gave me—so that they may be one, as we are one.

"While I was with them, I protected them in Your name that You have given me. I guarded them, and not one was lost except the son of perdition, in order for the Scripture to be fulfilled. Now I am coming to You, and I say these things while I am still in the world so that my apprentices may be filled with my joy.

"I have given them Your word, and the world has hated them because they are not of the world, just as I am not of the world. I do not ask that You take them out of the world but that You protect them from the evil one. They are not of the world, just as I am not of the world.

"Make them holy in the truth—Your word is truth. Just as You sent me into the world, I have sent them into the world. And for their sake I consecrate myself so that they also may be made holy in truth.

"I pray not only for these disciples but also for the ones who will believe in me through their message, so that all of them might be one. Just as You, Father, are in me, and I am in You, may they also be in us, so that the world may believe that You have sent me. I have given them the glory You gave me, so they may be one just as we are one—I in them and You in me. May they become completely one, so that the world may know that You sent me and have loved them just as You have loved me.

"Father, I want those You have given me to be with me where I am, so they can see my glory, the glory that You have given me because You loved me before the foundation of the world.

"Righteous Father, even though the world does not know You, I know You, and these disciples know that You have sent me. I have made You known to them, and I will continue to make You known so that Your love for me may be in them, and I will be in them."

JESUS ENDS HIS prayer and begins walking up the Mount of Olives. The men make their way slowly up the hill. There are hundreds of pilgrims camped in the shadows of the ancient trees.

They eventually come to a large walled orchard and garden. Named Gethsemane because of the oil press in it, the garden is familiar to the disciples. They have been here frequently with Jesus, and the eleven assume they will be spending the night here and not returning to Bethany.

When they enter the garden gate, Jesus invites Andrew, Phillip, Bartholomew, Matthew, Thomas, James, Simon, and Thaddaeus to find a place to rest, and asks Peter, James, and John to accompany him further for prayer.

It is obvious to the three that Jesus is troubled. They walk a short distance, and he turns to them. "My soul is extremely sorrowful—to the point of death. Stay here and keep watch with me."

Peter, James, and John are concerned about their master's anguish, but they are emotionally and physically exhausted. When Jesus asks them to pray for God to strengthen and prepare them for the ordeal ahead, the three agree, find a comfortable place to sit under a tree, and are soon sleeping soundly.

Jesus, his energy sapped and his steps leaden, walks a short distance and falls to his knees. "Abba, Father, everything is possible for You. Remove this cup from me. Nevertheless, I want Your will to be done, not mine."

Jesus knows the cup of God's wrath is full, and he has no death wish. As he prays, he is visited by an angel; there is no message of deliverance, only encouragement.

Eventually, he rises and goes to check on the disciples.

"Simon," he asks, "are you sleeping?"

The three disciples wake up to find Jesus kneeling beside them. "You couldn't stay awake with me for a single hour? Watch and pray that you will not give in to temptation. The spirit is willing, but the flesh is weak."

The apostles rub their eyes and try to wake up as Jesus walks away, but soon they drift back to sleep. Jesus continues praying. He has known this day was coming, but now that it's here, he struggles to comprehend the enormity of what is before him. Yet his resolve is unshakable.

"My Father, if this cup can't be taken away unless I drink it, may Your will be done."

After a few minutes, Jesus notices Peter, James, and John are asleep. He wakes them and exhorts them to watch and pray with him. The disciples are embarrassed and vow to themselves to stay awake, but when Jesus goes away a third time, they again fall asleep.

Jesus resumes praying, but soon his attention is drawn to the city. The Father has answered his prayer. A crowd carrying torches and weapons tumbles out the eastern gate, down into the valley, and straight up the Mount of Olives toward Gethsemane.

He returns to Peter, James, and John. They have slumbered through their opportunity to be strengthened. "Sleep on and rest!" he says.

The apostles stir and open their eyes.

"Look!" Jesus says. "The time has come—the Son of Man is betrayed into the hands of sinners. Get up. Let's go. Look, my betrayer has arrived."

The urgency in Jesus's voice startles the apostles to consciousness. They look around groggily, not comprehending. Their eyes grow wide when the see a large group of men with swords and clubs walking up the hill toward them.

Peter, James, and John scramble to their feet. The rabbi is already striding toward the gate. The apostles follow. In the torchlight, they see more than two hundred men approaching, an unusual alliance of priests, Pharisees, elders, scribes, temple police, and Roman soldiers.

The eleven are terrified when they see the angry mob, but horrified to see a trusted friend leading them.

The apostles brace for an attack, but the throng stops a short distance away, and Judas Iscariot meekly approaches alone. Jesus steps forward; he knows the signal Judas prearranged with the leaders, and as his former apprentice walks toward him, Jesus says, "Judas, are you betraying the Son of Man with a kiss? Friend, do what you came to do."

Judas smiles nervously and says, "Greetings, Rabbi!" He embraces Jesus and affectionately kisses him on the cheek.

As Judas pulls away, Jesus is looking directly into his eyes, but rather than acknowledging the kiss, he turns to the mob and asks, "Who are you looking for?"

"Jesus of Nazareth," a voice calls out.

"I am he," Jesus says.

As the words are spoken, a great fear strikes the men, and they fall back, shaken—by what, they are not sure.

Jesus asks again, "Who are you looking for?"

The men regain their composure and answer, "Jesus of Nazareth."

"I told you that I am he." Then gesturing toward the eleven, he adds, "So if you're looking for me, let these others go their way."

The arresting officers have no interest in the eleven so long as they do not get in the way. Swords drawn, the soldiers move toward Jesus. Near the front is Malchus, one of the high priest's most trusted slaves, sent to ensure that the arrest goes as planned and Jesus is brought directly to his home.

The apostles realize their master is about to be taken prisoner and ask, "Lord, shall we strike with the sword?"

Before Jesus can answer, Simon Peter draws a sword and slashes wildly. Malchus sees the steel coming and moves quickly; the blade misses his skull but slices off his right ear. The man curses as he clutches his head to staunch the bleeding.

"No more of this!" Jesus commands.

He walks over to the high priest's slave and touches the wound. It is instantly healed. Malchus, speechless, wonders where this man they are arresting got the power to restore a severed ear.

Jesus turns to Peter. "Put your sword back in its place, for all who draw the sword will die by the sword. Don't you realize that I could call upon my Father, and He would immediately send me more than twelve legions of angels? But how then would the Scriptures be fulfilled that say it must happen this way? Shall I not drink the cup the Father has given me?"

Peter, numb and confused, drops his sword. Jesus turns to the leaders of the alliance. "Have you come with swords and clubs to arrest me as if I were a bandit? When I was with you day after day teaching in the temple courts, you didn't arrest me. But this is your time—the time when darkness reigns."

When the apostles hear Jesus proclaiming that his arrest is part of God's plan, it sounds like foolishness. The story of the Messiah can't end this way. Why is the master meekly giving himself up? There are no answers. Convinced that all is lost, the eleven flee into the night.

Jesus, now alone before the mob, does not resist being bound and pushed down the hill.

The priests and leaders who have been frustrated in their attempts to silence Jesus are jubilant but eager to move quickly; dawn is only a few hours from now, and there is much to be done. The hard part, however, is behind them. The wily Nazarene is finally under their control, and if all goes as planned, he will be dead by nightfall.

# 28

# CONDEMNED

APRIL 3, AD 33

*"It is better for you that one man die for the people than the whole nation perish."*

—Joseph Caiaphas, High Priest, AD 18–36

A LARGE GROUP of city elders, lawyers, priests, and Roman soldiers escort the prisoner through the eastern gate. They climb the steep stairway to the Court of the Gentiles and walk across the temple plaza.

Their destination is the Hasmonean Palace on the hill west of the temple. It is too early to formally try Jesus before the Sanhedrin—the law demands all trials be held during the day. Still, there is much that can be accomplished before dawn, and if all goes well, that trial will be a mere formality.

The soldiers escort the accused to the home of the high priest and transfer authority to the temple police. Then they and most of the crowd hastily depart to get some sleep. Tomorrow will be a busy day.

In the shadows watching the transfer is Simon Peter and another disciple who knows the high priest. The other disciple slips into the small crowd escorting Jesus into the palace compound. A few minutes later he reappears, says a few words to the servant girl watching the gate, and Peter is granted entrance.

Peter walks into a large courtyard filled with dozens of slaves, servants, and policemen. It is a cold Nisan night, and the men and women are huddled around charcoal fires awaiting orders. He joins one of the groups to listen for news about Jesus, but soon senses he is being watched. The gatekeeper is staring at him. She's trying to remember where she has seen him before. When the chief apostle looks at her, she says, "You, too, were with that Nazarene, Jesus. Aren't you one of the man's disciples?"

Peter frowns. "I don't know what you're talking about—I don't know him, woman."

The apostle's voice is confident, but the servant girl's question unnerves Peter, and he walks away from the fire. In the distance a cock crows.

JESUS IS NEARBY in a large ornately furnished room in the heart of the palace. He is bound in thick ropes and standing before a well-dressed elderly man. Annas, son of Seth, was appointed high priest of Israel by Quirinius when Jesus was a child, and the old man would still hold the office if not for the political machinations of the Romans. According to the Torah, the appointment to high priest is for life, but Pilate's predecessor, Valarius Gratus, found Annas uncooperative and ousted him after nine years. Little changed, however, because the office remained in the family. Currently his devoted son-in-law, Joseph Caiaphas, is high priest, and Annas is grooming five more sons to take over after him.

Jesus has been brought to Annas for questioning and to allow Caiaphas time to gather enough councilmen to form a quorum. The savvy old politician has heard much about the Galilean and hopes to learn some of the sorcerer's secrets. Two things are of particular interest: the size of Jesus's forces and the secret teachings he is dispensing.

"I have spoken openly to the world," Jesus tells his inquisitor. "I have always taught in synagogues and in the temple, where all the Jews come together, and I have said nothing in secret. Why do you ask me? Ask those who have heard me—they know what I said."

No one in the room is accustomed to hearing Annas challenged. One of the minor officials who is standing near Jesus slaps him hard in the face. "Is that how you answer the high priest?"

Jesus looks the man in the eye and says, "If what I said is wrong, point out the wrong; but if what I said is right, why did you hit me?"

The wizened politico has seen enough fanatics in his day to know he will get nothing from this one. He orders the Levites to take Jesus to his son-in-law for final disposition.

OUTSIDE IN THE courtyard the temperature has dropped to near freezing. The soldiers, servants, and slaves draw closer to the charcoal fires and one another. Peter again walks near one of the fires. The servant girl who questioned him earlier is also at the fire and still suspicious. She points at Peter and says, "This man is one of them."

Another woman agrees. "This man was with Jesus of Nazareth."

The men take a closer look at the stranger. One finally nods and says, "You also are one of them."

Peter senses he is about to be exposed and swears, "Man, I am not!"

Throwing his arms up in disgust, Peter stomps away from the fire. But some are not convinced; they detect a Galilean accent. They watch the stranger go to the forecourt and stand for a long time near the gate. When Peter eventually walks over to another charcoal pit, several suspicious Jerusalemites follow.

They squeeze into the circle and stare across the coals at the outsider. Peter barely notices them. He is looking at Jesus. His master, bound and surrounded by temple police, has been brought into the courtyard. He looks unharmed; it appears they are moving him to a different part of the palace.

Peter's attention is brought back to the fire pit by familiar voices. "Surely you too are one of them—your accent betrays you—you are a Galilean."

Another man standing at the pit squints, straining to see the newcomer's features in the coal's faint light. He had been in Gethsemane when his kinsman, Malchus, had his ear cut off and miraculously restored. He, too, thinks the stranger looks familiar. "Didn't I see you in the garden with him?"

Fear grips Peter, and all he can think to do is save himself. "Man, I don't know what you are talking about—I do not know the man."

As Simon Peter denies knowing Jesus for the third time, he hears a rooster crow in the distance. His eyes grow wide. He turns and sees Jesus looking at him. The awful prophecy—the one that could never happen—has come to pass.

The apostle stands by the coal fire, his mind moving slowly, erratically. Was it just a few hours ago he cursed Judas for betraying the Master?

Peter stumbles away from the fire, out of the courtyard, and into the street, weeping inconsolably.

INSIDE THE PALACE, Caiaphas has not yet gathered a quorum, but there are sufficient councilmen to hold an inquiry and establish the facts of the case.

Jesus is brought into a large crowded room. The law demands the testimony of reliable witnesses in order to establish guilt, but Caiaphas can't find two whose stories agree.

Witness after witness appears, but their testimony is inconsistent. Several allude to comments Jesus made about the temple three years earlier. One says, "This man said, 'I am able to destroy the temple of God and rebuild it in three days.'"

Another testifies, "We heard him say, 'I will destroy this temple made with hands, and in three days I will build another made without hands.'"

The allegations pile up, but the high priest knows that none will survive formal court. Frustrated, he stands and glares at Jesus. "Have you no answer to these men's testimony against you?"

Jesus does not reply.

Caiaphas realizes that he must find a way to force Jesus to incriminate himself. He uses his authority as high priest to put Jesus under oath. "I adjure you by the living God—tell us if you are the Messiah, the Son of God."

"You say that I am," Jesus says.

He then quotes David and Daniel and seals his fate. "Indeed I tell you, from now on you will see the Son of Man seated at the right hand of power and coming on the clouds of heaven."

The informal hearing disintegrates into a sea of angry voices. Caiaphas grabs the collar of his robe and rips it, signifying a guilty verdict, and shakes his finger at Jesus. "He has blasphemed! What further need do we have for witnesses? You've heard his blasphemy—what is your judgment?"

The response is immediate. "He deserves death!"

Jesus has claimed to be God's co-regent. The inquiry is over; Caiaphas has more than enough evidence to convict when the Sanhedrin convenes. As he walks from the room, he tells the guards to prepare the condemned man for transport.

The temple police tie the prisoner's hands and blindfold him. The Galilean has cost them a night's sleep, and they are ready to return the favor. One of the men spits in Jesus's face and slams a fist to his head. "Prophesy to us, Messiah—who was it that hit you?"

The other guards laugh and join in the taunting and beating. It stops only when daylight comes and they are forced to transfer the prisoner to the council chambers. A quorum of the Sanhedrin is present, and they listen to a summary of the high priest's findings. Following the report, they turn to the accused. "If you're the Messiah, tell us."

Jesus shakes his head and says, "If I tell you, you will not believe, and if I question you, you will not answer. But from now on the Son of Man shall be seated at the right hand of the power of God."

"Are you, then, the Son of God?" they ask.

"You say that I am."

This is enough evidence for the Sanhedrin. "What further testimony do we need? We've heard it ourselves from his own mouth."

The council members prepare an indictment they are confident will get Jesus convicted of sedition, but the charges must be formulated quickly; Pilate only listens to court cases early in the morning.

LISTENING NEARBY IS the betrayer. Remorse sets in, and Judas realizes he made a mistake. The chief priests and elders he had originally negotiated with are standing outside the door of the temple. Judas walks up to them, his cupped hands filled with silver. "I have sinned by betraying innocent blood."

The men laugh. "What's that to us? That's your problem."

The ex-apostle, humiliated and out of ideas, hurls the coins to the temple floor and flees, his thoughts dark and confused. Iscariot heads toward the outskirts of town and contemplates his options. He can see only one. He finds a rope and a tree and hangs himself.

IN THE CITY, Jesus is being transferred to the prefect's headquarters. Caiaphas assumes that since Pilate had authorized his soldiers the night before to assist in the arrest, the governor will simply endorse their decision to execute him. The indictment must be changed, of course; blasphemy is not punishable by death under Roman law. Political charges must be substituted, but the Jewish leaders are confident they can use the prisoner's own words to prove he is a revolutionary and a threat to Rome.

A large delegation of chief priests accompanied by scribes and elders lead Jesus to the governor. Many of Pilate's troops are barracked in the Antonio Fortress on the temple mount, but he and his wife prefer the comforts of the old palace built in the upper city by Herod the Great.

When the religious leaders arrive at the governor's residence, they turn Jesus over to the Roman guard and request Pilate come outside to hear their case. Today is the first full day of the festival, and the priests are scheduled to oversee important ceremonies. If they enter the home of a Gentile, they will become ceremonially unclean and unable to participate in the Passover.

Pilate has lived long enough among the Jews to understand some of their peculiar customs. He normally accommodates them to avoid conflict, but when he walks out onto his porch to meet the Sanhedrin that morning, he knows they are being deceitful. The Jews aren't about to hand over one of their own simply to help Rome. There is something they aren't telling him.

"What accusation do you bring against this man?"

The question catches the leaders off guard. They were expecting a cursory endorsement, not a reopening of the trial. Their reply is surly. "If this man were not doing evil, we would not have delivered him over to you."

Pilate grimaces—it's far too early in the morning to put up with such insolence. "Take him yourselves and judge him by your own law."

The leaders look quickly at their sandals and are abruptly reminded how much they need the governor's cooperation. Sufficiently humbled, they reply, "It is not lawful for us to put anyone to death."

When Pilate does not respond, they bring an indictment against Jesus containing three cleverly devised charges. "We found this one perverting our nation and forbidding us to pay tribute to Caesar and saying that he himself is an anointed one—a king."

Pilate can see their charges are motivated by envy, but he is interested in the third accusation and goes inside to interrogate Jesus. When he sees the prisoner, he wonders why there is such animosity toward him. The man standing bound before him looks anything but royal or powerful. His peasant garb is torn and grimy. His face is swollen and cut. His hair is tangled and caked with blood. Pathetic, certainly, but not a threat.

"Are you the king of the Jews?"

"You are saying so," Jesus replies. "Do you say this of your own accord, or did others talk to you about me?"

Pilate is astounded. "Am I a Jew? Your own nation and the chief priests handed you over to me!" Pilate glares at the accused. "What have you done?"

"My kingdom," Jesus says, "is not of this world. If my kingdom were of this world, my servants would have fought so that I would not have been handed over to the Jews—but my kingdom is not from here."

"So you are a king?"

"You say that I am a king. For this purpose I was born and for this purpose I have come into the world—to testify to the truth. Everyone who is of the truth listens to my voice."

Pilate shakes his head and mutters, "What is truth?" This is the most unorthodox defense he has ever been offered. "Don't you hear how many charges they are bringing against you? Have you no answer?"

Jesus offers none. Pilate turns and paces the floor, thinking. He knows little about the accused, but it is clear the charges have no merit. The prefect walks back out onto the porch and announces, "I don't find this man guilty of anything."

The religious leaders throw up their hands and protest, "He stirs up the people, teaching throughout all Judea—from Galilee, where he began, even to this place."

When Pilate hears Jesus is a Galilean, he grows quiet. Perhaps there is a way he can avoid condemning the man after all. Herod Antipas is also in Jerusalem for the Passover. Since Jesus is from the province Herod governs, perhaps Herod will accept jurisdiction. The governor instructs his soldiers to take the prisoner to the tetrarch and hopes he has seen the last of Jesus.

ANTIPAS IS EXCITED when he learns that Jesus is coming. For years he has heard rumors about the Nazarene wonder-worker. Perhaps Jesus can be persuaded to perform a miracle for his lord.

Herod's spirit deflates when the prisoner is brought into the room. Can this gaunt and bleeding little man be the one he has heard so much about? How very average. How very unimpressive.

Accompanying Jesus are representatives from the Sanhedrin who repeat the charges they made before Pilate. The tetrarch listens carefully to the indictment, then turns to hear Jesus's defense.

The prisoner says nothing. More charges are brought. Herod pleads with Jesus to answer, but every accusation is met with silence.

After numerous attempts, Antipas grows bored and frustrated. It is clear to him that the charges have no merit, but he has no interest in getting involved in a messy political situation—what he wants is a demonstration from a famous magician. When it becomes clear that the accused will not cooperate, Herod decides he must make his own entertainment, so he begins taunting the raggedy mute. Soon everyone in the room is playing along. When he tires of the game, Herod drapes a beautiful cloak around the harmless fool who would be king and returns him to the governor.

MOST OF THE city is now awake, and many are already worshipping in the temple plaza. The large group of dignitaries escorting a prisoner to the governor's residence draws a crowd, and when Pilate walks out onto his porch to meet the delegation from the Sanhedrin, he sees a number of townspeople have joined them.

He addresses the high priests. "You brought this man to me claiming he is misleading the people. I have examined him here in your presence, and I find no basis for any of your accusations against him. Neither did Herod, for he sent him back to us. Look, he has done nothing deserving death, so I will punish and release him."

As Pilate pronounces the verdict, the chief priests stiffen, then huddle together to confer. A few minutes later they begin whispering into the crowd. A murmur fills the courtyard. People are discussing the governor's custom of releasing one Jewish prisoner at Passover, and Jesus isn't the only famous man under arrest. He's not even the only famous Jesus in custody. The Romans are holding a man named Jesus Barabbas, who many consider to be a hero because he advocates armed rebellion and has himself killed for the cause.

Pilate overhears the conversations in the crowd and is amazed. The nation's spiritual leaders are so filled with envy and hatred, they are encouraging the crowd to condemn a harmless rabbi and free a known robber and murderer. The governor reflects on the irony and laughs. He despises the Jews and decides to have some fun at the expense of the Sanhedrin. He throws his arms open to the crowd and asks, "Which of the two do you want me to release for you: Jesus Barabbas, or Jesus who is called Christ?"

Pilate looks toward the religious leaders and sneers. "Do you want me to release for you the king of the Jews?"

The priests, scribes and elders scowl and again begin whispering among the crowd. As Pilate waits, an aide brings him a message from his wife. It is a warning: "Have nothing to do with that righteous man, for I have suffered much because of him today in a dream."

Pilate nods grimly. He has no desire to participate, but sees no way to remove himself. Hopefully the people of Jerusalem will vindicate the Galilean. He looks over the sea of faces and repeats his offer. "Which of the two do you want me to release for you?"

This time there is no hesitancy. "Barabbas!" the crowd shouts. "Away with this fellow, and release to us Barabbas."

Pilate sighs and asks, "Then what shall I do with the one you call the king of the Jews?"

The people have requested grace for a terrorist; surely they will seek mercy for the gentle teacher as well.

The people cry out, "Let him be crucified!"

Pilate sees the crowd turning into a mob, and he blunders by trying to reason with them. "Why, what evil has he done?" Pilate says. "I have found no crime in him deserving death. I will therefore punish and release him."

Loud shouts drown Pilate out; the mob is gripped by bloodlust. "Let him be crucified!" they demand.

Pilate stands and walks back inside. The morning is passing, the mob is growing, and the situation is deteriorating. To appease the crowd, the governor orders his men to take the prisoner to an adjacent courtyard and punish him. The soldiers drag Jesus out, strip him naked, and throw him facefirst against a rough-hewn olivewood post. His bound wrists are tied high to the pillar, exposing his back and sides.

One of the soldiers picks up a scourge and walks slowly toward the condemned. He is skilled with the whip and knows just how much pain to inflict to accomplish the desired effect.

The Romans have three levels of whippings: the *fustigatio*, the least severe and usually prescribed for minor offenses, the *flagellatio*, for more serious offenses, and the *verberatio*, a life-threatening scourging normally reserved for those on their way to execution.

Pilate sentences Jesus to the fustigatio, but even this mildest of the beatings extracts a terrible price. The whip is made of multiple leather thongs plaited around found objects—pieces of jagged metal and bone shards and lead weights and fishhooks. In skilled hands, it is an instrument capable of delivering anything from a warning to a death sentence.

When the soldiers are satisfied the prisoner has received a worthy fustigatio, they release him from the post; it is time for the games to begin, and this prisoner will be the perfect pawn for a popular soldier's game. After all, what could be more fun than playing the game of *king* with a man who thinks he is a king?

Props are needed. One of the soldiers fashions a circlet that mimics the one worn by Caesar but is made of thorns. His mates roar with laughter as he forces the crude crown on Jesus's head. Another finds a spare tunic to serve as his royal robe. They encircle Jesus and begin slapping and pushing and taunting him. "Hail, king of the Jews!"

When the soldiers are finished, they inform Pilate. The governor evaluates the work his men have done on Jesus and is confident the crowd will be appeased.

Pilate walks back outside and the people grow quiet. He gestures toward the doorway and says, "Look, I am bringing him out to you so that you may know that I find him not guilty." Jesus is ushered to the porch wearing his new crown and wrapped in his mock regal robe. A loud murmur ripples through the crowd, and Pilate assumes they have seen the foolishness of their indictment. He points toward the impotent prisoner and says, "Behold the man!"

But Pilate has underestimated the Sanhedrin's hatred. When the chief priests see Jesus, they begin shouting, "Crucify him! Crucify him!" Soon the chant is picked up by the mob, and all are clamoring, "Crucify him!"

Pilate tells the soldiers to take the accused back inside. He waits for the din to subside, but for several minutes the crowd continues to shout, "Crucify him! Crucify him!"

Pilate turns to the priests who incited the riot. "Take him yourselves and crucify him—I find no fault in him."

For a third time the governor has pronounced Jesus not guilty, but the Sanhedrin refuses to accept the verdict. One of the councilmen reminds Pilate, "We have a law, and according to that law he ought to die because he claimed to be the Son of God."

The charge of blasphemy is being made, but all Pilate hears is that Jesus professes to be a son of God, and to Pilate that conjures images from his own religious beliefs. He is convinced there are divine men who walk the earth—mortals endowed by the gods with supernatural abilities.

Pilate recalls Jesus mentioning he had a kingdom in another world, and fear grips him—the last thing he wants to do is answer to the gods for harming one of their chosen ones. He quickly walks inside and within moments is in Jesus's face. "Where are you from?" he whispers.

Jesus looks into Pilate's eyes but says nothing.

The uncomfortable silence frustrates the prefect. "You refuse to speak to me?"

Jesus says nothing, and Pilate walks away even more afraid. After reflecting for a few moments, he turns back toward Jesus. His eyes narrow and he asks, "Do you not realize that I have authority to release you and authority to crucify you?"

Jesus nods and says, "You would have no authority over me at all unless it had been given you from above. Therefore he who handed me over to you has the greater sin."

Pilate has no idea what Jesus is talking about, but the answer disturbs him; he is now convinced he wants nothing to do with any of this. He walks back onto the porch and pleads with the mob to change their mind. All his requests are met with angry howls. The confrontation climaxes when a politically savvy council member delivers a veiled threat. "If you release this man, you are not Caesar's friend. Everyone who makes himself a king opposes Caesar."

This is a prospect Pilate cannot dismiss. He knows Tiberius Caesar is by nature a suspicious man, and a report from a distant land that the prefect is allowing someone to call himself a king will not be ignored. The emperor wants peaceful territories that produce crops to fill Rome's larder, not hotbeds of rebellion, and the governor knows that if he can't maintain the Pax Romana, he will be deposed.

Pilate realizes that justice in this case may have to give way to political expediency, but he desperately wants to avoid that if possible. At the same time, he loathes the Jews and loves to disturb them. He brings the accused out again and taunts, "Behold your king!"

Outraged, the religious leaders cry, "Away with him! Away with him! Crucify him!"

Pilate can't resist goading them. "Shall I crucify your king?"

One of the chief priests answers angrily, "We have no king but Caesar."

Pilate is tempted to laugh at the thought of Jewish allegiance to the emperor, but he knows he is trapped in an impossible situation. He ceremoniously walks over to a basin and begins washing his hands, imitating the Jewish rite of purification. "I am innocent of this man's blood," he tells the crowd. "See to it yourselves."

The mob roars in approval, "His blood be on us and on our children!"

Pilate marvels. In the name of God these people request the release of a known insurrectionist and murderer, yet they demand the life of an innocent man accused of the same crime. The exasperated governor instructs the guards to free Barabbas and begin the crucifixion process with the Galilean. He will join two other criminals condemned to die today.

The Roman troops are disgruntled by the addition; they know this third man is popular, and that means crowd control and more work. There is one consolation though: they will have another turn at the whip with him. The first part of the crucifixion process is a dreadful scourging known as the verberatio. When done properly, the criminal is flayed to the bone but remains alive enough to experience the agony of the cross and a lingering death.

Blow after blow falls on Jesus's already lacerated body. When the scourging stops, the soldier is dripping with sweat, and Jesus's back is an indefinable red mass. His face, torn and bleeding before the verberatio began, has taken numerous blows; his visage is now so marred that he barely looks human.

They lift the prisoner to his feet. Jesus attempts to stand, but his legs buckle. The soldiers catch him and prop him against the post to assess the damage they have inflicted. They determine he will survive the scourging and is good for a little more sport. They drape a red tunic over Jesus's shoulders and place a wooden staff in his hands to serve as his scepter. The soldiers then close in around him and begin pushing him around the circle, slapping him and spitting in his face. Several snatch the staff from his hand and bring it down upon his head; others kneel in homage and salute with a mock *ave Caesar*. "Hail, king of the Jews!"

The abuse continues until Jesus's weakened condition forces them to stop. They don't want to have to carry the laughingstock king to the cross. They strip him of the blood-soaked tunic and dress him in his own clothes, but for fun they leave the king his crown.

# 29

# CRUCIFIED

NISAN 14, 3793

*Christ redeemed us from the curse of the law by becoming a curse on our*
*behalf, for it is written, "Cursed is everyone who is hung on a tree."*

—Galatians 3:13

A CROWD HAS gathered in the street outside the old Herodian palace
that serves as the Praetorium when Pilate is in Jerusalem. It is rumored
that the controversial teacher from Galilee has been arrested for sedition
and blasphemy. The details are few, but some say he is being tried by
the Roman governor this morning.

When the onlookers see Jesus being dragged into the street by a
four-man execution squad, several gasp. The gentle teacher who
preached daily at the temple has been scourged so severely that he is
barely recognizable. Many shake their heads as the soldiers lead the
condemned man to a large crossbeam, place one end of it on his shoulder, and push him into the street.

Jesus staggers a few steps and falls on his face. The soldiers curse and
lift him to his feet. He stumbles forward and makes it as far as the city
gate before collapsing again. The guards kick him in the side and order
him to stand. Jesus tries to rise but slumps under the weight.

The soldiers start grumbling; at this pace they will be all morning
with this wretched assignment. They look into the crowd and conscript a

young man to carry the *patibulum*. Simon, a native of Cyrene who is in town to celebrate the Passover, dutifully shoulders the beam and follows.

An audience trails the procession. Some are curious pilgrims, some are enemies, some are sympathizers, and some are family. A small but vocal minority are women from Jerusalem who are lamenting the Galilean's fate.

Jesus stops and turns to the women. "Daughters of Jerusalem, do not weep for me—weep for yourselves and your children. For behold, the days are coming when they will say, 'Blessed are the barren and the wombs that never bore and the breasts that never nursed!' Then they will cry out to the mountains, 'Fall on us,' and to the hills, 'Cover us.'"

*Daughters of Jerusalem* is a phrase used in the Scriptures to refer to the entire population of the city. Jesus says their mourning is misdirected; they need to be concerned about themselves and their families. A judgment will overtake this generation that will be so terrifying that the residents of Jerusalem will plead for creation itself to end their misery. Jesus wants Israel to realize something far worse than a crucifixion can come upon a nation.

Jesus asks an enigmatic question. "If they do these things when the wood is green, what will happen when it is dry?"

He is asking them to consider what they are seeing. If God will allow a fiery judgment to fall on one who is full of life, what will be the fate of a nation whose faith is dead?

The soldiers prod Jesus to continue walking, and they are soon at their destination: a hill north of the city that the locals call Golgotha because of its eerie resemblance to a skull. The Romans like the site. In addition to being conveniently close to the Praetorium, it is on a well-traveled road and thus is an effective venue to demonstrate what happens to those who challenge the emperor.

Crucifixion is an indescribably painful and humiliating way to die, but the Jews have a further incentive to abhor the cross: the Torah says that anyone who is hanged on a tree is accursed by God.

The priests who follow the procession know this passage well and are gloating. Once Jesus is crucified, the people of Israel will be scandalized by the suggestion that a gallows bird is the Messiah.

When the execution detail reaches Golgotha, the other condemned men are already hanging, but there is an empty stake between them reserved for the day's most infamous criminal.

Simon of Cyrene is relieved of the beam and dismissed. One of the soldiers pours a cup of wine mixed with myrrh and puts it to Jesus's lips to torment him. He tastes the bitter liquid, winces, and turns away.

The men laugh, strip off his clothing, and throw him to the ground. One holds his arm to the patibulum while another drives a six-inch iron spike through the base of his palm and into the olive wood. His other arm is stretched out, and the process is repeated.

Two of the soldiers lift the beam to their shoulders, and then the other two come from beneath with forked poles and boost the spar high so that passersby can see where following this rebel will take them.

As he is lifted up, Jesus's body pitches forward; he groans as the nails take the weight of his body. His legs are placed together and turned to the side with knees slightly bent. Another long spike is hammered just under the ankles of both heels and deep into the tree.

He is now crucified and enduring one of the most exquisite tortures ever devised.

Jesus looks into faces filled with hatred and prays, "Father, forgive them, for they know not what they do."

One of the soldiers props a ladder to the cross, climbs it, and nails a *titula* with three inscriptions to the top of the upright. The charge of sedition is written in Aramaic, Greek, and Latin so that all will know his offense: "Jesus of Nazareth, the King of the Jews."

When the priests see the title, they are furious. They demand the soldiers remove the sign, and when they are told it is there by order of the governor, they rush down the hill and inform the high priest. Caiaphas immediately goes to the Praetorium to request the sign be changed.

"Do not write 'The King of the Jews,'" he tells Pilate, "but rather 'This man said I am King of the Jews.'"

Pilate hears the complaint but is unsympathetic. The danger of being reported to Caesar is now past, and the governor is not about to miss an opportunity to goad the men who threatened him. "What I have written," he tells Caiaphas, "I have written."

The high priest is livid but can only turn and walk away.

At the execution site, the four soldiers are bored and begin dividing up the meager spoils they are inheriting from the condemned. The items are few and of little value, but the men still quarrel over who gets what. When they come to Jesus's seamless tunic, they decide to gamble for it. Things are quiet on the hill, and the men are soon lost in their dice game.

Oblivious to the soldiers is a small group of Jesus's family and friends who have moved close to the cross. All but one are women from Galilee who have been a key part of Jesus's ministry since the beginning.

They have given money and supplies; they have cooked and cleaned; they have run errands and drawn water; they have ministered to women and children in crisis, but there is much they have been unable to do because of their gender. Nevertheless, the women do what they can— they faithfully follow Jesus and minister to him whenever they see a need. And they are committed to doing this regardless of what happens.

Jesus looks down from the cross. His vision is blurred, but he recognizes the familiar faces of his loved ones. He is particularly interested in one woman who is present—his mother.

Mary is biting her lip and weeping silently. She is now a widow in her fifties, and Jesus wants to assure her that she will want for nothing. He looks into his mother's anxious eyes, then to John, then back to Mary.

He smiles weakly and says, "Woman, behold, your son!"

Then he looks at his apprentice. "Behold, your mother!"

Others standing near the cross hear Jesus speaking and join in, but they want to take the conversation in a different direction.

"You who would destroy the temple and rebuild it in three days, save yourself! If you're the Son of God, come down from the cross."

Several onlookers begin laughing, and the group from the Sanhedrin wants to provoke the crowd. "He saved others," one says, "but he can't save himself."

Another crows, "Let him save himself if he's the Messiah of God, His Chosen One!"

Another man snickers and says, "Let this Messiah, the king of Israel, come down now from the cross so that we may see and believe in him.

He trusts in God; let God deliver him now—if He desires him. For he said, 'I am the Son of God.'"

This brings guffaws and more derision. One of the soldiers offers Jesus some *posca*, the vinegar wine the soldiers are allowed to drink while on duty, and says, "If you're the king of the Jews, save yourself!"

The ridicule becomes so widespread that even the two insurrectionists hanging on either side of Jesus join in. Eventually, one of them begins thinking about what he is doing and becomes silent. He has heard of Jesus, but until now has given Jesus's teachings little consideration.

The man on the other cross, however, continues to mock. "Are you not the Messiah? Save yourself—and us!"

This hypocrisy is too much for the criminal now repenting of his earlier remarks, and he rebukes the scoffer. "Do you not fear God? Are you not under the same condemnation? And indeed we are punished justly—we're getting what we deserve for our deeds. But this man has done nothing wrong."

He then pauses and looks to the man in the middle. He knows he doesn't deserve to ask, but he musters the courage to say, "Jesus, remember me when you come into your kingdom."

Jesus, himself near death, looks into the fearful man's eyes and assures him, "I tell you truly, today you will be with me in Paradise."

While Jesus is speaking to his new disciple, the people on Golgotha notice something strange happening. It is noon, yet the sun is growing dim. Within minutes, the entire land is immersed in an eerie twilight.

The preternatural darkness is unnerving. Several onlookers determine it is a bad omen and quickly walk down the hill to seek refuge within the city walls. Those who spent the morning mocking Jesus are now quiet, hoping the gloom will lift.

It doesn't. Three hours pass, and still a pall hangs over the land. The ominous silence is broken by a loud cry from the cross. "My God, my God, why have you forsaken me?"

Several bystanders say, "Listen, he's calling Elijah."

They have misunderstood Jesus. They hear his cry to *Eli* (the Aramaic word for God) and think he is a calling Elijah. Many believe that God sometimes sends the prophet to rescue the righteous from suffering.

They think they hear Jesus say something about being forsaken and strain to hear him talk more about who has abandoned him, but when he finally speaks, all he says is, "I thirst."

One of the women runs to the bucket of *posca*, dips a sponge in it, and puts it to Jesus's lips. Others try to stop her. "Wait!" they say, "let's see whether Elijah will come to save him."

But the ancient prophet does not appear. Instead, Jesus moistens his lips with the vinegar and cries out, "It is finished! Father, into Your hands I commit my spirit."

With these words, Jesus bows his head and dies.

As Jesus releases his last breath, a violent earthquake rocks Jerusalem.

At the temple, it is time for the afternoon sacrifice and the slaughter of the lambs for the Passover. The priests at the altar are jolted by the quake and hear a loud ripping sound coming from inside the Holy Place. They run to investigate the damage but stop in the doorway and stare in disbelief into the Holy of Holies. The thick curtain that keeps the most sacred space in perpetual darkness has been torn from top to bottom—a tear not unlike the way a judge rips his robe to pronounce guilt.

Light now streams into the Holy of Holies. The Levites, trembling, run to find the high priest, but travel in the city is difficult. The streets have sustained extensive damage; foundation stones have been moved, and numerous roofs have collapsed. In the Kidron Valley, where there are a large number of tombs, the quake is so strong that many of the graves lie open, the stones once covering them in pieces on the ground.

The only good news many in Jerusalem can see is that the darkness has receded, and the sun is once again shining.

The Roman centurion overseeing the execution detail is awestruck. He shakes his head and says, "Certainly this man was innocent—truly he was the Son of God!"

It is now midafternoon and only a few hours remain before sunset and the beginning of the Sabbath. The Jews petition Pilate to hasten the death of the men on the crosses; the living corpses will defile the paschal Sabbath about to begin.

The governor, familiar with Jewish idiosyncrasies, has no objections and orders a *crurifragium*—with their legs broken, the condemned can't push themselves up to free their diaphragm, and they will quickly asphyxiate.

A stout iron club is used to crush the shinbones of the first two, but when the executioners come to the man in the middle, they find he has already expired. To confirm he is dead, one of the soldiers thrusts his lance between the malefactor's ribs, piercing his heart. As he withdraws the blade, blood and water pour from the wound. The centurion supervising the detail officially pronounces Jesus dead and walks back into town to report the task is complete.

The centurion is not the only one on his way to the governor's residence. Soon after Jesus dies, Pilate receives an unexpected visit from Joseph of Arimathea. The wealthy councilman is requesting permission to give Jesus an honorable burial. Joseph knows his petition could be misconstrued and have him branded a rebel sympathizer, but he will not stand idly by while Jesus's body is thrown into a criminal's grave.

Until now, few have known Joseph's sympathies, but he is not Jesus's only friend in the Sanhedrin. Nicodemus, the Pharisee who visited Jesus three years earlier, is also now ready to identify himself as a disciple. While Joseph is petitioning Pilate for the body, Nicodemus is hastily gathering the supplies they will need. He has little time, but much money, and doors open to him.

At the Praetorium, Pilate is considering Joseph's request. Ordinarily the governor grants appeals by family and friends for a criminal's body. Except in one circumstance—when the crime is sedition. Roman policy throughout the empire is to leave the bodies of rebels and revolutionaries hanging on the cross to rot and become carrion, and when their bones are picked clean, they are tossed on the refuse heap to be burned.

In Israel, however, the execution process has been altered to placate Jewish convictions about ritual cleanness; a body hanging on the cross during the Sabbath will defile the land.

After Pilate consults the centurion and confirms Jesus's death, Joseph's petition is granted. The governor has no qualms about releasing the body to the prominent Sanhedrist; he knows the indictment against

Jesus was false. Pilate watches the old man hurry away and laughs; this is sure to infuriate Joseph's peers.

ON GOLGOTHA, THE soldiers are packing their gear; they're ready for a hot meal and more *posca*. When Joseph informs them of the governor's authorization, the soldiers are barely interested. They gesture toward the body and continue working.

Joseph and his servants carefully take Jesus down from the cross and to a freshly hewn tomb in a nearby garden. Joseph had purchased the grave for himself and his family; now it will be Jesus's final resting place.

The sepulcher, like others nearby, is cut into a sheer rock face, a remnant of the quarry that was here centuries earlier. The entrance is small, perhaps three feet in height, and leads into an antechamber tall enough to stand in and prepare the body. Because family tombs must be entered numerous times over the years, a large boulder is placed at the entrance to dissuade hungry animals.

For the tombs of the wealthy there is a more secure seal: A track several inches deep is notched in the ground at the entrance. In the slot sits a four-foot stone disk that serves as the door. The track is cut on an incline, making the door easy to close but difficult to open; several men will be needed to roll the heavy stone back up the slope once it is sealed.

Joseph instructs his servants to place Jesus's body on the stone slab in the antechamber. Nicodemus soon arrives with the necessary supplies. In accordance with Jewish custom, the body is carefully washed and then wrapped in clean linen.

In the tomb, the aroma is intense. Nicodemus, wanting to honor his Lord in death in a way he did not in life, has purchased more than sixty-five pounds of powdered myrrh and aloes—thirty thousand denarii worth of spices—an amount fit to bury a king.

Watching from a distance are two disciples, Mary Magdalene and Mary, wife of Clopas. The two women have not let Jesus out of their sight since he was thrown into the street at the Praetorium, but they do not speak to the two wealthy strangers. The women recognize them only as members of the council that condemned their Lord to death.

It will be Sabbath within an hour, and the two Marys know there is little they can do for Jesus until the Sabbath has passed, but there is one thing—they can purchase and mix the spices they will use to anoint his body. The two women are grieving as they leave the tomb, but they are comforted to know where their master's body will be when they return Sunday morning.

The sun sets and the paschal Sabbath begins. Because the Sabbath this year falls on the first day of the festival of Unleavened Bread, it is a Great Sabbath. Ordinarily this would be a time of heightened celebration, but many in the city are thinking about today's events. First there was the strange darkness that enveloped the land from noon until three. Then came the earthquake. Then tonight, when the full moon rose, it was blood red. Some attribute the events to coincidence. Others suspect they are signs from heaven and wonder what God is telling them.

Sunrise finds the temple plaza filled with thousands of people, but not everyone is worshipping. Dozens of Jesus's followers are huddled in small groups, grieving and confused and struggling to be thankful.

The nation's religious leaders are also not worshipping. They are discussing a prediction Jesus made that he would rise from the dead. The Sadducees who dominate the Sanhedrin find the notion of resurrection laughable, but they are not naive. What is to stop the deceiver's disciples from vandalizing the grave site and spreading lies? Priests and Pharisees are dispatched to the governor's residence to request that a Roman security detail be assigned to the tomb.

The emissaries go to Pilate and say, "Sir, we remember that when that impostor was still alive he said, 'After three days I will be raised.' Therefore order the tomb be made secure until the third day so that his disciples can't come and steal him and then tell the people, 'He has been raised from the dead.' That last deception would be worse than the first."

Pilate smiles and wonders what kind of dread this man instilled in them that they fear him even in death. But the governor has no interest in wasting good men on a fool's errand.

"You have a guard of soldiers. Go make it as secure as you can."

This is not the answer the leaders want, but at least they will be able to seal and stand guard at the tomb. The priests and Pharisees thank the governor and depart. Within an hour the grave site is swarming with temple police. The Levites roll away the stone, confirm the body is in the sepulcher, and roll the stone over the door. To assure no one breaks in undetected, the tomb is sealed, and a guard is set.

With the body of the impostor now secure, the priests and Pharisees decide they can finally relax. Tomorrow will be the third day. The Nazarene will be proven a liar and left to rot in his grave, and they can get on with the business of serving God.

# 30

# RAISED

APRIL–MAY, AD 33

*"I will put enmity between you and the woman, and between your offspring and her offspring; he will bruise your head, and you will bruise his heel."*

—Genesis 3:15

IN THE PREDAWN darkness, a group of Galilean women quietly dress and make their way toward the Gennath Gate. Mary Magdalene, Joanna, Mary the mother of James, Salome, and several others are bringing aromatic oils to anoint Jesus's body. They saw the abundance of spices brought to the tomb by the wealthy Sanhedrists who buried him, but these women have faithfully served Jesus since the early days in Capernaum, and they want to anoint their master with fragrances they have lovingly mixed with their own hands.

The women know nothing about the guard posted at the sepulcher; their concern is the large rock that blocks the entrance. They wonder aloud, "Who will roll away the stone for us from the door of the tomb?"

At the grave site, the Levites are nearing the end of their watch. The night has been uneventful, and the men are looking forward to some hot food and a bed.

Just before dawn, the earth begins to quake, and a brilliant light appears in the garden. The guards stand motionless and gape—the brightness is a person.

The luminous presence effortlessly rolls away the stone and perches atop it. The Levites guarding the tomb are no-nonsense professionals, but they have no defense against angels. Their weapons fall to the ground, and they faint from fear.

When the earthquake strikes, the women are nearing the city gate. Mary Magdalene senses something is amiss and bolts toward the garden. When she reaches the open sepulcher, she abruptly stops. She sees the guards lying unconscious near the entrance and assumes someone has stolen the body. Peter and the apostles must be alerted. Mary Magdalene flees the garden, running as fast as she can.

A few minutes later the other women arrive. Seeing the stone rolled away and the men on the ground, they assume the worst but decide to assess the damage inside the tomb before reporting the theft. Joanna, Salome, Mary, and the other women enter and are amazed to find that while the body is missing, the grave clothes and a fortune in precious spices rest undisturbed on the table. It appears the body has simply vanished.

As they stand looking at the empty grave clothes, they are joined by two angels. The disciples fall to their knees with their faces to the ground.

"Do not be afraid," one of the messengers says. "You seek Jesus of Nazareth, who was crucified. Why do you seek the living among the dead? He is not here but has risen! Remember how he told you while he was still in Galilee, 'The Son of Man must be delivered into the hands of sinful men and be crucified and on the third day rise.'"

The women slowly nod their heads as they recall the Master's predictions. Everything has happened just as he foretold.

"Come." The angel points toward the table of linen and spices. "See the place where they laid him. Then go quickly and tell his disciples and Peter that he has been raised from the dead and is going ahead of you to Galilee—there you will see him just as he told you."

The angel becomes very still and says, "This is my message to you." Then both angels disappear.

The women immediately set out to find the apostles, but as they are leaving the garden they are met by the last person they would expect to meet.

Jesus walks up to them and says, "Greetings!"

The women fall to the ground and clutch his feet. They want to touch him to be sure he is really there.

"Do not be afraid," Jesus says. "Go and tell my brothers to go to Galilee—that's where they will see me."


AT THE SEPULCHER, the guards are reviving. They stand on wobbly legs and stagger toward the city to report the empty tomb. When they tell the priests they were assaulted by an angel, a hasty meeting of the Sanhedrin is called.

The leaders aren't interested in discussing the implications of a divine visitation—their goal is to control the story. Several options are discussed, and ultimately they decide to bribe the witnesses.

The Levites are called before the ruling council. The men are fearful—if it is determined that they have lied, they will be executed for dereliction of duty. The policemen are pleasantly confused when a priest begins handing out leather pouches. They open the bags, look at one another, and smile.

One of the priests explains what they must do to earn the money: "Tell people, 'His disciples came by night and stole him away while we were asleep.' And if this comes to the governor's ears, we will satisfy him and keep you out of trouble."

The Levites pocket the bribe and vow to keep the truth to themselves.


IN ANOTHER PART of town, Mary Magdalene has found Peter and John.

"They've taken the Lord out of the tomb, and we don't know where they put him!"

The two apostles are quickly out the door and running toward the grave site. Mary Magdalene follows, weeping disconsolately.

John arrives at the sepulcher first but hesitates to enter. He bends down and peers into the shadows. He can see the grave clothes, but no body.

Peter arrives and immediately enters; John follows cautiously. The men are not ready for what they find. The linen cloths and spices lie untouched, but the napkin that was placed over Jesus's face has been neatly folded and is sitting to the side.

As the men leave the tomb, they are struggling to understand what has happened, but in John a change is taking place. He knows Jesus has somehow done what he promised. Lost in thought and considering an impossibility, the men say little to one another as they walk back to town.

Mary Magdalene sees the apostles leave. Sobbing, she walks to the tomb and stoops to look inside. Sitting on the table are two angels in bright raiment. "Woman," they ask, "why are you weeping?"

Mary Magdalene repeats what she told Peter and John. "They've taken my Lord away, and I don't know where they put him!"

Mary hears a noise and turns to see a man standing behind her. He asks her the same question the angels asked.

"Woman, why are you weeping? Whom are you seeking?"

Mary Magdalene doesn't recognize the man and assumes he is the caretaker. "Sir," she pleads, "if you've carried him away, tell me where you've put him—I will take him!"

Embarrassed by her boldness, she blushes and looks to the ground.

The stranger gently says, "Mary."

She looks up and cries, "Teacher!" and falls to his feet.

"Do not cling to me," Jesus tells her, "for I have not yet ascended to the Father. But go to my brothers and tell them, 'I am ascending to my Father and your Father, to my God and your God.'"

Mary Magdalene, her strength renewed, rises and runs from the garden. When she arrives at the home where the apostles are gathered, she discovers her friends have also seen the angels and spoken to Jesus. Mary tells everyone what happened at the tomb and gives them the message Jesus gave her.

Peter and John listen carefully but say nothing; they are still trying to make sense of what they saw in the tomb. The other apostles aren't as ambivalent; they believe the women are suffering from grief-induced delirium. Jesus is dead.

There is disagreement among the men and women who have been following Jesus. Some are hopeful, but others are discouraged and convinced the cause is lost. Later that day, two disciples decide to go home to the village of Emmaus. As they walk, they get into a heated debate about what happened to Jesus.

Soon they are overtaken by another pilgrim who is leaving Jerusalem. They assume he's headed home early from the festival as they are.

The man comes alongside them and asks, "What were you discussing with each other as you walked?"

The two stop and turn to the stranger. One of them, a man named Cleopas, is astounded.

"Are you the only visitor to Jerusalem who doesn't know the things that have happened there these last few days?"

"What kind of things?" the stranger asks.

"Things concerning Jesus of Nazareth, who was a prophet mighty in deed and word before God and all the people, and how our chief priests and leaders handed him over to be condemned to death and crucified him. We were hoping that he was the one to redeem Israel, but it has already been three days since all this happened.

"Then some women in our group amazed us. They were at the tomb early this morning, and when they didn't find his body there, they came back and told us they had seen a vision of angels who said that he was alive. Some of those who were with us went to the tomb and found it just as the women had said, but they didn't see Jesus."

The stranger looks into the eyes of Cleopas and his companion and gently replies, "Oh how foolish you are, and how slow of heart to believe all that the prophets spoke! Was it not necessary for the Messiah to suffer these things and enter into his glory?"

When the men do not answer, the stranger launches into a long explanation of how everything that had happened over the past three days had been foretold in the Scriptures.

As the mysterious traveler explains the necessity of the cross, the gloom in the disciples lifts. By the time they reach Emmaus, Cleopas and his companion are renewed and wanting to hear more from the peculiar teacher.

"Stay with us," they plead, "evening is near, and the day is already spent."

The stranger agrees, and they go to one of the men's homes for dinner. A simple meal is prepared, and the visitor is asked to offer thanks. He takes a loaf of bread, prays, then breaks it and gives some to Cleopas and his friend. As the disciples take the bread, they realize they are dining with Jesus. Their mouths drop open, and the men look at each other in disbelief, but when they turn back to Jesus, he is not there.

When the men recover from the shock, they ask each other, "Did not our hearts burn within us as he talked to us on the road and opened up the Scriptures to us?"

There is no question in their minds—Jesus has risen. They jump up from the table and return to Jerusalem. Night has fallen by the time Cleopas and his companion reach the city.

Ten of the eleven apostles are there when they arrive. The two disciples describe their encounter with Jesus on the Emmaus road and discover they are not the only ones who have seen him. One of the apostles says, "The Lord has risen indeed, and has appeared to Simon!"

The men become excited as they discuss what all this might mean, and they don't notice that their circle has grown by one. The new arrival says, "Peace be with you!"

The men are startled and step back, unsure how the one before them got past the locked door. They assume they are in the presence of a ghost.

"Why are you frightened?" the visitant asks. "Why do doubts arise in your hearts? Look at my hands and my feet—see that it's really me. Touch me and see for yourselves. A spirit doesn't have flesh and bones as you see I have."

Jesus then offers his hands for their inspection and shows them his pierced side. The men are overcome by astonishment and can't believe they are speaking with Jesus.

Jesus knows they are having trouble believing their eyes and asks, "Do you have anything here to eat?"

The men nod and offer him a piece of broiled fish. As Jesus eats, the apostles marvel. This is too good to be true.

Jesus smiles and says, "Peace be with you. As the Father has sent me, even so I am sending you."

He then takes a large breath and exhales, saying, "Receive the Holy Spirit. If you forgive anyone's sins, they are forgiven; if you do not forgive them, they are not forgiven."

Like the washing of the apostles' feet at Passover, this is an acted parable. Soon the Holy Spirit will indwell and empower the Lord's church to preach the good news, and the new community will be used to both comfort the broken and confront the proud.

When Jesus concludes his instructions, he leaves as mysteriously as he arrived.

The ten sit in silence trying to process what happened. By the time the apostle Thomas returns, they are convinced they did not imagine Jesus's visit.

"We've seen the Lord!" they tell Thomas.

Thomas frowns and shakes his head. "Unless I see the nail marks in his hands and put my finger where the nails were and put my hand into his side, I will never believe."

Thomas is convinced that Jesus is dead, and the ten say no more.

The apostles remain in Jerusalem another week until the festival ends. Most of their time is spent behind locked doors awaiting arrest as coconspirators, but the time passes uneventfully.

On the first day of the week, the apostles are preparing to go home to Galilee. Jesus again appears in their midst and says, "Peace be with you."

He walks over to Thomas, stretches forth his palms, and says, "Put your finger here and look at my hands. Put your hand into the wound in my side—stop doubting and believe!"

But Thomas no longer wants to probe the wounds. He falls to his knees and confesses, "My Lord and my God!"

"You believe because you've seen me," Jesus says. "Blessed are those who haven't seen, yet have come to believe."

With these words, Jesus vanishes from their sight.

THE DISCIPLES ARE soon on their way to Galilee. When they arrive in Capernaum, they are unsure how to proceed. They were told to go home and wait, and they have. Now what?

A week passes with no sign of Jesus. Simon Peter announces, "I'm going fishing."

Six of the apostles join him. The men spend all night on the lake. Time and again they pull in empty nets. By sunrise they have had enough and head in.

They see a stranger standing on the shore.

"Young men," he calls, "have you no fish?"

The apostles are too tired to engage in conversation, and simply answer no.

"Cast the net on the right side of the boat," the stranger tells them. "You will find some."

It's been a long and futile night, but they humor the stranger and halfheartedly cast the net one more time. When they begin to pull it in, the weight tells them the net is full. All hands begin feverishly pulling in the catch, but as they haul in the fish, the apostle John realizes this is all too familiar. When he looks again at the man on shore, he recognizes him. He nudges Peter and says, "It's the Lord!"

Peter turns and recognizes Jesus. He leaps into the water and begins swimming. The other disciples pull in the overflowing net and row in. When they land, they find Jesus has built a small charcoal fire and is cooking fish and heating bread.

"Bring some of the fish you've just caught," he tells them.

Peter retrieves several fish, and Jesus adds them to those already on the coals. When the fish are cooked, Jesus invites the apostles to have breakfast with him. The disciples walk over timidly. They know it is Jesus who is serving them, but they don't understand why, and none have the courage to ask.

They take the food and eat in silence. When they're finished, Jesus turns to Peter. He gestures toward the other disciples and asks, "Simon bar Jonah, do you love me more than these?"

Peter is not expecting the question. He has often boasted of his faithfulness in the past, but this morning he is content to appeal to Jesus's knowledge.

"Yes, Lord," he stammers, "you know that I love you."

"Feed my lambs," Jesus responds.

A few minutes later Jesus repeats his question. "Simon bar Jonah, do you love me?"

Peter, deeply grieved, again relies on Jesus's knowledge. "Yes, Lord. You know that I love you."

"Tend my sheep."

Jesus then asks a third time, "Simon bar Jonah, do you love me?"

Peter doesn't know what to say and can only repeat himself. "Lord, you know everything. You know that I love you!"

Jesus nods and says, "Feed my sheep. Truly, truly I tell you, when you were young, you dressed yourself and went wherever you wanted, but when you grow old, you'll stretch out your hands, and another will dress you and take you where you don't want to go."

As Jesus turns and walks toward the lakeshore, Peter follows. His mind is racing. Three times Peter stood at a charcoal fire and denied Jesus. Now at another fire he has thrice been challenged with a similar question.

The good news for Simon Peter is that he is right about Jesus knowing the condition of his heart. Jesus knows Peter has repented and is ready to serve God whenever and wherever God wants.

Jesus smiles at his apprentice and says, "Follow me."

Peter is relieved that he will be allowed to remain in the fold despite his apostasy, but he's concerned about Jesus's prediction that when he is old he will "stretch out his hands"—a common metaphor for crucifixion. Peter accepts Jesus's prediction without questioning the implications, but when he notices his friend John walking close behind them, he asks, "Lord, what about him?"

Jesus stops and looks into Peter's eyes. "If I want him to remain alive until I return, what is that to you? You follow me!"

Jesus tells the eleven to organize a meeting of those who believe in him. He will be leaving soon and has some parting instructions for his apprentices.

The apostles spread the message, and several days later more than five hundred people gather on a hillside in Galilee. Some are convinced Jesus has risen from the dead, and they worship him. Others are skeptical.

Jesus looks over the multitude and proclaims, "All authority in heaven and on earth has been given to me. Therefore, go and make apprentices of all nations, baptizing them in the name of the Father and of the Son and of the Holy Spirit, teaching them to observe all that I have commanded you. And behold, I am with you always, to the end of the age."

The commission is simple. The apostles are to *matheteusate*—make apprentices. They are to train any who are willing to walk in the Way. They are to pass on what they were taught by Jesus to faithful men and women who will then proclaim it to future generations. They are to baptize people in water, but more importantly, they are to immerse them in an environment where they can experience life with the Father, Son, and Spirit.

When Jesus finishes his message, he instructs the eleven to return to Jerusalem and wait.


WITHIN A WEEK the apostles are in the city, but their time with Jesus in Galilee has changed them. They no longer cower in fear behind locked doors. Daily they are in the temple plaza worshipping and praising God.

Jesus visits the eleven often during the next few weeks. When the festival of *Pentecost* (held fifty days after Passover) draws near, Jesus reminds them, "This is what I told you while I was still with you— everything written about me in the Law of Moses and the Prophets and the Psalms must be fulfilled. It was written that the Messiah would suffer and rise from the dead on the third day, and that repentance and forgiveness of sins are to be proclaimed in his name to all nations, beginning in Jerusalem.

"You are witnesses of these things. Behold, I am sending the promise of my Father upon you, but stay in the city until you are clothed with power from on high, for John baptized with water, but you will be baptized with the Holy Spirit not many days from now."

Jesus concludes his teaching and invites the apostles to walk with him. The route is familiar. They walk out of the city into the Kidron

Valley and take the road east. They walk past the Garden of Gethsemane and up the Mount of Olives. When they reach the summit, Jesus stops and turns toward the temple. The colorful Babylonian tapestries that adorn the entrance are slowly undulating in the breeze.

The disciples can sense something dramatic is about to happen, and they assume Jesus is finally going to assert his messianic authority. All their lives they have been taught from the Scriptures that the pouring out of the Spirit will accompany the reign of the Messiah and will reestablish Israel's wealth and power.

"Lord," the eleven ask, "has the time come to restore the kingdom to Israel?"

Jesus shakes his head. "That is not for you to know. The Father alone has the authority to set those dates and times. But you will receive power when the Holy Spirit comes upon you, and you will be my witnesses in Jerusalem and throughout Judea and Samaria and to the ends of the earth."

Jesus then lifts his hands and begins pronouncing blessings on them. As he speaks, he begins to rise. The apostles watch, dumbstruck, as Jesus drifts upward and is enveloped by a cloud.

As the men stand gazing into the heavens, they are joined by two angels who say, "Men of Galilee, why are you standing here staring into the sky? Jesus has been taken from you into heaven, but one day he will return from heaven in the same way you saw him go."

# EPILOGUE

*"Now Jesus did many other signs in the presence of the disciples which are not recorded in this book. Were every one of them to be recorded, I suppose that the world itself could not contain the books that would be written, but these are written so that you may believe that Jesus is the Christ, the Son of God, and that by believing you may have life in His name."*

—John 20:30–31; 21:25

# A BIBLICAL CHRONOLOGY OF JESUS'S MINISTRY

## CHAPTER 1: A VOICE FROM THE WILDERNESS

1) **John the Baptist and Scripture:** Matthew 3:1–6; Mark 1:2–6; Luke 3:1–6; Luke 1:5–19; Isaiah 40:3–5; Hosea 2:14–15; Malachi 3:1–3; 4:5–6
2) **John's preaching of repentance:** Matthew 3:7–10; Luke 3:7–9
3) **John's reply to questioners:** Luke 3:10–14
4) **John's messianic preaching:** Matthew 3:11–12; Mark 1:7–8; Luke 3:15–18
5) **Baptism of Jesus:** Matthew 3:13–17; Mark 1:9–11; Luke 3:21–22; Psalm 2:7; Isaiah 42:1

## CHAPTER 2: INCEPTION

1) **The temptation:** Matthew 4:1–11; Mark 1:12–13; Luke 4:1–13; Exodus 17:1–7; Deuteronomy 6:13, 16; Psalm 91:9–15; Ezekiel 28:12–19; Isaiah 14:12–15
2) **John the Baptist's testimony:** John 1:15, 19–34; Isaiah 40:3
3) **Jesus's first contact with five of the twelve:** John 1:35–51; Genesis 27:34–36; 28:10–13
4) **The first sign—water to wine:** John 2:1–12; Amos 9:13

## CHAPTER 3: THE FIRST PASSOVER

## CHAPTER 4: THE GOD OF ALL CLANS

## CHAPTER 5: GALILEE OF THE GENTILES

## Chapter 6: Authority

1) **The cleansing of a leper:** Matthew 8:2–4; Mark 1:40–45; Luke 5:12–15; Leviticus 13:45–46; 14:1–20; Numbers 12:1–10
2) **The healing of the paralytic lowered through the roof:** Matthew 9:2–8; Mark 2:1–12; Luke 5:17–26
3) **The calling of Matthew Levi:** Matthew 9:9; Mark 2:13–14; Luke 5:27–28; Isaiah 53:2–12

## Chapter 7: Lord of the Sabbath

1) **Sabbath healing at the pool of Bethesda:** John 5:1–18
2) **Jesus's defense of the Sabbath healing:** John 5:19–47
3) **Sabbath grain-picking dispute:** Matthew 12:1–8; Mark 2:33–28; Luke 6:1–5; 1 Samuel 21:1–6; Exodus 25:30; Leviticus 24:5–9; Numbers 28:9–10; Hosea 6:6
4) **Synagogue Sabbath healing of a man with a withered hand:** Matthew 12:9–15a; Mark 3:1–6; Luke 6:6–11
5) **Jesus heals multitudes by the lake:** Matthew 12:15b–16; Mark 3:7–12; Luke 6:17–19

## Chapter 8: The Divine Conspiracy

1) **The choosing of the twelve:** Matthew 10:2–4; Mark 3:13–19; Luke 6:12–16
2) **Setting of the Sermon on the Mount/Plain:** Matthew 5:1–2; Luke 6:17–20a
3) **Blessings and woes:** Matthew 5:3–12; Luke 6:20b–26; Isaiah 57:15
4) **Salt of the earth, light of the world:** Matthew 5:13–16
5) **Fulfilling the Law of Moses:** Matthew 5:17–48; Luke 6:27–36
6) **True and false religion:** Matthew 6:1–18
7) **Wealth and worry:** Matthew 6:19–34
8) **How to treat others:** Matthew 7:1–12; Luke 6:37–42
9) **The two ways:** Matthew 7:13–27; Luke 6:43–49

## Chapter 9: Wisdom's Children

1) The healing of the centurion's servant: Matthew 8:5–13; Luke 7:1–10; Isaiah 25:6

2) The raising of the widow's son in Nain: Luke 7:11–17; 1 Kings 17:17–23

3) John the Baptist's question and Jesus's answer: Matthew 11:2–6; Luke 7:18–23; Isaiah 35:4–6

4) Jesus's witness about John: Matthew 11:7–19; Luke 7:24–35; Malachi 3:1; Jeremiah 31:31–34

5) Woes pronounced on Galilean cities: Matthew 11:20–24

6) Thanksgiving and invitation: Matthew 11:25–30

7) A sinful woman anoints Jesus at a Pharisee's table: Luke 7:36–50; Song of Songs 6:5

8) Death of John the Baptist: Matthew 14:6–13a; Mark 6:21–29

## Chapter 10: Dark Sayings from of Old

1) Jesus's family seeks to protect him: Mark 3:20–21

2) Collusion with Beelzebul accusation: Matthew 12:22–30; Mark 3:22–27; Luke 11:14–23; Isaiah 49:23–25

3) The sin against the Holy Spirit: Matthew 12:31–37: Mark 3:28–30; Numbers 15:29–31; Isaiah 5:20

4) The sign of Jonah: Matthew 12:38–42; Luke 11:29–32; Jonah 1:17; 3:4–10; 2 Chronicles 9:1

5) The return of the evil spirit: Matthew 12:43–45; Luke 11:24–28

6) Jesus defines his true family: Matthew 12:46, 48–50; Mark 3:31–35; Luke 8:19–21

7) Parable of the sower: Matthew 13:1–9; Mark 4:1–9; Luke 8:4–8

8) Parable of the seed growing secretly: Mark 4:26–29

9) Parable of the wheat and the weeds: Matthew 13:24–30

10) Parable of the mustard seed: Matthew 13:31–32; Mark 4:30–32

11) Parable of the leaven: Matthew 13:33

12) Two parables: the hidden treasure and the pearl: Matthew 13:44–46

13) Parable of the net: Matthew 13:47–50

14) **The reason Jesus speaks in parables:** Matthew 13:10–17; Mark 4:10–12; Luke 8:9–10; Isaiah 6:9–10

15) **Explanation of the parable of the sower:** Matthew 13:18–23; Mark 4:13–20; Luke 8:11–15

16) **Explanation of the parable of the wheat and the weeds:** Matthew 13:36–43

17) **Revelation as light to be heeded:** Mark 4:21–25; Luke 8:16–18

18) **Kingdom scribes and treasures old and new:** Matthew 13:51–52

## CHAPTER 11: IDENTITY

1) **Jesus stills a storm:** Matthew 8:23–27; Mark 4:35–41; Luke 8:22–25

2) **The Gadarene demoniacs:** Matthew 8:28–34; Mark 5:1–20; Luke 8:26–39

3) **Levi's banquet:** Matthew 9:10–13: Mark 2:15–17; Luke 5:29–32; Hosea 6:6

4) **A question about fasting:** Matthew 9:14–17: Mark 2:18–22; Luke 5:33–39; Isaiah 54:5–6; 62:4–5; Hosea 2:16–20

5) **Jairus's daughter and the woman with a hemorrhage** Matthew 9:18–26; Mark 5:21–43; Luke 8:40–56

6) **Two blind men healed:** Matthew 9:27–31

7) **The mute demoniac:** Matthew 9:32–34

## CHAPTER 12: HOMECOMING

1) **Rejected in Nazareth:** Matthew 13:54–58; Mark 6:1–6a; Luke 4:16–30; Deuteronomy 6:4–9; Isaiah 61:1–2; 1 Kings 17:1–24; 18:1; 2 Kings 5:1–14

2) **The commissioning of the twelve:** Matthew 9:35–38; 10:1, 5–42; Mark 6:6b–13; Luke 9:1–6

## CHAPTER 13: THE BREAD OF LIFE

1) **Opinions About Jesus:** Matthew 14:1–2; Mark 6:14–16; Luke 9:7–10

2) **Return of the twelve:** Mark 6:30–31; Luke 9:10a

3) **Feeding of the five thousand:** Matthew 14:13–21; Mark 6:32–44; Luke 9:10b–17; John 6:1–15; 2 Kings 4:42–44; Exodus 16:4; Nehemiah 9:15; Deuteronomy 18:15–19; Isaiah 54:13; Jeremiah 31:33–34

4) **Jesus walks on water:** Matthew 14:22–33; Mark 6:45–52; John 6:16–21

5) **Healings at Gennesaret:** Matthew 14:34–36; Mark 6:53–56

6) **The Bread of Life discourse:** John 6:22–59

7) **Reaction to the discourse:** John 6:60–71

## CHAPTER 14: TRADITION

1) **Conflicts about the traditions of the elders:** Matthew 15:1–20; Mark 7:1–23; Isaiah 29:13; Deuteronomy 23:21–23; Numbers 30:1–16; Exodus 20:12; 21:17

2) **The Syrophoenician woman:** Matthew 15:21–28; Mark 7:24–30

3) **Heals a deaf mute and many others:** Matthew 15:29–31; Mark 7:31–37

4) **Feeding of the 4,000:** Matthew 15:32–39a; Mark 8:1–9

5) **The Pharisees seek a sign:** Matthew 15:39b–16:4; Mark 8:10–13

6) **The leaven of the Pharisees:** Matthew 16:5–12; Mark 8:14–21

7) **A blind man is healed in Bethsaida:** Mark 8:22–26

## CHAPTER 15: THE TURNING POINT

1) **Peter's confession:** Matthew 16:13–20; Mark 8:27–30; Luke 9:18–21

2) **Jesus foretells his death and resurrection:** Matthew 16:21–28; Mark 8:31–9:1; Luke 9:22–27

3) **The transfiguration:** Matthew 17:1–8; Mark 9:2–8; Luke 9:28–36a; Psalm 2:7; Isaiah 42:1; Deuteronomy 18:15–19

4) **The coming of Elijah:** Matthew 17:9–13; Mark 9:9–13; Luke 9:36b; Isaiah 53:2–12; Malachi 4:5–6

5) **Jesus heals a demon–possessed boy:** Matthew 17:14–20; Mark 9:14–29; Luke 9:37–43a

## CHAPTER 16: A KINGDOM OF CHILDREN

1) **Jesus again foretells his death:** Matthew 17:22–23; Mark 9:30–32; Luke 9:43b–45

2) **Payment of the temple tax:** Matthew 17:24–27; Exodus 30:12–16; Nehemiah 10:32–33

3) **True greatness:** Matthew 18:1–5; Mark 9:33–37; Luke 9:46–48

4) **The outsider exorcist:** Mark 9:38–41; Luke 9:49–50

5) **Warnings about temptations:** Matthew 18:7–9; Mark 9:42–50; 2 Kings 23:10; Isaiah 66:24; Jeremiah 7:31–32; Malachi 3:1–3

6) **Parable of the lost sheep:** Matthew 18:10–14

7) **On reproving a fellow disciple:** Matthew 18:15–18; Leviticus 19:17; Deuteronomy 19:15

8) **Two or three gathered in my name:** Matthew 18:19–20

9) **On reconciliation:** Matthew 18:21–22; Amos 1:3–13; Genesis 4:23–24

10) **Parable of the unforgiving servant:** Matthew 18:23–35

11) **Jesus's unbelieving brothers:** John 7:1–9

12) **Decision to go to Jerusalem secretly:** Luke 9:51; John 7:10

13) **Jesus is rejected by the Samaritans:** Luke 9:52–56; 2 Kings 1:1–17

14) **On Following Jesus:** Matthew 8:19–22; Luke 9:57–62

## CHAPTER 17: LIGHT OF THE WORLD

1) **Jesus at Sukkoth—mixed reactions:** John 7:11–52; Leviticus 23:33–43; Numbers 29:12–39; Deuteronomy 16:13–17; Nehemiah 8:13–18; Psalm 78:16; 118:1–29; Isaiah 58:11

2) **Jesus claims to be the light of the world, the truth, and Abraham's superior:** John 8:12–59

## CHAPTER 18: PRIDE AND PREJUDICE

1) **Jesus heals a man born blind:** John 9:1–41

2) **Jesus the Good Shepherd with a new flock:** John 10:1–21; Ezekiel 34:2–16; Jeremiah 3:17; Isaiah 49:6; 56:7

5) Parable of salt: Luke 14:34–35
6) Parable of the lost sheep: Luke 15:1–7
7) Parable of the lost coin: Luke 15:8–10
8) Parable of the forgiving father: Luke 15:11–32
9) Parable of the unjust steward: Luke 16:1–9
10) On faithfulness in what is least: Luke 16:10–12
11) On serving two masters: Luke 16:13
12) Jesus rebukes the Pharisees: Luke 16:14–15
13) Parable of the rich man and Lazarus: Luke 16:19–31
14) Parable of the dutiful servant: Luke 17:7–10
15) The cleansing of ten lepers: Luke 17:11–19
16) The kingdom is in the midst of you: Luke 17:20–21

## CHAPTER 21: DEATHLESS

1) Parable of the unjust judge: Luke 18:1–8
2) Parable of the Pharisee and the tax collector: Luke 18:9–14
3) Departure to Judea: Matthew 19:1–2; Mark 10:1
4) On divorce and celibacy: Matthew 19:3–12; Mark 10:2–12; Genesis 1:27; 2:24; Deuteronomy 24:1; Malachi 2:16
5) Jesus blesses the children: Matthew 19:13–15; Mark 10:13–16
6) The rich young ruler: Matthew 19:16–22; Mark 10:17–22; Luke 18:18–23
7) On riches and the rewards of discipleship: Matthew 19:23–30; Mark 10:23–31; Luke 18:24–30; Daniel 7:13–14, 27
8) Parable of the laborers in the vineyard: Matthew 20:1–16
9) The raising of Lazarus: John 11:1–44

## CHAPTER 22: THE PASSOVER PLOT

1) The Jewish reaction to the raising of Lazarus: John 11:45–54
2) Jesus again foretells his death and resurrection: Matthew 20:17–19; Mark 10:32–34; Luke 18:31–34
3) The request for precedence by the sons of Zebedee: Matthew 20:20–28; Mark 10:35–45; Luke 22:24–27; Isaiah 53:1–12

4) **Healing of the blind men at Jericho (Bartimaeus):** Matthew 20:29–34; Mark 10:46–52; Luke 18:35–43

5) **Zacchaeus the tax farmer:** Luke 19:1–10

6) **Parable of the ten minas:** Luke 19:11–28

7) **The hostility of the Sanhedrin:** John 11:55–57

8) **The anointing in Bethany:** Matthew 26:6–13; Mark 14:3–9; John 12:1–11

## CHAPTER 23: ON A DONKEY'S COLT

1) **The triumphal entry into Jerusalem:** Matthew 21:1–9; Mark 11:1–10; Luke 19:29–44; John 12:12–19; Exodus 12:3–6; 2 Samuel 15:30–32; Ezekiel 11:22–23; Zechariah 9:9; 14:3–4

2) **Jesus curses a fruitless fig tree:** Matthew 21:18–19; Mark 11:12–14; Jeremiah 8:13

3) **Second temple cleansing:** Matthew 21:10–17; Mark 11:15–19; Luke 19:45–48; Isaiah 56:7; Jeremiah 7:11; Psalm 8:2

4) **Jesus explains the significance of his death:** John 12:20–50

5) **Explanation of the withered fig tree:** Matthew 21:20–22; Mark 11:20–25; Jeremiah 8:13

6) **The woman caught in adultery:** John 7:53—8:11; Deuteronomy 17:7

## CHAPTER 24: CONFRONTATION

1) **A question about authority:** Matthew 21:23–27; Mark 11:27–33; Luke 20:1–8

2) **Parable of the two sons:** Matthew 21:28–32

3) **Parable of the wicked tenants:** Matthew 21:33–46; Mark 12:1–12; Luke 20:9–19; Isaiah 5:1–7; 8:14–15; Psalm 118:22–23

4) **Parable of the great supper:** Matthew 22:1–14

5) **On paying tribute to Caesar:** Matthew 22:15–22; Mark 12:13–17; Luke 20:20–26

6) **A question about the resurrection:** Matthew 22:23–33; Mark 12:18–27; Luke 20:27–40; Exodus 3:1–6

7) **A question about the greatest commandment:** Matthew 22:34–40; Mark 12:28–34

8) **A question about the Messiah:** Matthew 22:41–46; Mark 12:35–37a; Luke 20:41–44

9) **Jesus publicly denounces the religious leaders:** Matthew 23:1–36; Mark 12:37b–40; Luke 20:45–47

10) **Jesus's lament over Jerusalem:** Matthew 23:37–39

11) **The widow's mite:** Mark 12:41–44; Luke 21:1–4

## CHAPTER 25: A SECOND COMING

1) **Prediction of the destruction of the temple:** Matthew 24:1–2; Mark 13:1–2; Luke 21:5–6

2) **Events before the end:** Matthew 24:3–8; Mark 13:3–8; Luke 21:7–11

3) **Persecutions foretold:** Matthew 24:9–14; Mark 13:9–13; Luke 21:12–19

4) **The Desolation:** Matthew 24:15–22; Mark 13:14–20; Luke 21:20–24; Daniel 2:44–45; 9:27; Isaiah 13:10; 34:4; Joel 2:31; Ezekiel 10:3, 18; 11:23

5) **False christs and false prophets:** Matthew 24:23–27; Mark 13:21–23; Luke 17:23–24

6) **The Second Coming:** Matthew 24:29–31; Mark 13:24–27; Luke 21:25–28

7) **Parable of the fig tree:** Matthew 24:32–36; Mark 13:28–32; Luke 21:29–33

8) **Watchfulness enjoined:** Luke 21:34–36

9) **Be ready, for the Day will come suddenly:** Matthew 24:37–42; Luke 17:26–37

10) **Parable of the Ten Virgins:** Matthew 25:1–13

11) **Parable of the talents:** Matthew 25:14–30

12) **The sheep and the goats:** Matthew 25:31–46

13) **Plot to kill Jesus:** Matthew 26:1–5; Mark 14:1–2; Luke 22:1–2

14) **Judas's betrayal:** Matthew 26:14–16; Mark 14:10–11; Luke 22:3–6; Exodus 21:32; Zechariah 11:7–13

## CHAPTER 26: THE LORD'S SUPPER

1) **Preparation for the Passover:** Matthew 26:17–19; Mark 14:12–16;

Luke 22:7–13

2) **The last supper:** Matthew 26:20; Mark 14:17; Luke 22:14–17; John 13:1–2
3) **Jesus washes the disciples feet:** John 13:3–20; Psalm 41:9
4) **Jesus foretells his betrayal:** Matthew 26:21–25; Mark 14:18–21; Luke 22:21–23; John 13:21–30
5) **The Lord's Supper:** Matthew 26:26–29; Mark 14:22–25; Luke 22:15–20; 1 Corinthians 11:24–25; Exodus 24:8; Jeremiah 31:31–34; Isaiah 53:12
6) **The new way of greatness:** Luke 22:24–30
7) **A new commandment:** John 13:31–35
8) **Peter's denial predicted:** Matthew 26:31–35; Mark 14:26–31; Luke 22:31–34; John 13:36–38
9) **The two swords:** Luke 22:35–38
10) **The way, the truth, the life:** John 14:1–14
11) **The promise of the Paraclete:** John 14:15–26
12) **Peace pronounced:** John 14:27–31
13) **Meal conclusion and departure:** Matthew 26:30; Mark 14:26; Luke 22:39; Psalm 118:21–29

## CHAPTER 27: BETRAYED

1) **The true vine:** John 15:1–8; Isaiah 5:1–7
2) **Love, obedience, abiding:** John 15:9–17
3) **The world's hatred:** John 15:18–25; John 13:16; Matthew 10:24; Psalm 35:19; 69:4
4) **The witness of the Paraclete:** John 15:26–27
5) **On persecutions:** John 16:1–4
6) **The work of the Paraclete:** John 16:5–15
7) **Sorrow turned to joy:** John 16:16–22; Isaiah 66:14
8) **Access to the Father:** John 16:23–28
9) **Tribulation is coming, but Jesus has overcome the world:** John 16:29–33
10) **Jesus's intercessory prayer:** John 17:1–26

11) **Gethsemane:** Matthew 26:36–46; Mark 14:32–42; Luke 22:39–46; John 18:1

12) **Jesus is arrested:** Matthew 26:47–56; Mark 14:43–52; Luke 22:47–53; John 18:2–12

## CHAPTER 28: CONDEMNED

1) **Jesus examined by Annas and Peter's first denial:** Matthew 26:69–70; Mark 14:66–68; Luke 22:56–57; John 18:12–24

2) **Peter's second denial:** Matthew 26:71–72; Mark 14:69–70a; Luke 22:58; John 18:25

3) **Peter's third denial:** Matthew 26:73–75; Mark 14:70b–72; Luke 22:59–62; John 18:26–27

4) **Examined by Caiaphas:** Matthew 26:57–68; Mark 14:53–65; Luke 22:63–65; Psalm 110:1; Daniel 7:13

5) **Formally condemned by the Sanhedrin and delivered to Pilate:** Matthew 27:1–2; Mark 15:1; Luke 22:66—23:1

6) **Judas commits suicide:** Matthew 27:3–10; Jeremiah 19:1–13; Zechariah 11:12–13

7) **First examination by Pilate:** Matthew 27:11–14; Mark 15:2–5; Luke 23:2–7; John 18:28–38

8) **Examination by Herod:** Luke 23:8–12

9) **Pilate declares Jesus innocent:** Luke 23:13–16

10) **The trial and the choice—Jesus or Barabbas:** Matthew 27:15–23; Mark 15:6–14; Luke 23:18–23; John 18:39—19:15

11) **Pilate delivers Jesus to be crucified:** Matthew 27:24–26; Mark 15:15

12) **Jesus mocked by the soldiers:** Matthew 27:28–31; Mark 15:17–20; John 19:2–3 (see 10 for context)

## CHAPTER 29: CRUCIFIED

1) **Journey to Golgotha:** Matthew 27:32; Mark 15:21; Luke 23:26–32; John 19:16b–17; Galatians 3:13; Deuteronomy 21:22–23

2) **The crucifixion:** Matthew 27:33–37; Mark 15:22–26; Luke 23:33–34; John 19:18–27

3) **Jesus is mocked on the cross:** Matthew 27:38–43; Mark 15:27–32a; Luke 23:35–38

4) **The two thieves:** Matthew 27:44; Mark 15:32b; Luke 23:39–43

5) **Death of Jesus:** Matthew 27:45–56; Mark 15:33–41; Luke 23:44–49; John 19:28–37; Psalm 22:1

6) **The burial of Jesus:** Matthew 27:57–61; Mark 15:42–47; Luke 23:50–56; John 19:38–42

7) **The guard at the tomb:** Matthew 27:62-66

## Chapter 30: Raised

1) **The women come to the tomb (Mary runs ahead, then quickly leaves):** Matthew 28:1; Mark 16:1–3; Luke 24:1; John 20:1–2

2) **The other women arrive and are met by two angels:** Matthew 28:2–7; Mark 16:4–7; Luke 24:2–8

3) **Jesus appears to the women after they leave the garden:** Matthew 28:8–10; Mark 16:8

4) **The report of the guard:** Matthew 28:11–15

5) **Peter and John go to the tomb:** John 20:3–10; Luke 24:12

6) **Mary returns after Peter and John leave:** Luke 24:9–11; John 20:11–18

7) **The Emmaus road appearance:** Luke 24:13–35

8) **Jesus appears to the apostles (without Thomas):** Luke 24:36–43; John 20:19–23

9) **Jesus appears to the apostles (with Thomas):** John 20:24–29

10) **Further appearances over forty days:** John 21:1–23; Acts 1:3; 1 Corinthians 15:5–6

11) **The great commission:** Matthew 28:16–20

12) **Parting instructions and ascension:** Luke 24:44–53; Acts 1:4–11

# ABOUT THIS BOOK

*Son of Man* harmonizes the four Gospels to tell the story of Jesus's ministry years. No fictionalized elements or dialog have been added. All events and quotations are taken from the texts of Matthew, Mark, Luke, and John. All of Jesus's recorded words and actions are included, and duplicate accounts have been harmonized.

Several widely respected harmonies were consulted to establish the chronology of events: *Synopsis of the Four Gospels* by Kurt Aland (Editor), *A Harmony of the Gospels: New American Standard Edition* by Robert L. Thomas and Stanley N. Gundry, *A Harmony of the Gospels: The New International Version* by Orville E. Daniel, and *Jesus according to Scripture: Restoring the Portrait from the Gospels* by Darrell L. Bock.

# About the Author

**HENRY H HARRIS** knows Jesus. He has been Henry's constant companion for more than fifty years.

In addition to being a pastor and a church planter, Henry is an award-winning author who has published more than 500 articles about life in Christ. For thirty years he has taught the in-Christ lifestyle to both large and small groups in churches, conferences, and retreats, de-mystifying what it means to be an apprentice to Christ, clarifying the discipleship process, and helping people understand how we can become more like Jesus.

Henry has been happily married to his wife, Lauren, since 1976. They live in San Juan Bautista, California.

Ingram Content Group UK Ltd.
Milton Keynes UK
UKHW021132180423
420361UK00015B/1031

9 780996 393317